Social Media in Asia

Social Media in Asia:

Changing Paradigms of Communication

Edited by

Azman Azwan Azmawati
and Rachel E. Khan

Cambridge
Scholars
Publishing

Social Media in Asia: Changing Paradigms of Communication

Edited by Azman Azwan Azmawati and Rachel E. Khan

This book first published 2016

Cambridge Scholars Publishing

Lady Stephenson Library, Newcastle upon Tyne, NE6 2PA, UK

British Library Cataloguing in Publication Data
A catalogue record for this book is available from the British Library

ISBN (10): 1-4438-9692-6
ISBN (13): 978-1-4438-9692-4

This book is a peer-reviewed, academic publication of the Asian Congress for Media and Communication, an international, not-for-profit, professional organization of mass communication and languages academe.
Website: <www.asianmediacongress.org>
Email: <info@asianmediacongress.org>

CONTENTS

Chapter One 1
Introduction
Rachel E. Khan

Chapter Two 8
In Search of Theoretical Foundations for Social Media
Rachel E. Khan

Chapter Three 25
Crisis Communication in Social Media:
The Singapore Airlines and Air New Zealand Story
Khairiah A Rahman and Tracey Ann Jury

Chapter Four 76
The Role of Internet Memes in Public Discourse:
The Case of the Philippine Pork Barrel Scam of 2013
Karen Y. Varona

Chapter Five 107
Investigating Malaysian Youth's Social Media Practice for Crime Prevention
Jamilah Ahmad and Nurzali Ismail

Chapter Six 130
Building a Digital Counterpublic: Civic Affordances of Twitter under Thai Authoritarian Governance
Chanon Adsanatham

Chapter Seven 154
On-line Dating: Exploring the Digital Ways of Finding Love in Indonesia
Tony Chalkley

Chapter Eight 170
Ambient News in Vietnam: Opportunities, Risks, and Influences
in the Emergent Use of Social Media
Bradley Freeman and Hoang Thi Kim Khanh

Chapter Nine 195
New Freedom of Expression in Media:
An Analysis of 'Dissent' on Facebook Wall Posts
Pushpika Kumari Ganegoda and Nisansala Subhasini Jayawardhana

Annex 213
The Southeast Asian Region at a Glance

About Us 216

CHAPTER ONE

INTRODUCTION

RACHEL E. KHAN

If Facebook were a country, it would have the third largest population in the world, following China at 1.3 billion and India at one billion. A 2012 report from the Wall Street Journal (Scott, 2012) noted that the number of Facebook users was a little over 900 million and still growing.

This statistic is a telltale sign of the growing influence of social media, and this number accounts for only one social media network among many. Social media refers to interaction among people in which they create, share, and/or exchange information and ideas in virtual communities and networks (Kaplan and Haenlein, 2010). Its terminology comes from the fact that, like traditional media, it serves as an instrument for sharing information—whether public or private—and content such as photos, videos, audio files, or text. However, it also exhibits social characteristics such as conversation, community, collaboration, and connectedness. As its name indicates, social media relies on user-generated content (UGC), i.e., on-line material that has been provided by an on-line user, rather than an established on-line company or institution. Conversely, UGC has also been defined as the 'sum of all ways in which people make use of social media' (Kaplan and Haenlein, 2010).

According to Nielsen's 2012 Social Media Report, internet users continue to spend more time with social media sites than any other type of website. According to the United Nations-affiliated International Telecommunications Union (ITU), Singapore and Brunei have the highest internet penetration vis-à-vis the population in Southeast Asia (see Figure 1A). This corresponds to their social networking statistics as well. However, their combined actual number of social media users is much less than that of India, which has 38 million people using Facebook (albeit an internet penetration of only three per cent). Facebook remains the most popular social networking site in all of Asia, including the countries covered in this book. In China and Taiwan, the most popular networking sites are *Qzone*, *Sino Weibo,* and *Tencent Weibo* (Kemp 2013).

One thing unique about the region, however, is that internet penetration, while indicative of technological development, does not necessarily translate to access to information. In six out of the ten Southeast Asian nations, as well as in Sri Lanka, freedom of speech and expression are still restricted. The 2015 World Press Freedom Report of the international organisation 'Reporters Without Borders', shows that this region is generally in the red when it comes to freedom of speech and expression. These are the ranking of nations in the region out of the 180 countries in the world survey (see Table 1A).

Some countries in the region have strict internet and press laws that restrict what an individual can do or can access on the internet. For example, Brunei has the so-called Internet Code of Practice that regulates bloggers; the Philippines has the Cybercrime Law, which penalises on-line libel; other nations, like Cambodia, Malaysia, Myanmar and Singapore practice media censorship.

Figure 1A: Internet Penetration in Southeast Asia

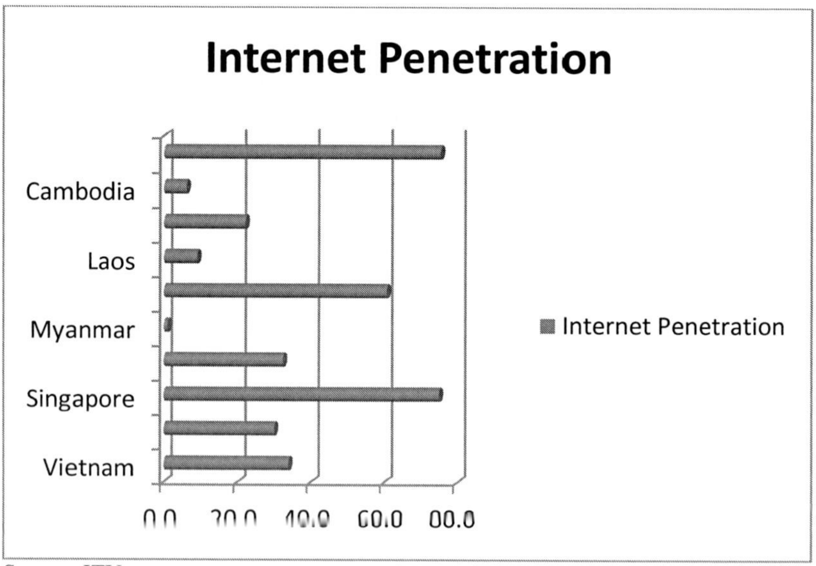

Source: ITU

Table 1A: 2015 World Press Freedom Ranking

	Overall rank	Difference in rank from 2014
Brunei	121	-4
Cambodia	139	+5
Laos	171	0
Indonesia	138	-6
Malaysia	147	0
Myanmar	144	+1
Philippines	141	+8
Singapore	153	-3
Sri Lanka	165	0
Thailand	134	-4
Vietnam	175	-1

Source: Reporters Without Borders

A Brief History of Social Media

While social media history should be traced from the initial phase of the internet in 1957, the actual beginnings of social media as we know it began in the 1990s as part and parcel of the evolution of the World Wide Web (Khan, 2006).

The earliest form of social media platforms are blogs, made popular by the on-line journal sites in the mid-1990s. Among internet geeks, the acknowledged father of blogs is David Winer, a software developer, who popularised blogging in two ways: firstly through Scripting News [scripting.com], a precursor of the blog, because it was the first popular on-line journal that recorded Winer's trials into software development 'as it was happening'. And secondly, through the free blog service, EditThisPage.com, which encouraged the growth of the early blogging community. He is also credited for pioneering podcasting, i.e., an audio application for audio blogging (Scott, 2009).

The term 'weblog' is credited to Jorn Barger, another early blogger, who popularised the term through his blog, 'Robot Wisdom'. The short form, 'blog', was coined by another blogger, Peter Merholz (Wortham, 2007). This was picked up by Evan Williams of Pyra Labs in 1999 as the name of the very popular free blogging site, Blogger.com.

The blog, as we know it today, is part of the social media universe, which is made possible by the so-called Web 2.0 platform, i.e., application developments within the World Wide Web that enables real-time interaction and participatory sharing of information and content.

Technically, there is no internet infrastructure difference between Web 1.0 and 2.0. The development lies in the users' dependency on applications such as *Java*, *Adobe Flash,* and *RSS* (Really Simple Syndication). These technologies emerged in the late 1990s, but became popular with the emergence of the first generation social media networks, such as *Six Degrees* (1997), *Friendster* (2002), and *LinkedIn* (2003).

A study by Andreas Kaplan and Michael Haenlein (2010) of the Kelly School of Business, Indiana University, categorised social media into six different types:

- Collaborative projects – A website or portal that allows the joint and simultaneous creation of content by many social media users as exemplified by *Wikipedia*.
- Blogs and microblogs— Applications such as *Wordpress.com* and *Blogger.com* provide the venues for these earliest forms of social media. Short for 'web logs', blogs are personal web pages that provide a venue for interaction by other social media users with the creator of the site. On the other hand, microblogs are those with limited file allotment, such as *Twitter*, which allows only 140 characters per message, and *Snapchat*, a mobile app that allows users to send and receive 'self-destructing' photos and 10-second videos.
- Content communities – Platforms that allow the sharing of a whole range of media types, from photographs as exemplified by *Flickr*; video, *YouTube*; and even PowerPoint presentations, *Slideshare*.
- Social networking sites – Platforms that enable users to create a social media profile and connect with family, friends (both real and virtual), and share experiences and content as exemplified by *Facebook* and *LinkedIn*.
- Virtual game worlds – Platforms wherein the user is represented by an avatar, which enables him/her to interact with other players in real-time. Applications are operated via game consoles such as Microsoft's X-Box and Sony's PlayStation, which simulates a three-dimensional environment in an imaginary setting. An example of this is the popular *Ragnarok*.

- Virtual social worlds – Portals that replicate real-life scenarios in a virtual platform without the restraint of social conventions or constraints of the real world, such as the ability to travel to exotic destinations. They allow users to create their own content and their own avatars. An example of this is the application dubbed *Second Life*.

Kaplan and Haenlein (2010) contend that social media can be categorised and classified based on application, as stated above, and based this on their media richness and their self-disclosure, which represent 'the two key elements of social media' (see Table 1B).

Table 1B. Classification of Social Media by Characteristic

		SOCIAL PRESENCE/ MEDIA RICHNESS		
		LOW	*MEDIUM*	*HIGH*
SELF PRESENTATION/ SELF DISCLOSURE	*HIGH*	Blogs	Social networking sites	Virtual social worlds
	LOW	Collaborative projects	Content communities	Virtual game worlds

Source: Kaplan and Haenlein, 2010

Media richness is the amount of information or multi-media elements that may be transmitted within a given time; social presence is the level of intimacy (interpersonal vs. mediated) enabled by the medium as well as the degree of presence as defined by the acoustic, visual, and physical contact achieved between two communication subjects (Kaplan and Haenlein, 2010).On the other hand, self-disclosure or self-presentation assumes that people have a desire to control the impressions other people form of them and a desire to create an image that is consistent with their personal identity. Moreover, social media services allow social network aggregators, such as *Pipl*, to integrate data provided by users to come up with a profile of the user.

According to a Nielsen report, the continuous growth of social media is directly proportional to the fast growing mobile industry and the development of smartphones and mobile applications. However, statistics in the United States still differ from those of Asia. The Nielsen report noted that of the time spent using social media, only 20 per cent of Americans used a personal computer, while 80 per cent of total time on-line is via mobile. In Asia, on the other hand, around 90 per cent of the population still prefer the computer to access social media; although some 60 per cent also use smartphones (Nielsen, 2012). The report also said that top on-line purchases in the Asian region were entertainment, travel, and clothing.

About this book

As part of the advocacy of the Asian Congress for Media and Communication to promote regional studies into the global academic discourse, this book aims to contribute to a better understanding of social media within the context of Southeast Asian countries with the addition of Sri Lanka. Reading through the chapters, the reader will discover that social media has changed the paradigm of communication in the region. The next chapter discusses communication theories that can help elucidate the role of social media in society and the third chapter looks at the use of social media as a tool for reaching the public. Chapters Four, Six, and Nine examine the use of social media as a liberating channel in nations that have limits on their citizens' freedom of expression and as a venue to voice grievances against government. On the other hand, Chapters Five and Eight examine the use of social media as tools for making the world a better place, whether for crime prevention or news gathering. And last but not least, Chapter Seven explores the potential of social media for relationship-building, in this particular case the search for a lifelong partner.

For non-Asian readers, the editors added an annex that provides a summary of social media statistics in the region to help readers locate the countries mentioned in this book within the global context.

References

Kaplan Andreas M and Haenlein Michael (2010). Users of the world, unite! The challenges and opportunities of social media, *Business Horizons* 53 vol. 1. Indiana: Kelley School of Business, Indiana University, pp. 59-68

Kemp, Simon (26 March 2013) *The State of Social in Asia* from We are Social blog, downloaded from <wearesocial.net>

Khan, Rachel E. (2006). Internet 101: The New Mass Medium for Filipinos. Mandaluyong: Anvil Publishing, Inc.

Nielsen (2012). *State of the Media: Social Media Report*. Downloaded from <http://www.nielsen.com/us/en/reports/2012/state-of-the-media-the-social-media-report-2012.html>

Scott, Austin (April 23, 2012). Facebook Passes the 900 Million Monthly Users Barrier. *WSJ.com* downloaded from <http://blogs.wsj.com/digits/2012/04/23/facebook-passes-the-900-million-monthly-users-barrier/>

Scott, Rosenberg (June 16, 2009). The unedited voice of a person: Dave Winer. *Say Everything: How Blogging Began, What It's Becoming, and Why It Matters* (eBook ed.). New York: Crown. p.58.

Wortham, Jenna (2007). After 10 Years of Blogs, the Future's Brighter Than Ever. *Wired.com*. Downloaded from <http://archive.wired.com/entertainment/theweb/news/2007/12/blog_anniversary>

CHAPTER TWO

IN SEARCH OF THEORETICAL FOUNDATIONS FOR SOCIAL MEDIA

RACHEL E. KHAN

Overview

- Old theory, new media. There are some mass communication theories that continue to be a good fit to the new media and social media scenario, albeit there is a need to adapt them to the present time. However, scholars are slowly coming up with theories that can catch the multifaceted new medium.
- Gaining popularity in analysing social media phenomena are Kietzmann, Hermkens, and McCarthy's Honeycomb Theory and the Social Network Theory.
- Many existing media theories may also be applied to social media. Among these are the basic Sender-Message-Channel-and-Receiver model, McLuhan's technological determinism and Wilson's cultural determinism.
- Roger Fidler, on the other hand, believed that both technological and cultural determinism combine to produce a 'mediamorphosis', a term he coined to demonstrate that the evolution of technology and history are interdependent.

When Your Fingers Do the Talking

While accessing the virtual world can be as simple as a click of a mouse, the influx of social media network sites on the World Wide Web has resulted in new ways of using the internet. Social media is altering how people do their jobs and how we communicate in a Web 2.0 world.

Unlike the one-way model of communication of traditional mass media, social media adopts the two-way communication that the internet has enabled and has taken to an even more personal level. It facilitates conversations between and among consumers as well as between consumers and producers, suppliers, and/or marketers. Social media—one can argue—is the digital version of 'by word-of-mouth'. With social media, it is your fingers that do the talking but it is more potent because it also serves as a record and storage of word-of-mouth content.

Despite its growing personalisation, however, the fact that it runs on virtual platforms that the internet provides, social media allows users the large-scale and anonymous reach of traditional media minus its cumbersome structure. Analysing social media can be as varied as people's need for communication and information. For example, from a media producer's point of view, it represents a new medium that opens up more opportunities for independent work that makes him less dependent on multi-millionaire publishers and network owners. On the other hand, for a media consumer, it allows him not only to have real-time long-distance conversations, but also gives him the means to become a producer of content as well.

Thus, understanding it as a medium of information and communication has been a slow and challenging process in terms of the development of scholarly research. In-depth theoretical and behavioural understanding of this content is crucial for making sense of these new media. While there is a need to develop new models, this chapter discusses new concepts such as the Honeycomb model as well as new approaches to social media research using existing theories and concepts.

Moreover, unlike traditional media, which have fixed patterns of communication, modes of internet communication are virtually unlimited through new and social media platforms. Therefore, the amount of possibilities for scholarly examination of communicating on the internet is impossible to exhaust.

Honeycomb Model of Social Media

Among the pioneers in social media theory, Jan Kietzmann, Kristopher Hermkens, Ian McCarthy, and Bruno Silvestre of the Simon Fraser University in Vancouver, Canada, have developed a framework for understanding the social media phenomenon.

Dubbed as the *Honeycomb of Social Media*, the theory purports that there are seven functionalities of social media that help deconstruct it, which they presented in the form of blocks within a honeycomb structure (see Figure 2A). These blocks represent identity, conversations, sharing, presence, relationships, reputation, and groups (Kietzmann et al., 2011).

Figure 2A: Honeycomb Functionality of Social Media

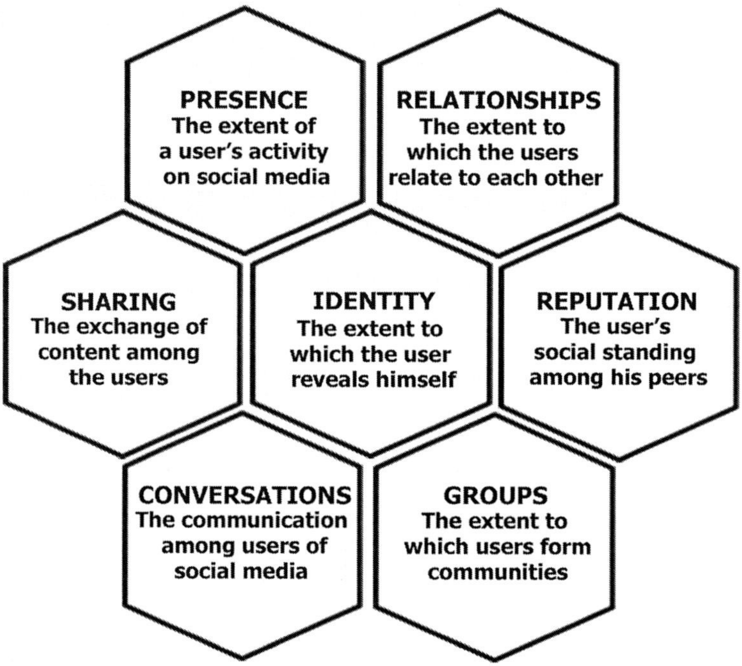

Source: Kietzmann et al 2011, p.243

Each block allows the social media researcher to examine a specific facet of the social media user's experience and its implications (Kietzmann *et al.* 2011). 'They are constructs that allow us to make sense of how different levels of social media functionality can be configured', said the authors (Kietzmann *et al.*, 2011). Utilised individually and together, these blocks can help researchers interpret the social media ecology, and understand social media audiences and their interactions.

'Identity', the central block of the honeycomb, represents the 'extent to which users reveal their identities in a social media setting', such as their name, age, profession, location, likes and dislikes.

'Conversations', on the other hand, represent the extent to which users communicate with others in a social media setting. Many social media sites, such as Facebook and Twitter, are designed primarily to facilitate conversations between individuals and groups. Under this block, the social media researcher can study several factors in a conversation; for example, the diversity or similarity of the participants within a conversation, the emerging public opinion, and so on.

'Sharing' denotes the extent to which users exchange, distribute, and receive content, such as pictures, music, or video or even Web links.

The block labelled 'Presence' represents the extent to which friends or the public at large know that particular user can be found on a particular site. Do his/her friends know that he/she has a Facebook page? Are they connected to a particular person through that site? At the same time, Presence could also denote the amount of exposure a person has in the social media networks. For example, one person could have an account on Facebook, Twitter, Orkut, Flickr, MySpace, and YouTube.

The 'Relationships' block, on the other hand, denotes the extent to which users are related to other users, i.e., they can be related by blood, by affinity, by profession or organisation, and so on. Consequently, this block can also be harnessed to determine how social media builds relationships that previously did not exist in the real world. Kietzmann *et al.* (2011) noted that some social media services trace relationships between individuals by degrees. For example, LinkedIn indicates connections through referral systems of a chain of friends.

Meanwhile, 'Reputation' refers to the extent to which users know how they are perceived by others or by their popularity or notoriety. Kietzmann *et al.* (2011) noted that on social media, Reputation refers not only to the person but also 'to the content', i.e., one's endorsements from others, views or hits, and ratings given by mechanical tools that aggregate content such as Technorati.com and Klout.com.

Finally, the block labelled 'Groups' signifies the sub-communities social media users form within the network. To illustrate: on Facebook, the alumni of various universities worldwide have formed semi-private groups through which they can communicate, while various professions also have networks on-line. Kietzmann *et al.* (2011) noted that there are generally two types of groupings: 1) self-created groups formed by the users to categorise themselves, such as a group of family or people with the same hobby; and 2) those analogous to organisations and institutions in the real world. These Groups can be public, private, or secret.

Kietzmann *et al.* noted that the successful social media sites are those that have been able to strike a balance among the different blocks of the honeycomb, even if some could focus more on a particular block such as identity, sharing, or conversations. At the same time, effective users of social media are those who are able to maximise their networking potential as categorised in these blocks.

Social Network Theory

A number of scholars, especially in the fields of marketing and advertising, are adopting the Social Network Theory (SNT) in their study of social media.

The SNT is a concept used in the study of relationships between individuals, groups, organisations, societies, and even nations. A ‘social network’ is used to describe a structure determined by interactions and/or relationships rather than hierarchy. It views these social relationships in terms of nodes and ties. *Nodes* represent the individual actors within the networks while *ties* are the relationships between the actors. The ties through which individual actors connect or intersect are called dyads, representing the linkages formed by the actors in the network.

These are usually mapped or graphed for analysis wherein nodes are represented by points and ties by lines. Mathematical calculations and analyses on these dyads could be done using the following parameters:

- Betweenness: the extent of a node lying between other nodes;
- Centrality: how connected is a node to the network;
- Closeness: how one node is near all other nodes in the network;
- Density: all the ties in a network in proportion to all the possible ties; and
- Ociomatrix: age, education, and other socio-economic data of actors.

These measurements determine the importance and structural positions of individual actors, and the characteristics of the partial or whole networks. The measurements could be used to study the social network, improve the network structure, and help increase the efficiency of information flows within the network. Network analysis software (such as *NetMiner*, *UCInet* for Windows and *Pajek*) could be used to measure those indices (Everett, M. G., & Borgatti, S. P., 1999; Hanneman, Robert A. and Mark Riddle, 2005).

A popular example of this theory (although largely unproven) is the *Six Degrees of Separation* concept of Harvard University psychology professor Stanley Milgram, which was a part of his 'small world experiment' in the late 1960s. The concept posits that everyone and everything is no more than six steps away; i.e., the chain of '*a friend of a friend*' can be made to connect any two people in a maximum of six steps. This was later popularised by SixDegrees.com, a pioneering social networking site that existed from 1997 to 2001, pre-dating more popular networking sites such as Friendster and Facebook.

While SNT has been used since the late 1960s in social science studies, it's slowly gaining popularity in social media marketing studies. Unlike traditional marketing studies, which attempt to pinpoint attributes of individual actors, the social network theory produces an alternate view and focuses on ties with other actors within the network. This approach has turned out to be useful for explaining many real-world phenomena, such as the spread of gossip and the informal links between individuals in different fields or competing companies and the like. However, it leaves out knowledge regarding an individual's motives for acting and other sociological data.

Revisiting the SMCR Model

Some scholars tend to see social media as a complex system in need of complex communication theories. In reality, the Internet can very well be analysed using the model by Wilbur Schramm (Heinich, 1996), who, taking off from the traditional source-message-receiver communication (SMCR) model of Claude Shannon and Warren Weaver (Shannon and Weaver, 1949), added the concepts of field of experience and feedback (see Figure 2B).

In developing his theory, Schramm emphasised that communication cannot occur unless the fields of experience of both the sender and receiver overlap. With the internet serving as both the 'encoder' and the 'decoder' of the message, communication ceases to be a one-way process as in the Shannon model. In fact, the success of a communication is the ability and ease with which the receiver gives his/her feedback to the sender once the message has been transmitted.

Figure 2B. The Schramm Model of Communication

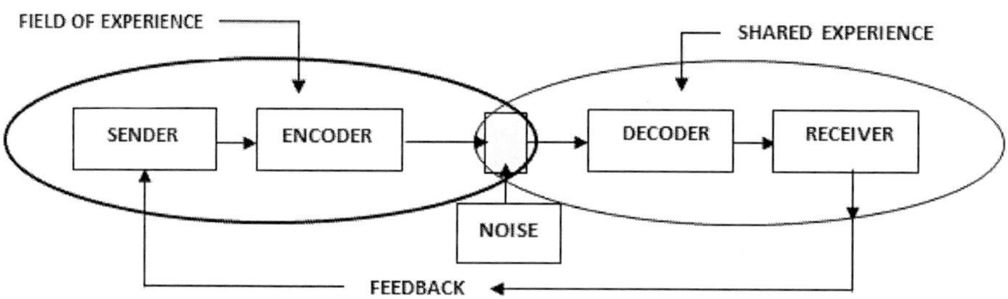

The Schramm model can be used to measure computer-mediated communication (CMC) from the interpersonal level, such as emails, to mass messages, such as blogs and YouTube videos. The traditional concept of interpersonal communication changes with the internet. Email (like texting on a cellular phone) allows non-face-to-face and non-voice immediate communication.

'Field of experience' places an important role in internet communication. For example, an internet user can sign on to a chat room because of shared qualities; e.g., a chatroom for the '30-something' or for 'Star Wars fans'. Similarly, the vast field of information available on-line obliges the user to choose where he wants to go. Thus, a Blogger who wants to increase his page views must find a way to build a relationship with his viewers. One way of doing this is for the Blogger to check his web statistics and 'cookies' (i.e., decoders) to get a glimpse of the users' profiles. On the other hand, the kind of feedback usually given by an internet user is not merely a receiver's reaction to the message. For example, blog viewers often enhance the original message through their shared experiences or contribute new information to the content of the message.

Uses and Gratification Model

With social media being relatively new in relation to traditional media (such as newspapers and television), one theory that has regained popularity is the Uses and Gratification (U&G) model. Unlike other media theories, U&G is more audience-centred. It examines what people do with media rather than what media does to people.

According to Blumler and Katz (1974), an individual's choice of media usually depends on his/her needs for information and stimulation. Thus, it is important to consider the psychological and socio-cultural needs that contribute to his/her media choice or, in this case, website choice (ibid.). Communication researchers using this model can also help better understand the effects of the internet on its users. For example, Wallace in her book, *The Psychology of the Internet*, claims that time spent on the internet results in a decline of interpersonal communication that eventually leads to feelings of isolation and depression (Wallace, 1999). In a similar manner, Paladin *et al.* (2015) used U&G as their foundational theory for exploring the usefulness of Twitter as a disaster communication tool during typhoons in the Philippines.

The Users and Gratification theory takes a more humanistic approach to media use. According to the theory, media users freely decide how they will use media and how it will affect them. Unlike other theories, U&G recognises the individual's capacity as well as responsibility in using and choosing media instead of treating him as a passive subject to media manipulation. This bodes well for a medium that thrives on interactivity.

Interactivity, which has been defined as 'the degree to which participants in the communication process have control over, and can exchange roles in, their mutual discourse' (Williams, Rice, and Rogers, 1988) significantly strengthens the core notion of U&G users as being pro-active in their choice of medium. This interactivity has five dimensions applicable to internet studies; i.e., playfulness, choice, connectedness, information collection, and reciprocal communication (Ha and James, 1998). It has also been suggested that for 'self-indulgers' and 'Web surfers', the playfulness and choice dimensions of interactivity fulfil self-communication and entertainment needs (Ha and James, 1998).

Elihu Blumler and Hadassah Haas (West and Turner, 2010) noted that the people's need for media can be divided into five basic categories. These were adopted by West and Turner (2010) for internet and social media research. The five 'need' categories are:

- *Cognitive need*: The use of social media for knowledge and information; e.g., a buyer looking for the latest computer models and their prices;
- *Affective need*: The use of social media to satisfy emotional needs; e.g. watching inspiring videos on YouTube;
- *Integrative need*: The need for self-esteem; i.e., when people use media to reassure their status, gain credibility and stabilise relationships, such as the need for others to 'like' their status on Facebook;
- *Social Integrative need*: This is the need to socialise with family, friends and acquaintances via social networking sites like Myspace, Facebook, Weibo, and so on; and,
- *Tension free need*: The use of media as a means of escapism and tension-relief.

The explanatory power of the theory emerges on the assumption that, given certain needs, only some media will be able to satisfy those needs. Gratification is predictable at some degree of certainty if the researcher is aware of the needs being served by a particular media. The connection between the characteristic of the medium and the satisfaction of a need is also directive and, to a certain extent, necessary (West and Turner, 2010).

However, Ruggiero (2000) noted that one potential problem of the U&G model for internet research is the 'practical impossibility of probability sampling on the internet'. Because of the almost unlimited number of internet users, studies may only be able to tentatively generalise very specific populations—for example, the youth sector in a specific country. At the same time, Web-administered surveys may pose problems with tracking precise and reliable response rates. Additionally, a current lack of standardisation among browsers, servers, and operating systems may create a serious challenge to methodically sound quantitative research (Ruggiero, 2000).

Medium as Message

On the opposite spectrum of the UGM is Marshall McLuhan's concept of Technological Determinism, more popularly known as 'the medium is the message'. McLuhan contended that people organised their lives as a result of the way they communicated with others. For McLuhan, as elaborated by Fordham University professor Paul Levinson in his book *Digital McLuhan: A Guide to the Information Millennium* (1999), 'the mere use of a medium has a more profound impact upon society than what individuals may do specifically with the medium'.

Believing that media was anything that extended the sensory organs of man; i.e., the wheel as the extension of the foot and clothing as the extension of the skin, McLuhan was the first media theorist who dubbed the telephone and the computer as media, two decades before their potentials were unleashed. He considered them so because 'all media, from the phonetic alphabet to the computer, cause deep and lasting changes in [man] and transform his environment' (Norden, 1969).

McLuhan asserted that all of human history could be subdivided into four major periods, or epochs. Each epoch, he said, began with a technological development in communication. These periods did not gradually evolve into each other, he claims. Rather, the entry of a technology wrenched the world from one era into the next one.

McLuhan dubbed the first epoch as the Tribal Age and noted that the primary medium was oral communication. Without the benefit of technology to extend man's faculties, the primitive man depended on his auditory senses for receiving information. The ear was the key organ. Thus, during this period, primitive man's knowledge largely depended on his connection with the tribe. To move away from the tribe was to exclude oneself from the information chain. Because of the dependence on oral communication, one could assume that the information among individuals was more or less at the same level. But this, he noted also meant that there was little individualism and specialisation, the hallmarks of modern man (McLuhan, 1964).

McLuhan was emphatic in naming the invention of the phonetic alphabet as the turning point of the next epoch and he dubbed this as the Age of Literacy (2000/1500 BC). The 'phonetic alphabet fell like a bombshell, installing sight at the head of the hierarchy of senses', said McLuhan (as quoted in Norden, 1969). He argued that early forms of writing, such as the Egyptian hieroglyphics or ancient Chinese ideograms, did not remove primitive man's dependence on the tribe. These writing forms were pictorial expressions of reality, which needed the tribe's interpretations of the wide number of symbols that covered an equally wide range of information. On the other hand, the phonetic alphabet is made up of a few semantically meaningless letters, which by virtue of abstracted concepts could represent a wide range of information. The alphabet was a technological breakthrough, he said, because primitive man could now explore other lands without being cut off from the flow of information.

Gutenberg's invention of the printing press brought in the Print Age (AD 1450). For McLuhan, the printing press was the ultimate extension of phonetic literacy, maintaining the predominance of the sense of sight. It pushed out the mediaeval man and paved the way for the renaissance man, even as knowledge—through the written word—no longer remained in the hands of a few. As books became more available, more people naturally became literate. Independent thinkers could now spread their ideas more rapidly. Moreover, because books are portable, men could now live farther from the centre of society and still gain knowledge. He also went as far as to say that because the movable type made possible the mass production of written words, the Print Age was the precursor of the industrial revolution.

McLuhan said that the last historical epoch was ushered in by the invention of the telegraph in 1844. The Electronic Age and the Rise of the Global Village, he contended, made the printed word a thing of the past. For McLuhan, electric media—i.e., the telegraph, radio, films, telephone, television, and the computer—have greater influence on man because they do not serve as an extension of only one sense organ as in the case of print, but use all the senses. Of these, he believed the television the most influential because it enhanced and externalised our entire central nervous system. The Electronic Age which relies on visual and aural senses, claimed McLuhan, has re-shifted man's thinking process back to the nonlinear mode and acoustic of tribal man.

In the Print Age, the literate man was aloof and could disassociate himself from the world even as he gained knowledge. During this period, rationality was superior to emotionality. But radio and television reversed this and re-tribalised man because they returned us to the pre-alphabetic oral tradition. That is, we don't need to be literate to gain information since we again depend on the other senses.

However, McLuhan did not mean that we all went back to our local tribes. Rather, because of the farther reach of television, we became one tribe: a global village. Through cable television images and live website feeds we witnessed the nuclear plant disaster in Fukushima, Japan, in 2011 and the devastation of southern Philippine provinces during the Haiyan super typhoon in 2013. People felt compassion for the families of the victims and were in shock at the destruction caused. The electronic media have kept us informed about events across the globe without us having to leave the comfort of our own homes. Through social media, people the world over can also actively participate in world events. During Typhoon Haiyan in the Philippines, Twitter feeds were used to track the devastated provinces and locate people who needed rescue. Facebook was used by private organisations and individuals to raise funds for the victims and rescue missions.

Levinson (1999) argues that the internet is a continuum of the fourth epoch. Cyberspace, said Levinson, is acoustic space. He argues that the printed word in cyberspace cannot be compared with the printed word in a book or magazine. He notes that the internet has brought us back to the tribal acoustic way of thinking where emotionality is superior to rationality, where what we feel is more important than what we think.

Cultural Determinism

Opposing McLuhan is the theory of Cultural Determinism. Leading the group is Brian Winston, who asserted that technology should be placed within its cultural context. He argued that the cultural context is the key to the development of both media technology and content. Contrary to McLuhan, technology is seen as human-made, carrying the imprint of the social and historical circumstances that formed it.

McLuhan believed that new technology wrenched the world from one epoch to another without the benefit of a gradual shift. But Winston contends that the development of technology comes in the wake of societies' perceived needs and its influence in the realm of pure science.

In his book *Misunderstanding Media*, Winston (1986) held that supervening social necessities accelerate the development of media and other technologies and not vice-versa. For example, the development of the television was hindered and suppressed at the height of World War II so that all U.S. economic resources could be directed to the war effort.

For cultural determinists, the circumstances into which a technology is introduced and diffused through society, as well as the circumstances preceding its introduction, are what are deemed as significant to social change. Four factors (Winston, 1986) are of primary significance:

- Human engineers take into consideration the constraints of culture and the limits imposed by socio-economic forces. These affect their choices in terms of materials, design, purpose etc.;
- Market forces, such as the availability of investors, play a major role in the development of a media product, e.g. in the late nineties Wall Street was bullish over internet stocks, a corresponding boom in internet start-up companies followed;
- Consumer needs and demands, which are shaped by culture and the prevalent public opinion, influence the market for new products; also, advertising can influence us in telling us what we need; finally,
- Interaction of all individuals and groups who are also social products.

Technological determinists, on the other hand, focus on the so-called 'invention', referring to the new communication tool that changes society. But, cultural determinists believe that that word is inaccurate since the 'invention' of a new medium does not come as a result of one person's effort alone in an instantaneous moment in time. Rather, it is the fruit of a 'development' of several persons and various prototypes before it is accepted by society.

Moreover, Winston argued, if technological determinism is correct, then 'why are some prototypes abandoned while others are not? Why are some devices deemed 'inventions' and others not?' Sometimes, market forces come into play, such as what happened to Sony's 'Betamax', the first VCR to hit the market. After it was introduced in 1976, Universal Pictures and Disney filed a suit against Sony for copyright infringement. The film companies wanted the court to ban VCRs because of the threat they allegedly represented to their legitimate business interests. The suit dragged on for eight years and went all the way to the U.S. Supreme Court. While the court battle was raging, the head of the Motion Picture Association of America tried to persuade Congress to impose royalties on the sale of videotapes and VCRs. Meanwhile, American technological firms developed their own VCR, called the 'VHS', and tied-up with these big Hollywood firms. This led to the demise of the 'Betamax', although Sony eventually won the case in the Supreme Court in 1984.

For cultural determinists, the medium is NOT the message; rather, the market players such as Universal and Disney, as well as the users of media, have the last say on how we want to use a certain technology. As Paul Saffo, Director of the Silicon Valley-based Institute for the Future, said, 'Technology does not drive change at all. Technology merely enables change. It's our collective cultural response to the options and opportunities presented by technology that drives change' (as quoted in Fidler, 1997). Or, to put it succinctly, technology is in the eye of the beholder.

Media Metamorphosis

Roger Fidler, Head of the Institute of Cyberjournalism at Kent State University, believes that technological evolution is somewhat a marriage of both technological and cultural determinism theories. In his book entitled *Mediamorphosis: Understanding New Media* (1997), Fidler described 'mediamorphosis'—a term he coined in 1990—as the transformation of communication media, brought about by the complex interplay of perceived needs, competitive and political pressures, and social and technological innovations (Fidler, 1997).

The evolution of new media technologies, he noted, does not happen in a vacuum. Rather, when one medium changes, it affects the others, and vice-versa. 'By studying the communication system as a whole, we will see that new media do not arise spontaneously and independently—they emerge gradually from the metamorphosis of old media. And that when newer forms of communications media emerge, the older forms usually do not die—they continue to evolve and adapt', he said.

Borrowing a page of McLuhan's theory, Fidler claims that there are three great mediamorphoses in human communication: spoken language, written language, and the digital language. He further maintains that spoken language led to the formation of social groups, complex problem solving skills, and the development of 'broadcast' forms like storytelling and ritual performance. This in turn, he said, divided society into performers, gatekeepers, and audiences.

Written language, he asserted, ushered in the development of portable documents (such as books), mechanical printing, and mass media (specifically newspapers and magazines). Unlike spoken and written, however, digital language enables communication between machines, and mediated communication between humans. He quoted MIT's Nicholas

Negroponte, author of 'Being Digital', in asserting that human distinctions between text, images, and sounds are irrelevant; they are all represented as 'bits'. He noted that this last stage extended the power of the spoken and written language even as computer networks 'greatly extend human interactions throughout the world'.

Fidler further claims that the evolution of communications media can be depicted in six principles (1997):

- *Coevolution and coexistence*: The introduction of a new medium does not make the old media obsolete. Rather, they become coexistent. Moreover, as each new form emerges and develops, it influences, over time and to varying degrees, the development of every other existing form;
- *Metamorphosis*: New media do not arise spontaneously and independently. They emerge gradually from the metamorphosis of older media. When newer forms emerge, the older forms tend to adapt and continue to evolve rather than die;
- *Propagation*: Emerging forms of communication media propagate dominant traits from earlier forms, e.g., on-line news sites tend to be designed using the newspaper as model;
- *Survival*: All forms of communication media, as well as media enterprises, are compelled to adapt and evolve for survival in a changing environment. Their only other option is to die, e.g. with the advent of TV News, newspapers adopted a longer form of reportage, such as the so-called investigative reports;
- *Opportunity and Need*: New media are not widely adopted on the merits of technology alone. There must always be an opportunity, as well as a motivating social, political, and/or economic reason for a new media technology to be developed; and,
- *Delayed Adoption*: New media technologies always take longer than expected to become commercial successes. They tend to require at least one human generation (20-30 years) to progress from proof of concept to widespread adoption.

Essentially, the theory of Mediamorphosis argues that media, technology, and communication are all interconnected. Fidler claims that as a rule of thumb, 30 years is the amount of time it takes for a new technology to seep into a culture. He also said that new media do not develop overnight but instead morph into new usages as technology develops.

References

Blumler, J. and E. Katz (1974), *The Uses of Mass Communication*. Beverly Hills: SAGE Publications, Beverly Hills, CA.

Chandler, Daniel (1996). Shaping and Being Shaped, *CMC Magazine*, downloaded from <http://www.december.com/cmc/mag>.

Everett, M. G., & Borgatti, S. P. 1999. The centrality of groups and classes. *Journal of Mathematical Sociology*. 23(3): 181-201.

Fidler, Roger.*Mediamorphosis: Understanding New Media*. California: Pine Forge Press (1997).

Ha, L., & James, E. L. (1998). Interactivity reexamined: A baseline analysis of early business Web sites. *Journal of Broadcasting & Electronic Media*, 42, 457–474.

Kietzmann, J. H., Hermkens, K., McCarthy, I. P., & Silvestre, B. S. (2011). Social media? Get serious! Understanding the functional building blocks of social media. *Business Horizons*, *54*(3), 241-251.

Levinson, Paul (1999). *Digital McLuhan: a guide to the information millennium*. London: Routledge.

McLuhan, Marshall (1964). *Understanding Media: The Extension of Man*. Toronto: McGraw Hill.

Milgram, Stanley (1967). The Small World Problem, *Psychology Today*, 1967, Vol. 2, 60–67 New York: Sussex.

Hanneman, Robert A. and Mark Riddle 2005. *Introduction to social network methods*. Riverside, CA: University of California, Riverside (downloaded from http://faculty.ucr.edu/~hanneman/)

Heinich, R. et al. (1996), *Instructional Media and Technologies for Learning*. Columbus, Ohio: Prentice Hall

Norden, Eric (1969). The Playboy Interview: Marshall McLuhan, *Playboy Magazine*, March 1969.

Paladin, Kristelle, Kris Anne Ramos and Rowena Capulong-Reyes (2015). Meron o Wala: A Study on the Usefulness of Twitter during Typhoon as Perceived by the Students of the Selected Intramuros-Based Schools. *International Journal of Social Science and Humanity*, Vol. 5, No. 1, January 2015. Downloaded from <http://www.ijssh.org/>

Ruggiero, T. (2000). Uses and gratification theory in the 21st century. *Mass Communication &Society, 3*(1), 3-37. London: Routledge Publishing, Inc.

Scott, J. (2000). *Social Network Analysis: A handbook*. Second edition. London: Sage.

Shannon, Claude and Warren Weaver (1949). *The Mathematical Theory of Communication*. Urbana: University of Illinois Press p.66.
West, Richard L. and Lynn H. Turner (2010). Uses and Gratification Theory. *Introducing Communication Theory: Analysis and Application*. Boston: McGraw Hill. p. 392-401.
Williams, F., Rice, R. E., & Rogers, E. M. (1988). *Research methods and the new media*. New York: Free Press.
Winston, Brian (1996). *Media Technology and Society, A History From the Telegraph to the Internet*. London: Routledge.

CHAPTER THREE

CRISIS COMMUNICATION IN SOCIAL MEDIA: THE SINGAPORE AIRLINES AND AIR NEW ZEALAND STORY

KHAIRIAH A RAHMAN
AND TRACEY ANN JURY

Overview

- Social media (SM) is now a permanent channel of human communication. With the marked growth in membership of SM users on sites such as Twitter and Facebook, SM has increasingly become today's preferred mode of daily communication involving large groups of people.
- Public relations practitioners must consider SM as a strategic communication tool, particularly in the event of a crisis situation, when the reputation of an organisation is called into question. Members of the public who are affected by crises involving organisations are likely to take to SM to air their grievances, often demanding an immediate response.
- Crisis communication strategies used are critically evaluated for their theoretical application and found to be wanting. Formulaic, prescriptive and controlled communication can no longer be supported in public relations crisis handling in SM.

The Challenge of a Crisis

By their very nature, crises are negative situations that present themselves unexpectedly, with often devastating consequences. They have the potential to ruin an organisation's reputation, which could cause long-term damage. In such situations, appropriate and accurate communication becomes critical, explaining the growing interest in crisis communication strategies within public relations research (Benoit, 1995; Coombs, 2007; Zaremba, 2010; Fearn-Banks, 2011). Traditionally, a crisis situation is followed by an adverse public reaction, which the organisation proceeds to immediately address through a series of planned communication approaches and actions. These planned steps suggest a strict adherence to protocol and controlled communication.

Research suggests that communication practitioners and organisations are generally hesitant to join the SM revolution out of fear of the new medium and loss of control of the communication situation (Deepti, 2010; McAllister-Spooner, 2009; Eikelmann, Hajj & Peterson, 2008). However, absence does not guarantee protection of reputation. If anything, it robs the organisation of authentic representation as the voices speaking on behalf of and against the organisation may not represent the facts of a crisis situation. Adcorp (2013) notes that audiences tend to congregate in SM platforms, expecting to engage with organisations. In an SM age, not responding to the voices that demand explanation, justification or change can be the peril that leads to an organisation's downfall. Traditionally, responding to collective criticisms on a crisis that affects an organisation's reputation in a timely, honest and transparent way has saved the day for many companies. One example in New Zealand is Mercury Energy's response to public outrage over the death of Mrs. Muliaga, a customer whose breathing aid was affected because of a power cut to her home due to payment issues. Another example relates to Z Energy apologising for their introductory advertisement that made fun of Asian call centres. Z Energy had also excluded Asians in their representation of the New Zealand national identity (Johnson, 2011) despite Asians making up 11.8% of the population with a projected growth to number more than the indigenous Maori by the 2020s (Ihaka, 2013).

The speed of viral sharing makes responding immediately to crises feedback on SM even more pertinent. SM conveys direct messages from affected members of the public, with many active and mindful members participating in and observing the crisis-handling. Sending the appropriate response that can alleviate and dissipate the tense situation should be at the forefront of every organisation's crisis-communication plan. SM is the ideal communication method to respond to affected people, as it reaches the target groups directly. One such media is Facebook (FB), now a permanent medium of communication, with FB membership growing at a steady rate of 19 % annually in addition to its already 829 million active users daily and 1.32 billion active users monthly (Facebook, 2014). FB's sheer volume of regular users makes it too big a communication method to ignore. Having an FB presence is not only advantageous but critical to an organisation's handling of crises in order to maintain, enhance and protect its reputation.

In Search of a Strategy

While many organisations today sense the urgency of SM communication and have taken up its use as a means to relate to the public, the communication is largely one way, informational and persuasive (Waters & Jamal, 2011; Grunig, 1992). Grunig's 1992 Excellence Theory suggests that for organisational communication to truly excel, organisations must move away from one-way communication practices and embrace a two-way symmetrical model of communication. Communication that follows the ideals of the Two Way Symmetrical Model allows the potential for dialogue between key members of the public, stakeholders and organisations.

Dialogue promotes understanding between the communicating participants. There is the act of exchanging feedback to understand the target audience and explain the organisation's position, which could result in a change of behaviour for either party (Kent and Taylor, 1998 & 2002). With dialogue, both the organisation and the public do not enter into the dialogic process with any planned outcome. In their seminal work on dialogic communication, Kent and Taylor (1998) suggest that dialogic communication is a negotiated communication process based on respect and guided by two principles – to reach a better understanding of the other's position, although this might not result in an agreement, and to maintain an ethical perspective, i.e. dialogue is about the 'intersubjectivity' of truths since participants are entering into a dialogic exchange with their own ideas and opinions.

SM provides opportunities for real-time, public conversations to occur between representatives of the organisations and affected members of the public, increasing the potential for dialogic exchanges held up as ideal in the Excellence Theory. However, some might argue that organisational-public relationships can never be truly dialogic due to the nature of participants (individual versus the company). Also, dialogue requires time and the main participants may change in the process of addressing an issue, which means something is lost in understanding. There is no continuity in the listening act when varied representatives of the company respond as the organisation's representative over time in a dialogic process.

Still, one cannot ignore the fact that fundamentally, two-way human communication involves two participants exchanging messages to convey meaning. At this basic level, communication between a company representative and a concerned member of the public has the potential to be dialogic.

Despite this, organisations with SM pages seem to prefer controlling information flow and participation, failing to fully utilise the dialogic potential of SM (Waters *et al.*, 2009). Observations of crisis handling on SM pages of two national airlines from Oceania and Asia indicate that the strategies used are far from satisfactory. Questions remain over whether these strategies are conducive to the SM environment, whether existing crisis communication strategies benefit this media, and what improvements are necessary to address any gap in theory and practice.

Prevailing studies in crisis communication strategies focus on image restoration and public perception (Benoit, 1995; Coombs, 2007). Benoit's (1995) Image Restoration Theory addresses the impact that perception has on organisational reputation and the communicative steps that may be taken to reduce the impact of negative perception. Image Restoration Theory relies on two key tenets: communication is a goal-driven activity and maintaining a positive image is one of the central goals of communication (Benoit, 1995). Image Restoration Theory is reactionary, outlining a typology of appropriately-themed responses dependent on the actions that pose a potential threat to reputation, as outlined in the below table. Image Restoration Theory has become a popular typology to allow case-by-case analysis of the implementation of crisis communication strategies employed in traditional media environments.

Table 3A: Benoit's (1995) message strategies as outlined in Image Restoration Theory.

Benoit's Image Restoration Theory Message Strategies		
Category	**Sub-Category**	**Explanation**
Denial		Used to absolve blame by denying the act occurred or denying responsibility.
	Shifting blame	Provide statements or evidence to suggest someone else committed the offensive action.
Evading Responsibility		If the act cannot be denied, the organisation may be able to use the following strategies to evade responsibility.
	Defeasibility	Organisation claims it lacked control over, or knowledge of, the event.
	Provocation	Organisations can claim that their action was in response to another more offensive action.
	Excuses based on accident	Organisations claim the act was an accident to lessen responsibility.
	Justify	Organisation accepts the act that occurred but asks the public not to hold it accountable, as the organisation had sound intentions.
Reducing Offensiveness		These strategies do not deny the occurrence but attempt to minimise the negative impact on reputation.
	Bolstering	Remind audience of past positive actions.
	Minimisation	Convince audience that the act isn't as bad as it first appeared.
	Differentiate	Compare act to similar, but worse, actions taken by other organisations.
	Transcendence	Place the act in a different context.
	Compensation	Offer monetary compensation.
Corrective Action		Either promise to make changes or promise to restore state of affairs prior to the act occurring.
Mortification		Organisation admits responsibility and seeks forgiveness.

Coombs's (2007) Situational Crisis Communication Theory (SCCT) addresses the limitations posed by Benoit's case-by-case focus by relying on experimental design. Instead of providing reactionary suggestions, SCCT provides a framework for crisis communicators to understand how communication can be used to protect reputation (Coombs, 2007). SCCT is receiver-orientated, prioritising the well-being of stakeholders over the aim of reputation management, and aims to allow prediction of how stakeholders will respond in any given crisis to allow pre-planning and preparation (Coombs, 2007). The table below outlines the message strategies proposed by SCCT.

Table 3B: SCCT Message Strategies (Coombs, 2007)

Coomb's SCCT Message Strategies		
Category	**Sub-Category**	**Explanation**
Deny Strategies	Attack the accuser	Confront those who are claiming something is wrong.
	Denial	Claim that there is no crisis.
	Scapegoat	Blame a person or group outside of the organisation for the crisis.
Diminish	Excuse	Claim organisation did not intend to cause harm or declare that events causing the crisis are beyond their control.
	Justification	Minimises perceived damage by explaining the crisis and damage caused.
Rebuild	Compensation	Offering gifts to the affected.
	Apology	Taking responsibility and seeking forgiveness.

Despite the apparent differences in perspectives between Coombs's (2007) SCCT and Benoit's (1995) Image Restoration Theory, they both share fundamental similarities in the prescription of ready-made responses that can be employed during crisis situations. These ready-made strategies aim to control communication and were designed on the basis of a one-way communication environment. SM developments have resulted in a change to this communication environment, where dialogic communication has become paramount. This change has led to the necessary examination of Coombs's (2007) and Benoit's (1995) communication strategies as control of media messages becomes less likely and organisations are required to negotiate collective meanings with their key customers on-line. The change in communication dynamic, brought about by SM, requires a thorough examination of the application of traditional techniques within the SM environment to ensure that organisations can continue to manage and protect a positive reputation. Examination of these traditional techniques enable insight into pertinent questions raised by SM, such as how crisis-communication can be managed within an environment that struggles with competing voices and which communication strategies can be recommended.

In light of the popularity of SM in contemporary communication, public relations practitioners must consider SM as a strategic communication tool, particularly in the event of a crisis situation, when the reputation of an organisation is at stake.

A Comparative Analysis

A study of comparative airlines' responses (Air New Zealand and Singapore Airlines) to complaints in a crisis situation on their FB pages aims to capture existing practices that will be critically evaluated for their theoretical application. For PR practitioners and organisations still formulating SM crisis-communication strategies, this work provides an introduction into an unchartered area, adding insight into this body of knowledge.

This study uses qualitative textual analysis to compare the crisis-communications issued in an SM environment by an airline from the Oceania market (Air New Zealand) with an airline from the Asian market (Singapore Airlines). Both of these airlines are national carriers in their respective nations and have long-standing reputations of providing premium air travel. Qualitative methods are favoured due to their ability to gain an in-depth understanding of conversation, motivations and perceptions (Baxter & Babbie, 2004; Branthwaite & Patterson, 2011; Lindloff & Taylor, 2011). In-depth insight into conversation is essential to understand the use and the effectiveness of crisis-communication strategies that are employed on SM.

In order to analyse crisis communication in an SM environment, a potential crisis situation that each airline faced was selected. The crisis event selected for Air New Zealand (Air NZ) was the June 2013 Antarctic weather storm that caused delays and cancellations to flights throughout

New Zealand over several days (19 June 2013 – 23 June 2013). For Singapore Airlines (SIA), the crisis event analysed was their use of Ukrainian Airspace following the shooting down of MH17 on 17 July 2014. Although these crisis situations differ in their severity, they both initiated negative public reaction that called for crisis-communication strategies to be employed in an SM environment. FB was chosen as the studied social medium as both airlines have a strong FB presence and because FB use is prevalent worldwide, with a total of 1.32 billion users active monthly (Facebook, 2014). SIA has 1,002,076 'Likes' on their FB page and AirNZ has 890,607.

Content for textual analysis was sourced from the airlines' respective FB pages two weeks before and after the event in order to gain an insight into crisis-communication strategies employed before, during and after the situation occurred. This content was then categorised following the tenets of thematic analysis. Braun and Clarke (2006) stated, 'thematic analysis is a method for identifying, analysing and reporting patterns [themes] within data' (p.79). Thematic analysis creates themes through inductive and deductive lenses by asking and answering questions of the research (Baxter and Babbie, 2004). Initial analysis of the data sourced and the literature has led to the development of four major themes within the research, as follows:

- The Organisation's Communication Strategies
- Consumers' Preferred Communication Strategies
- Emotion
- Impact of Prior Reputation and Crisis History

These themes enable a comparison of the use of crisis-communication strategies in an SM environment between both organisations to give insight into the relevance of traditional crisis-communication strategies for such platforms.

The Case of Air New Zealand

Textual analysis indicated that Air NZ most commonly used standardised replies to address queries and concerns made on their FB page. Figure 3C demonstrates the construction of these standardised replies, in which the airline offers an initial apology and then directs the complainant to another channel to have their concerns addressed.

In Figure 3A, Air NZ does not attempt to directly address the specifics of each complaint and attempts to direct the conversation from the public forum of SM onto the more private forum of email. Replies that appear to follow specific templates suggest that Air NZ may be ill-prepared or unwilling to address specific complaints on FB and may prefer to address complaints using other forums. Furthermore, the standardised nature indicates that the SM crisis communication plan currently employed by Air NZ may not let SM managers address complaints. Although redirection to a less public platform may be an appealing address for organisations who wish to protect their reputation, the use of such standardised replies could spark frustration in customers who see the organisation as uncooperative or unwilling to address concerns.

Figure 3B shows how SM managers working for Air NZ are unwilling or unable to reply to further queries made through FB once the initial standardised reply is given. By not responding to the complaints and queries made, Air NZ increases the level of frustration felt by the customer and leaves the situation unresolved. A lack of response could damage their reputation as both the complainant and others witness the issue that is left unaddressed. Figure 3B shows an unwillingness to engage beyond a superficial level, despite the fact that SM enables principles of dialogic communication to be easily followed by organisations. Lack of dialogic communication and a higher level of engagement may leave key stakeholders and affected customers aggrieved as they increasingly expect to be able to use SM as a platform to have concerns addressed, queries answered and to seek information. SM gives organisations an opportunity to provide their own voice within community debates, respond to queries and take on feedback (Veil et al., 2011; Perry et al., 2003; Gonzales-Herrero & Smith, 2010). If organisations choose not to participate in the debate by not engaging beyond initial replies, organisational reputation and perception will be defined without organisational input, potentially having negative ramifications.

Figure 3A: AirNZ issues a standardised reply to different complainants.

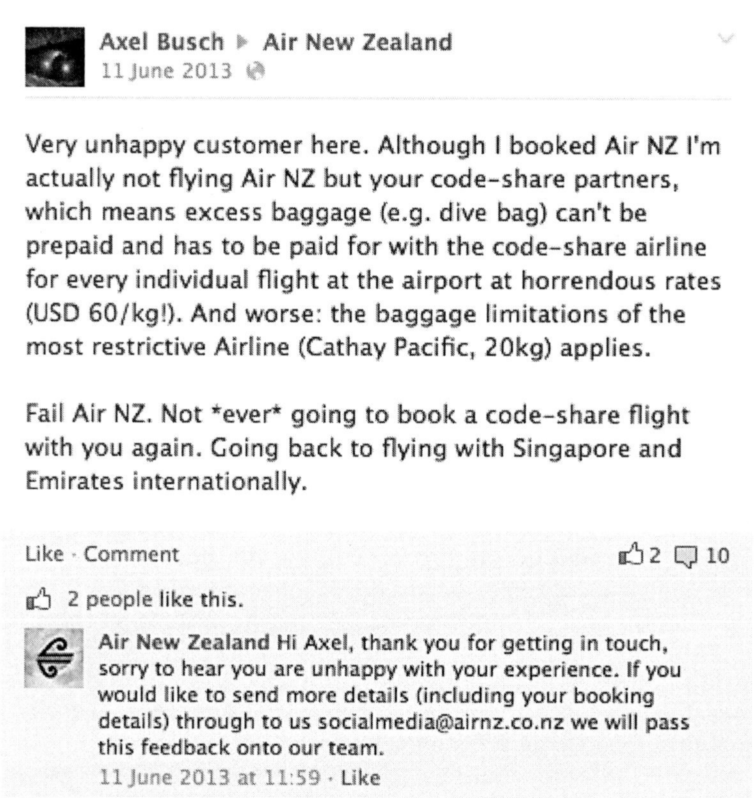

Axel Busch ▸ Air New Zealand
11 June 2013

Very unhappy customer here. Although I booked Air NZ I'm actually not flying Air NZ but your code-share partners, which means excess baggage (e.g. dive bag) can't be prepaid and has to be paid for with the code-share airline for every individual flight at the airport at horrendous rates (USD 60/kg!). And worse: the baggage limitations of the most restrictive Airline (Cathay Pacific, 20kg) applies.

Fail Air NZ. Not *ever* going to book a code-share flight with you again. Going back to flying with Singapore and Emirates internationally.

Like · Comment 2 10

2 people like this.

Air New Zealand Hi Axel, thank you for getting in touch, sorry to hear you are unhappy with your experience. If you would like to send more details (including your booking details) through to us socialmedia@airnz.co.nz we will pass this feedback onto our team.
11 June 2013 at 11:59 · Like

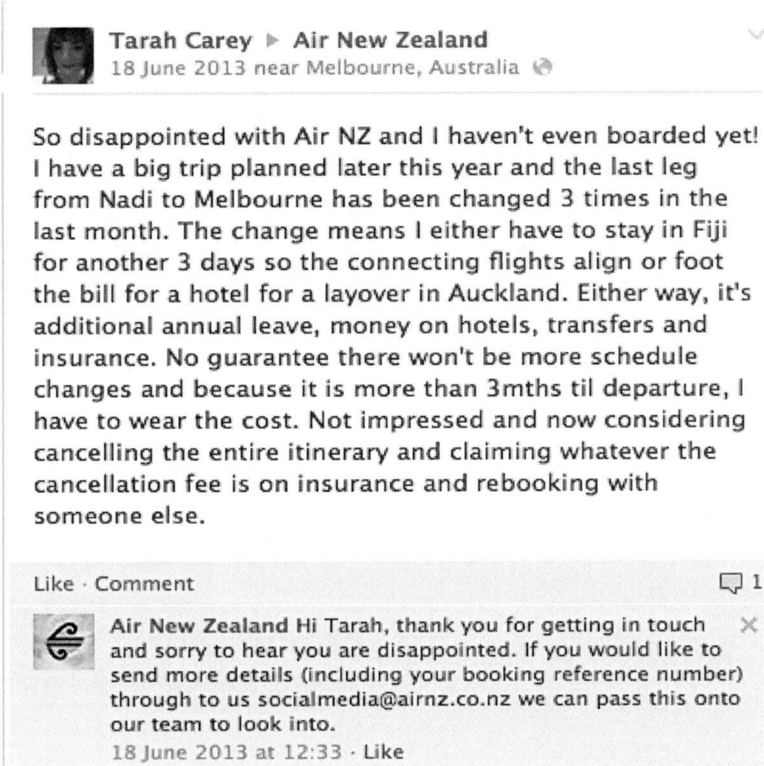
Tarah Carey ▸ Air New Zealand
18 June 2013 near Melbourne, Australia

So disappointed with Air NZ and I haven't even boarded yet! I have a big trip planned later this year and the last leg from Nadi to Melbourne has been changed 3 times in the last month. The change means I either have to stay in Fiji for another 3 days so the connecting flights align or foot the bill for a hotel for a layover in Auckland. Either way, it's additional annual leave, money on hotels, transfers and insurance. No guarantee there won't be more schedule changes and because it is more than 3mths til departure, I have to wear the cost. Not impressed and now considering cancelling the entire itinerary and claiming whatever the cancellation fee is on insurance and rebooking with someone else.

Like · Comment 1

Air New Zealand Hi Tarah, thank you for getting in touch and sorry to hear you are disappointed. If you would like to send more details (including your booking reference number) through to us socialmedia@airnz.co.nz we can pass this onto our team to look into.
18 June 2013 at 12:33 · Like

Figure 3B demonstrates the risk of using standardised replies, displaying how a standardised reply can cause further frustration and anger towards the organisation.

Figure 3B: Air NZ customer displays frustration after receiving a standardised reply.

Figure 3C displays the application of traditional crisis communication strategies in forming standardised replies. Using Benoit (1995) and Coombs (2007) as a lens for analysis, it becomes obvious that Air NZ's replies favour the use of Apology and Instructing Information and at times Justification.

Figure 3C: AirNZ uses Apology and Instructing Information during crisis.

The combination of an apology, a severely accommodating crisis-communication strategy, with the less accommodating strategies of instructing information and justification creates an insincere approach. This insincerity is caused by the fundamental juxtaposition between the severities of the strategies.

The insincerity is then escalated by the use of standardised replies that do not address specific complaints or give solutions, despite providing an apology that suggests acceptance of fault. The apology given in Figure 3C is not a traditional admission of wrong-doing. Instead it takes the form of a token gesture, before providing necessary information. The use of such rigid strategies may not be as effective in an SM environment, in which the participants expect solutions and answers in a timely manner. Strategies that allow organisations to provide information and communicate in a personable tone may be more effective than the use of these particular traditional strategies that create insincerity and are ineffective for the platform. The inadequacies of these message strategies are further demonstrated in Figure 3D.

Figure 3D: Air NZ used organisation replies that are inappropriate for the situation presented.

Figure 3D shows customer frustration at being redirected as the customer felt the organisation offered no solution. The lack of a specific and timely resolution, and the implementation of standardised replies indicate that Air NZ's communicators work within a rigid crisis-communication plan that only allows the provision of answers that follow a template. Autonomy is not given to the communicators, instead they are left to give responses that are inadequate and do little to protect and maintain a good reputation.

The Case of Singapore Airlines

An initial download of comments on Singapore Airlines's (SIA's) FB page indicates that SIA generated standardised replies but this might well have been an error in the system as the replies seemed identical and occurred at one (1) minute intervals (Figure 3E):

Figure 3E: Singapore Airlines' repetitive responses.

Singapore Airlines @Milind Nivendkar: Please elaborate some details about your concern to SQ_Social@singaporeair.com.sg. We will try to reply you as soon as possible.
Like · Reply · July 29 at 11:38am

Singapore Airlines @Milind Nivendkar: Please elaborate some details about your concern to SQ_Social@singaporeair.com.sg. We will try to reply you as soon as possible.
Like · Reply · July 29 at 11:37am

Singapore Airlines @Milind Nivendkar: Please elaborate some details about your concern to SQ_Social@singaporeair.com.sg. We will try to reply you as soon as possible.
Like · Reply · July 29 at 11:36am

Singapore Airlines @Milind Nivendkar: Please elaborate some details about your concern to SQ_Social@singaporeair.com.sg. We will try to reply you as soon as possible.
Like · Reply · July 29 at 11:35am

Singapore Airlines @Milind Nivendkar: Please elaborate some details about your concern to SQ_Social@singaporeair.com.sg. We will try to reply as soon as we can.
Like · Reply · July 29 at 11:32am

Singapore Airlines @Milind Nivendkar: Please elaborate some details about your concern to SQ_Social@singaporeair.com.sg. We will try to reply as soon as we can.
Like · Reply · July 29 at 11:31am

Singapore Airlines @Milind Nivendkar: Please elaborate some details about your concern to SQ_Social@singaporeair.com.sg. We will try to reply as soon as we can.
Like · Reply · July 29 at 11:30am

This and several other similar repetitive replies indicate that the airline was not immediately alerted to the crisis situation. These replies show a sense of carelessness and callousness. A subsequent download of SIA postings on 28 October showed that SIA had moderated its posts by removing all such messages. SIA minimises its communication with the public, allowing the many disgruntled voices to frame the debate against their airline. SIA's initial status update made on 18 July generated 1,304 shares querying the sincerity of the status and the accuracy of SIA's flight paths. SIA responded with an announcement on 19 July at 10.50 pm expressing their condolences to the families of MH17 (Figure 3F):

Figure 3F: Singapore Airlines's assurances

Singapore Airlines
July 18

Customers may wish to note that Singapore Airlines flights are not using Ukraine airspace.

Like · Comment · Share 1,304 Shares

Singapore Airlines We are deeply saddened by what has happened to Malaysia Airlines flight MH17. Our thoughts remain with the families and loved ones of the passengers and crew who perished on board. We are aware that our Facebook and Twitter update on Friday morning may... See More
Like · Reply · 98 · July 19 at 10:50pm · Edited

Singapore Airlines @Kristina Andersen: "We understand your concerns. Please allow us to share that we were using internationally approved air routes over parts of the Ukraine until last week. These were open for commercial flights by the national authority managing that airspace. We have since re-routed all our flights to alternative flight paths that are away from that region. We would like to assure you that the safety of our customers and crew is of utmost importance to us."
Like · Reply · 3 · July 22 at 12:15am

Letitia Martinez Perception is reality. SQ you have failed miserably at all levels.
Like · 1 · July 27 at 2:57am

It was not until 22 July at 12.15 am that SIA responded to a concerned member of the public:

They replied to another concerned user on 25 July 2014, demonstrating that their messages when posted were tailored to the concerns of individual passengers:

> **Singapore Airlines** @Goh Ws Tjc: Thank you for reaching out to us. Please allow us to share that SIA continuously reviews decisions on the use of airspace and these decisions are made based on numerous factors, such as weather, safety and security conditions, advisories from international and regional bodies, and any restrictions that may be imposed by the national authorities responsible for the airspace. We have not been routing our flights over Syria for some time now. Hope that clarifies.
> Like · Reply · July 25 at 10:07pm

These replies demonstrate the use of the Deny and Diminish strategies (Coombs, 2007) and the Denial and Evading Responsibility strategies (Benoit, 1995). SIA denied that lives were at stake and justified their actions by shifting the responsibility of passengers' safety to some other power—the 'international and regional bodies'. Unlike Air NZ though, SIA appears to address the concerns of their passengers individually. However, there is the question of timeliness, transparency and fairness. Unlike stock and prescribed responses, individually tailored ones require accuracy and tactful delivery; it takes time and requires a skilful communicator. Reliance on the same few trained people will result in limited queries receiving attention and creates a sense of abandonment and disregard for some members of the public. This is apparent in the following SIA post and responses (Figure 3G):

Figure 3G: Singapore Airlines addresses concerns

Singapore Airlines @Sim Sim: Hi, we were but have re-routed all our flights to alternative flight paths. see here for more info: http://bit.ly/1po4oUd . Hope this clarifies.
Like · Reply · July 20 at 3:36am

Rob van Albada The web page you mentioned unfortunately does not go into details, but I just saw on flight radar that now the route is much more to the South and over the Mediterranean Sea. A somewhat longer flight path but much safer. No planes at all over E-Ukraine.
Like · July 20 at 2:03pm

Fu Biaoliang Transparency is the best policy
Like · 1 · July 20 at 2:46pm

Wendy Kee Besides this undeclared war zone area, SQ please also review the safety of flying over other such areas of potential conflict, e.g. South / North Korea as we hear of intermittent firing of missiles for 'testing' purposes.....As a consumer, I do not study flight paths SQ takes. We place a lot of faith that SQ -a world class airline - does its due diligence (and even more) in ensuring the safety of its passengers. In such scenarios, it pays to be overly cautious.
Like · July 20 at 6:24pm

May Ong SIA, it seems you only have the courtesy to reply to ONE netizen call @ Sim Sim, please also answer to all others and don't practice double standard ??!!!
Like · 1 · July 21 at 3:53am

Another active FB user downloaded an earlier comment on 21 July by a disgruntled traveller whose query also went unanswered:

Claudio Facchini ▶ Singapore Airlines
7 hours ago

Besides Ukraine there are other active war zones. We flew above Iraq and Syria few days ago on our way to Milan. We will be flying back to Singapore in one week time. I have asked SIA for info about the planned route but no news

Like Comment Share

While SIA's current FB post on 18 July is empathetic towards the MH17 tragedy, the general public does not forget. This group is aware of SIA's management of their FB postings in terms of post deletions. In comparing later downloads of posts with earlier ones, it is evident that SIA has manipulated, or moderated, its page. Manipulation of dialogue shows an attempt to regain control over the conversation. However, such manipulation is often critically received by active users who are concerned with an issue and eager to engage in debate with the organisation. One FB user observed the change in postings, having captured both the earlier, arguably insensitive posting and the later post offering condolences to the grieving family of the MH17 victims:

Another user noted that SIA's display of empathy was delayed and should have come first, followed by agreement from other users. Inappropriate timing was blamed on inexperienced public relations, as shown below in Figure 3H.

Figure 3H: SIA's condolence message to MH17, captured three months after the incident.

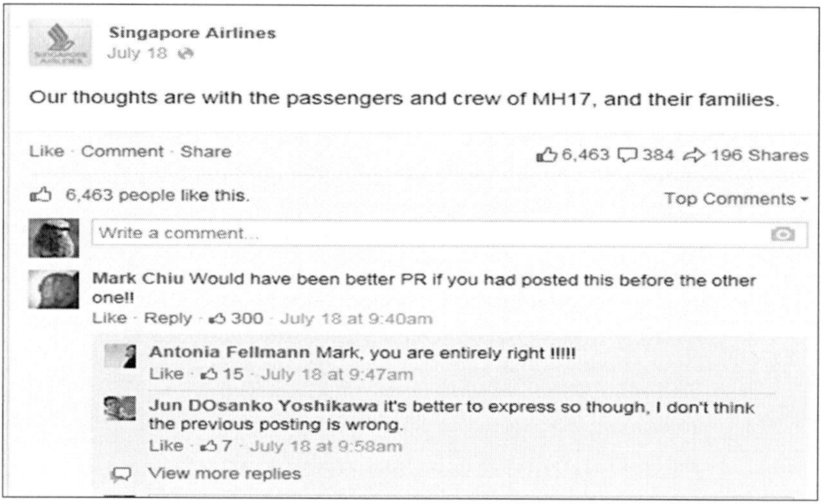

Figure 3H shows only 196 shares compared to the earlier record of 1,304 shares. Clearly, SIA has moderated its FB page on the matter, manipulating the number of shares and potentially negative feedback. SIA's lack of timely editing in the earlier insensitive post, while posting apologies for making them, suggests the importance of an empathetic tone. SM communities increasingly expect organisations to be accountable for their mistakes. Not addressing the community demonstrates a lack of sincerity, and callousness during a tragic situation.

Textual analysis indicates that both SIA's and Air NZ's current SM crisis-communication guidelines did not allow for the level of engagement and involvement that responsible participation in SM environments demand. Both airlines had delayed responses. The use of standardised replies and slow, tailored responses indicate that those who were responsible for the front-line SM communication worked within rigid communication guidelines that did not allow for either organisation to provide solution-based replies or quick, tailored responses. These findings suggest that both airlines did not appreciate the communicative opportunities that SM provides. Literature suggests that front-line communicators working with SM need to be given the autonomy to act and react in crisis situations, creating solutions and providing answers on the same platform that audiences had originally used to make their queries and complaints (Evans, 2011). Therefore, SM crisis-communication plans must allow for those on the front-line to provide timely, honest and accurate information to the community, providing solutions and offering help when appropriate. While such communication cannot follow a template, these communicators must be trusted to still display company values and its position in a personable manner, which is more appropriate to the medium. These provisions would allow organisations to avoid the use of standardised replies and over-reliance on ineffective traditional strategies that spark further frustration and anger. By allowing communicators to move beyond a script, organisations harness SM as a tool for conflict resolution, reducing the load on other communication mediums that may be more susceptible in crisis situations, such as phone lines.

Evidence of frustration and anger towards standardised replies also indicated the necessary change in tone that SM demands. There was strong evidence of cynicism and frustration to standardised replies, which is inevitably damaging to perception. SM communities expect engagement on a personable level; they provide an opportunity for the organisation to show its ‘human’ side. Therefore, engagement with an empathetic ‘human voice’ becomes key to the success of organisations participating in SM environments. As communities increasingly expect dialogue that goes beyond the traditional organisational-public engagement, it becomes imperative that crisis communicators responsible for SM pages are given the autonomy required to communicate in a more sensitive and personable nature.

While findings suggest that traditional crisis communication strategies cannot simply be transplanted into an SM environment, these strategies, and their theoretical basis, still have a role in the formation of new SM crisis communication strategies. SM users did not object to the application of Coombs’s (2007) and Benoit’s (1995) strategies. Rather, they objected to the tone of SM messages, their lack of sensitivity and consideration of the crisis situation, the absence of a human voice, the accuracy of information, and the timeliness of responses. The tenets of a pre-planning stakeholder reaction (Coombs, 2007) become even more important in an SM environment as SM crisis-communicators must be able to communicate within minutes of complaints and queries being made and therefore must prepare how they are going to respond to various situations in order to diffuse any potential negative repercussions.

Consumer Preferences

Key findings indicate that SM users expect engagement on SM platforms on a personal level. Findings validate claims made in earlier literature that SM platforms would be used by key customers to seek information during a crisis (Liu, Jin & Austin, 2013). Figure 3I demonstrates the type of information-seeking posts found on Air NZ's page during the crisis situation. Figure 3I shows Air NZ customers seeking information about time delays and weather conditions. Air NZ replies with a standard response and is unable to provide the necessary information that is sought. The inability or unwillingness to supply this information shows that crisis-communication plans may not allow for communicators to address specific queries and concerns via SM. Inability to provide information also indicates that those managing the SM pages did not have access to timely information above and beyond information already available to the public, resulting in the organisation not being able to use FB to provide the information that its community was seeking.

Figure 3I: Air NZ customers turn to FB to seek information and receive organisation replies.

Odette Sotheran ▶ Air New Zealand
19 June 2013

What are the chances of flights from Chch to Auckland being cancelled on Friday night due to the storm?

Like · Comment 1 2

Andrea Green likes this.

Air New Zealand Hi Odette, best to keep an eye out on our website for updated information http://www.airnewzealand.co.nz/flight-tracker
19 June 2013 at 12:35 · Like

Customers expect organisations to provide timely and accurate information in a clear and concise manner. If the organisation is unable to provide this information, or redirects the consumer to other media channels, key publics may become frustrated, as shown in Figure 3J, which may lead to further comments that have the potential to damage reputation.

Figure 3J: Air NZ FB community express frustration over slow replies.

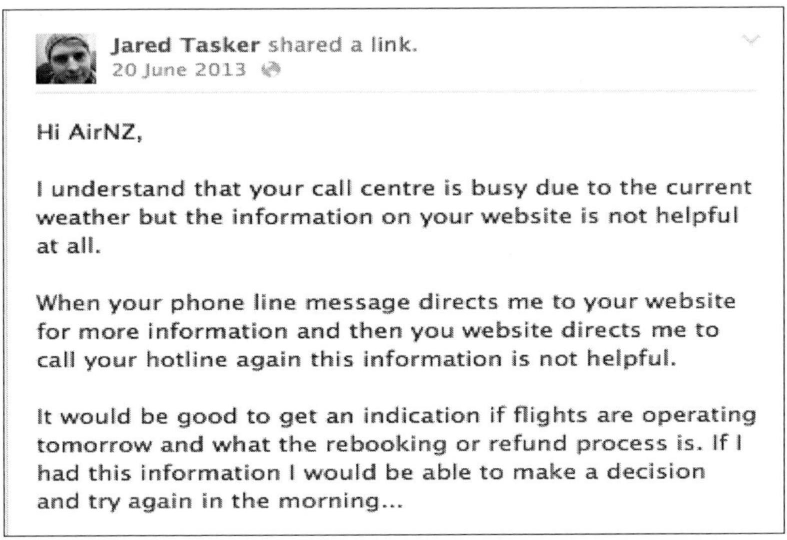
Jared Tasker shared a link.
20 June 2013

Hi AirNZ,

I understand that your call centre is busy due to the current weather but the information on your website is not helpful at all.

When your phone line message directs me to your website for more information and then you website directs me to call your hotline again this information is not helpful.

It would be good to get an indication if flights are operating tomorrow and what the rebooking or refund process is. If I had this information I would be able to make a decision and try again in the morning...

Jared Tasker Also I have no hold music or friendly indications to let me know that 'Your call is important to us, A customer service representative will be with you as soon as they become available'
20 June 2013 at 21:43 · Like · 1

Air New Zealand Hi Jared, the operation of flights today is determined on the weather. Unfortunately Wellington Airport remains closed this morning, Best to keep an eye on the following link for flight updates for Wellington http://www.ifids.airnewzealand.com/transform.... We will pass your feedback on. Thanks
21 June 2013 at 06:48 · Like

Arielle Kauaeroa Monk And the website is still actually incorrect!! All flights delayed until AT LEAST 10am.
21 June 2013 at 07:47 · Like · 1

Textual analysis demonstrates that affected members of the public required information through on-line forums and avoided other platforms that may become overloaded, such as phone lines. In Figure 3K, Air NZ customers suggest using the airline's on-line mediums as a way to overcome problems caused by overloaded phone lines in a crisis.

In the case of SIA, the importance of displaying empathy and providing accurate information in SM postings was highlighted by the backlash to SIA's original post made directly after the MH17 tragedy, as shown in Figure 3L.

Figure 3K: Air NZ customers suggest on-line mediums as a form of communication.

Aj Wade ▸ Air New Zealand
21 June 2013 near Christchurch

Can you at least update us as to how long people are waiting to speak to you? I've made 33 calls in the last 3 hours and still no joy – I'm running out of time as I'm sure many others are.

Like · Comment 2

Air New Zealand Hi Aj, we just checked with the team and the current wait time is between 12-15min.
21 June 2013 at 14:27 · Like

Aj Wade So you're aware of how difficult it was for your customers to contact you – it took 37 calls to connect and then a wait time of 17 mins to speak to someone. Maybe you should look at live chat?
21 June 2013 at 15:36 · Like · 3

Write a comment...

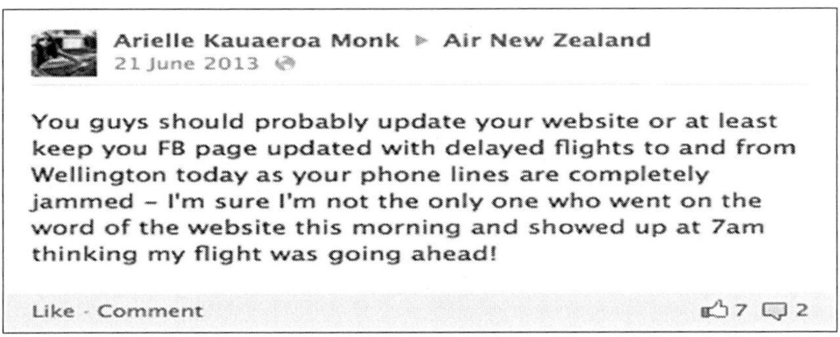

Arielle Kauaeroa Monk ▸ Air New Zealand
21 June 2013

You guys should probably update your website or at least keep you FB page updated with delayed flights to and from Wellington today as your phone lines are completely jammed – I'm sure I'm not the only one who went on the word of the website this morning and showed up at 7am thinking my flight was going ahead!

Like · Comment 7 2

Figure 3L: SIA receives backlash for what is perceived as an insensitive and misleading status update following the MH17 crash in the Ukraine.

Singapore Airlines
July 18

Customers may wish to note that Singapore Airlines flights are not using Ukraine airspace.

Like · Comment · Share 1,304 Shares

9,613 people like this. Top Comments

Write a comment...

Singapore Airlines We are deeply saddened by what has happened to Malaysia Airlines flight MH17. Our thoughts remain with the families and loved ones of the passengers and crew who perished on board. We are aware that our Facebook and Twitter update on Friday morning may... See More
Like · Reply · 98 · July 19 at 10:50pm · Edited

Hide 38 Replies

April Lim's Corner It is not just being insensitive, it actually sounds like you were trying to deceive or mislead us. I will soon be flying to Europe via your carrier, I was telling my worried family that "No worry, SIA said they are not using the same route." Your statement gave me the impression that you never use that route.......Well, "are not using" is not the same as "are no longer using", isn't it?
Like · 76 · July 20 at 1:28am

Alexander Knight They should fire their social media team
Like · 15 · July 20 at 2:08am

Ghea Santo Ghea Santo I think this page should be close down. If there is no sq page i think ppl would be doing more good things heh peace
Like · 1 · July 20 at 2:28am

Wasir Tao shame on you
Like · 3 · July 20 at 11:04am

David Ong Singapore Airlines, you have truly shown us what Singaporeans are typically like, selfish and self centered.
Like · 41 · July 20 at 12:36pm

Fu Biaoliang Still refusing to edit your original post to reflect that you stopped flying in Ukraine airspace ONLY AFTER the incident happened? Nvm, now everybody knows anyway. Even out in the papers. Clap Clap, well done SIA.
Like · 11 · July 20 at 1:30pm

Zan Oh SHAME ON YOU SIA!!!
Like · 7 · July 20 at 1:56pm

SIA's status update was seen by many to be lacking in empathy for those involved in the event and appeared to lack necessary levels of human compassion. While it could be argued that providing these types of informative posts displayed the correct use of SM to inform the public of key information following a crisis, the tone and implication of the message was unacceptable to the FB community. The response to the tone used in Figure 3L provides a strong indication of how these FB communities expect the organisation to behave. Figure 3M below clearly indicates the importance of communication on a human level, with appropriate tones, while still providing necessary information. On-line discussions following the posting indicate that while the community respected the need to use FB to provide information, the tone and lack of condolences meant that the information was provided in an insensitive way and showed a lack of community relations.

In addition to the apparent lack of sensitivity, active customers were also concerned over SIA's flight path as news media reported that an SIA plane was flying in the same flight corridor as MH17 and was only minutes away from the Malaysian carrier before the aircraft went down. FB users affected by the news did not take kindly to SIA's earlier post declaring that SIA was not using the Ukrainian airspace. This post was viewed as misleading and dishonest as it gave the impression that SIA was more concerned about passenger safety than was Malaysian Air System (MAS).

Figure 3M: SIA's FB community responds to their decision to no longer use Ukrainian Airspace.

Catherine Lim It's not about posting order it's about how it was posted .They could have mentioned about the tragedy and showed sympathy first and then announce not taking that route ! All that could have been on one post ...not post about being sorry ONLY after some people expressing their disappointment with the airline's insensitivity!
Like · Reply · 5 · July 18 at 12:57pm

Jeffery Yong Shame on you ! I am a PPS member and will definitely rethink flying with u again
Like · Reply · 10 · July 18 at 9:43am

Mark Francis yess right decision..!
Like · 2 · July 20 at 9:07pm · Edited

Dan Fitt Very disappointed with SIA over this & for the first time in 20 plus years I've been flying with you, I feel let down. My thoughts are with the families and friends of those on board MH17.
Like · Reply · 8 · July 19 at 10:20pm

Nooral Izainee Ibrahim Not going to fly with SIA, it's an insensitive airline.... Shame on you, SIA! After you've posted a silly statement, now you've come out with " let's clear the air" posting. Unfortunately, the damage has been done. You've shown us how insensitive your airline is
Like · Reply · 5 · July 19 at 1:32am

Jake Blissé

Like · Reply · 8 · July 20 at 4:14am

Figure 3N: SIA's FB community responds to news that SIA plane was using the Ukrainian airspace.

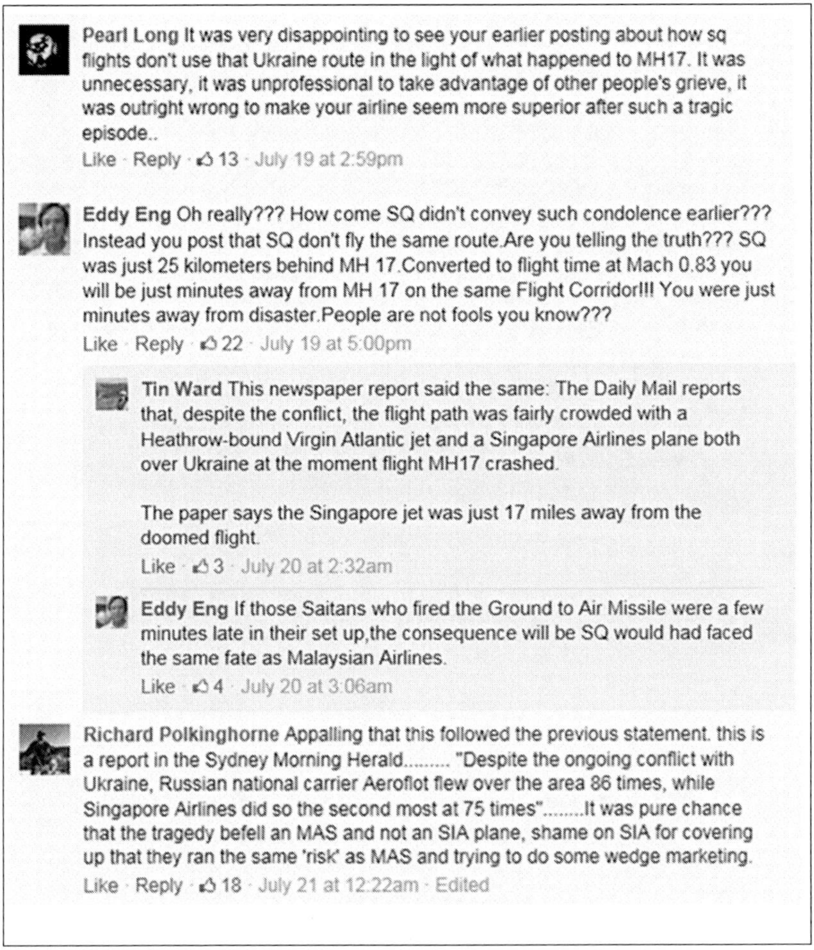

Pearl Long It was very disappointing to see your earlier posting about how sq flights don't use that Ukraine route in the light of what happened to MH17. It was unnecessary, it was unprofessional to take advantage of other people's grieve, it was outright wrong to make your airline seem more superior after such a tragic episode..

Like · Reply · 13 · July 19 at 2:59pm

Eddy Eng Oh really??? How come SQ didn't convey such condolence earlier??? Instead you post that SQ don't fly the same route.Are you telling the truth??? SQ was just 25 kilometers behind MH 17.Converted to flight time at Mach 0.83 you will be just minutes away from MH 17 on the same Flight Corridor!!! You were just minutes away from disaster.People are not fools you know???

Like · Reply · 22 · July 19 at 5:00pm

Tin Ward This newspaper report said the same: The Daily Mail reports that, despite the conflict, the flight path was fairly crowded with a Heathrow-bound Virgin Atlantic jet and a Singapore Airlines plane both over Ukraine at the moment flight MH17 crashed.

The paper says the Singapore jet was just 17 miles away from the doomed flight.

Like · 3 · July 20 at 2:32am

Eddy Eng If those Saitans who fired the Ground to Air Missile were a few minutes late in their set up,the consequence will be SQ would had faced the same fate as Malaysian Airlines.

Like · 4 · July 20 at 3:06am

Richard Polkinghorne Appalling that this followed the previous statement. this is a report in the Sydney Morning Herald......... "Despite the ongoing conflict with Ukraine, Russian national carrier Aeroflot flew over the area 86 times, while Singapore Airlines did so the second most at 75 times"........It was pure chance that the tragedy befell an MAS and not an SIA plane, shame on SIA for covering up that they ran the same 'risk' as MAS and trying to do some wedge marketing.

Like · Reply · 18 · July 21 at 12:22am · Edited

In light of proof and news reports that SIA was in fact guilty of using the risky airspace more often than MAS, members of the public displayed their sense of betrayal and unhappiness. The airline was accused of putting money before lives, failing to behave responsibly and honestly as well as lacking ethics. Many of the FB commentators debated the use of the progressive verb form 'are not using' and agreed that it gave the airline a sense of false superiority. Several accused the airline of lying and suggested that the airline should review its criteria for updates and edit its post to reflect the truth, as indicated in Figure 3N.

Figure 3N: SIA's FB community expresses their concern over SIA's lack of honesty, transparency and tact.

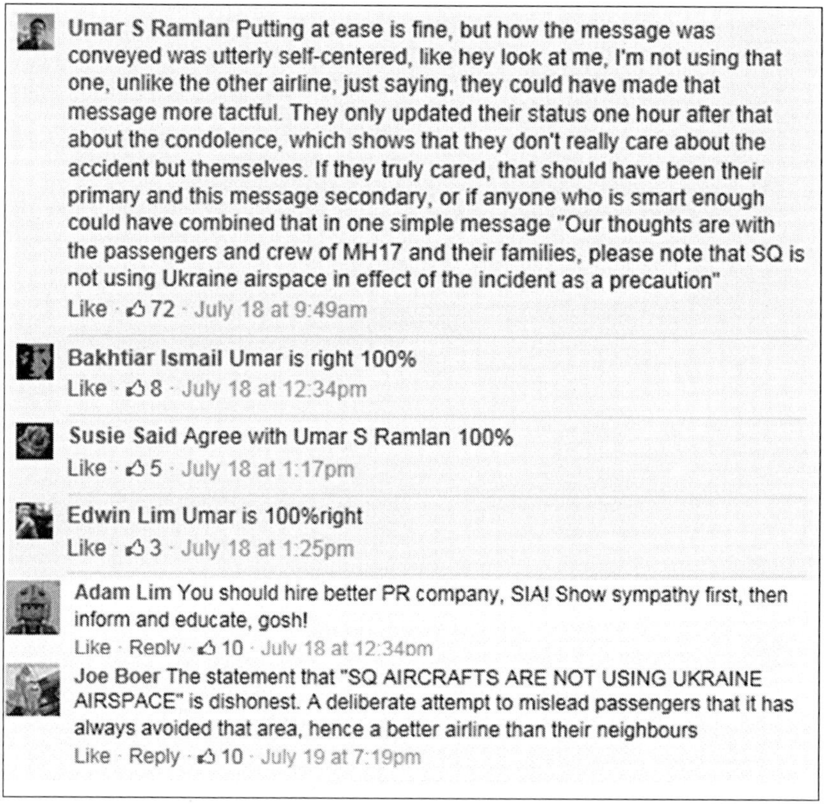

Umar S Ramlan Putting at ease is fine, but how the message was conveyed was utterly self-centered, like hey look at me, I'm not using that one, unlike the other airline, just saying, they could have made that message more tactful. They only updated their status one hour after that about the condolence, which shows that they don't really care about the accident but themselves. If they truly cared, that should have been their primary and this message secondary, or if anyone who is smart enough could have combined that in one simple message "Our thoughts are with the passengers and crew of MH17 and their families, please note that SQ is not using Ukraine airspace in effect of the incident as a precaution"
Like · 72 · July 18 at 9:49am

Bakhtiar Ismail Umar is right 100%
Like · 8 · July 18 at 12:34pm

Susie Said Agree with Umar S Ramlan 100%
Like · 5 · July 18 at 1:17pm

Edwin Lim Umar is 100%right
Like · 3 · July 18 at 1:25pm

Adam Lim You should hire better PR company, SIA! Show sympathy first, then inform and educate, gosh!
Like · Reply · 10 · July 18 at 12:34pm

Joe Boer The statement that "SQ AIRCRAFTS ARE NOT USING UKRAINE AIRSPACE" is dishonest. A deliberate attempt to mislead passengers that it has always avoided that area, hence a better airline than their neighbours
Like · Reply · 10 · July 19 at 7:19pm

Literature indicates that to successfully manage a crisis situation through SM, those that manage the SM pages must be given all available and accurate information to clearly communicate with key customers (Evans, 2011). Findings suggest that customers expect communication on-line to be timely, honest and accurate, delivering the latest information. On FB, stakeholders seek personalised, humanised replies to their SM comments, which directly address their concerns, without being re-directed to another communication platform, such as a phone number. They also expect the airlines to put relationships at the forefront with business decisions. These expectations help to shape communication strategies, as organisations actively work to provide key stakeholders with the information that they seek through their preferred communication medium, to effectively manage a crisis situation.

Findings indicate that the expectations for SM crisis-communication were not met by the airlines, which instead preferred to adopt message strategies that favoured token and limited levels of engagement and employed traditional controlled crisis communication techniques. While Air NZ's lack of timely information and solution signals a disconnect with the needs of their customers, SIA's insensitive and inaccurate statuses reveal a defensive agenda that lacked foresight. Both airlines' respective actions on FB have resulted in evident frustration and anger towards them, having a negative impact on reputation and perception. These findings suggest organisations may need to move toward communicative environments that foster open and honest conversation rather than controlled information dissemination that does not address public concerns or meet their needs. SM presents the opportunity for dialogue where both the organisation and the stakeholder could engage with each other as equals by putting aside their own motivations and support a process that involves listening, talking and providing feedback.

It can be argued that dialogue may not be possible as not all FB users enter into an exchange with the intention of listening to the organisation's views without their own agenda. However, there will be participants who are willing to put their own agenda and motives aside, particularly those who have displayed some level of respect in their comments. Using the SM environment as a dialogic platform and behaving as a dialogic participant, stakeholders and key members of the public can relate to the organisation, share issues and concerns, and give feedback in a way that may foster constructive exchanges that initiate positive change. Such an environment that, at the very least, encourages dialogic communication principles is a timely addition to today's media environment. In SM, the communications professional must be able to transition between informing, ethically persuading and engaging in dialogue so as to arrive at communication that is mutually satisfying to the participant and the organisation.

This communication does not need to end in complete agreement on an issue, but the process of communicating in such a manner, which builds trust and respect without the imposition of an agenda or views, is critical to the dialogic process. In an increasingly transparent environment, the practice of this dialogic process can be responsible for boosting reputation, as stakeholders see the prioritisation of ethical communication built on trust and respect. Therefore, in an SM environment, the priority needs to be on encouraging the organisation to engage in dialogue and to move away from the prescriptive strategies developed by Coombs (2007) and Benoit (1995). In doing so, the organisation will face the challenge of communicating with many voices, some of which may not always be as willing to engage in dialogue. However, due to the prevalence of SM and the changes it demands, the organisation needs to face the challenge by modelling dialogic communication behaviour on SM so that it becomes an accepted practice.

Examining Emotion

Various emotions were present in the SM commentary made by FB users and emotion acted as a motivating factor for sharing experiences on SM, which is consistent with previous literature (Liu et al., 2013; Coombs, 2007; Nabi, 2003; Kim & Cameron, 2011). These findings are pertinent because crisis situations, by their very nature, tend to give rise to a variety of emotions. Emotions in their own right present a major challenge to crisis-0communicators who must work to nullify negative emotions that may lead to a negative perception of an organisation. Anger, disappointment and frustration were all identified as negative emotions that were present in SM postings, which may cause a negative impact on reputation. Figure 3R indicates that those who expressed these negative emotions on the Air NZ FB page often accompanied these expressions with promises of never flying with the airline again as well as other indicators of negative repercussions for the airline's reputation. Motivating factors behind the sharing of such emotion displayed in Figure 3O included lack of communication or experiences of poor customer service.

Figure 3O: Air NZ customers air negative emotions after having negative experiences with the airline.

Philip James Dawrant ▸ Air New Zealand
21 June 2013

Not impressed with air nz's lack of help for their wellington service today. Have had three flight cancelled and transfered, which not once have we been notified about, we found out through their website. And then found out they were flying jet propelled aircraft only which they would not put on any additional flights to get the people who booked phantom of the opera tickets to wellington to see the production. Just a 'well sorry, we have flights on sunday' avaliable. (the day after the show!) Oh and by the way, we booked air nz over jetstar because they were the better more reliable company.......... except jetstar has been flying all afternoon!!!!!!!!!

Like · Comment 1 2

Possum Combes likes this.

Air New Zealand Hi Philip, thank you for getting in touch and your feedback. I am sorry to hear of your situation. Unfortunately due to the weather there have been many flight cancellations and disruptions. Our team on 0800 737 000 would be the best people to speak to in regards to your options and rebooking.
21 June 2013 at 19:22 · Like

Deharn Peffers ▸ Air New Zealand
10 June 2013

Let me start with saying how much I love Air NZ, because I do. You are my preferred airline. Today however the service I experienced whilst on the phone to one of the customer service staff was extremely poor. The girl on the other end of the phone had attitude from the start and to actually hang up on me was terrible. I did not raise my voice, nor did I use any abusive language at all, I merely questioned what she was saying and responded to her bad attitude. Not at all the type of service I would expect at all from you guys. Pretty annoyed!!!

Like · Comment 2 1

The hyperbolic nature of these comments and the strong presence of emotion as a primary motivating factor indicate that crisis-communicators are increasingly faced with a community that could be described as hyper-emotive. The imagined community created by SM further compounds the impact of the publicness of emotional content on these platforms. SM facilitates an imagined community in which users seek out SM platforms to share emotional experiences with each other and vent (Liu et al., 2013). This inevitably creates a space where negative experiences shared are more concentrated and are also more frequent as users seek to validate and support each other. This hyper-emotive situation creates a hyperbolised word-of-mouth that could be potentially damaging to reputation if not handled correctly.

Textual analysis also indicated that those who were expressing negative emotions were motivated to do so to gain recourse that they did not think was possible if their experiences were shared privately with the organisation. Figure 3P indicated that there is a strong belief in the power of word-of-mouth. The fact that the public believes in the strength of word-of-mouth is particularly pertinent in the SM environment as consumers may increasingly seek out social media, and other public forms of digital communication, to share negative experiences and seek resolution.

The perception that issues are more likely to be addressed if shared on SM creates a situation that may lead to increased negative feedback on SM platforms as people seek out the platform for recourse. To address this challenging situation, it is imperative that organisations respond to any and all complaints in a timely nature, providing solutions to diffuse the situation. Figure 3Q demonstrates the effectiveness of this strategy, where the provision of information and solutions in a timely manner diffuses the initial negative emotions displayed.

Figure 3P: Frustrated Air NZ Customer refers to the effectiveness of word of mouth via SM.

Tim Gardiner ▸ Air New Zealand
21 June 2013

As a Koru member 04341139 feel real ripped off at the moment. Needed to change my flight from Sunday to Monday and the difference was $22 in terms of the additional charges and the cost of a new ticket. In addition, wanted another $20 to book a seat. I really struggle with the cost of Koru membership and the poor value that Air NZ has for its Koru customers. A real dissatisfied customer. My sales team all have Koru which I will certainly be reviewing next year.

Like · Comment 4 6

4 people like this.

Air New Zealand Hi Tim, thank you for getting in touch with us with your feedback. It would be best to contact our team on 0800 737 000 as Koru Members should receive complimentary premium seating on most Air New Zealand flights. You can find out more information about seat select here including the conditions http://www.airnewzealand.co.nz/seat-select If you would like to send further feedback to socialmedia@airnz.co.nz we can pass this onto our team to follow up.
21 June 2013 at 21:32 · Like

Tim Gardiner Thanks for your feedback and if anyone from Air NZ wants to contact me, they have my details.....I'm done.

Michael Maitland Just go Sopranos on them! Works every time.
22 June 2013 at 09:11 · Like · 1

Tim Gardiner No Michael Maitland, these days word of mouth is far more effective. Really disappointed.
22 June 2013 at 10:31 · Like · 2

Figure 3Q: Air NZ addresses query promptly, diffusing frustration

Although the presence of negative emotions creates a significant challenge for crisis communicators, there was also strong evidence of the sharing of positive emotions and experiences. The types of comments in Figure 3R display how important positive commentary from the community is to building a good reputation. The frequency and nature of these types of comments would help counter negative comments and build a more positive perception and reputation. Figure 3S displays the importance of facilitating engagement and sharing of all experiences.

Figure 3R: Customers of AirNZ share positive experiences.

Agnes Hailes ▸ Air New Zealand
22 June 2013

Great flights from Vancouver to Auckland, then Auckland to Melbourne yesterday. Thanks to all the crew members.

Like · Comment 1 1

Marlaina Curtis ▸ Air New Zealand
4 June 2013 near New Plymouth

Wow I must congratulate the crew in Premium Economy on flight NZ1 coming from LA to Auckland 21 June. My legs blew up and they ran around found me a doctor on board and really looked after me. They organized wheel chairs as I couldn't feel my feet. Even Making the up-grade the man on the other end of the phone didn't go until I had sorted it all out and that took an hour and 20 minutes. Thank you so much Air New Zealand you've done it again.

Like · Comment 6 2

Due to the difference in crisis levels of the two airlines, it is likely that those using SIA's FB page may have been experiencing a higher level of emotion than those involved in the Air NZ delays. The loss of life caused by the MH17 tragedy and the implications for those due to fly over European airspace caused a situation where global emotions were high. The vitriolic responses to SIA's status update clearly display the presence of strong emotions in the community. Figure 3S shows highly emotive statements by those responding to the lack of emotion and empathy displayed by SIA.

Figure 3S: SIA's FB community responds to their lack of empathy with emotional responses.

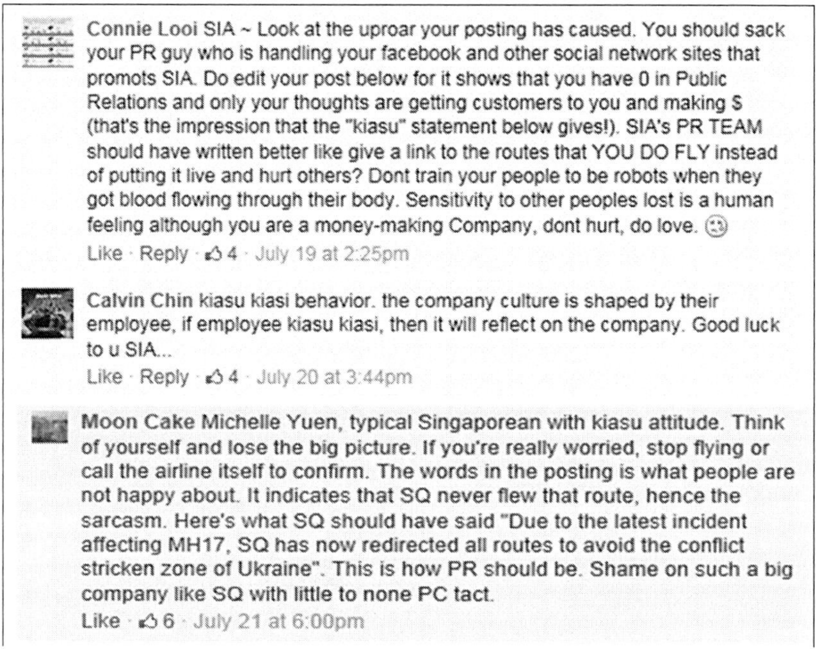

Connie Looi SIA ~ Look at the uproar your posting has caused. You should sack your PR guy who is handling your facebook and other social network sites that promots SIA. Do edit your post below for it shows that you have 0 in Public Relations and only your thoughts are getting customers to you and making $ (that's the impression that the "kiasu" statement below gives!). SIA's PR TEAM should have written better like give a link to the routes that YOU DO FLY instead of putting it live and hurt others? Dont train your people to be robots when they got blood flowing through their body. Sensitivity to other peoples lost is a human feeling although you are a money-making Company, dont hurt, do love.
Like · Reply · 4 · July 19 at 2:25pm

Calvin Chin kiasu kiasi behavior. the company culture is shaped by their employee, if employee kiasu kiasi, then it will reflect on the company. Good luck to u SIA...
Like · Reply · 4 · July 20 at 3:44pm

Moon Cake Michelle Yuen, typical Singaporean with kiasu attitude. Think of yourself and lose the big picture. If you're really worried, stop flying or call the airline itself to confirm. The words in the posting is what people are not happy about. It indicates that SQ never flew that route, hence the sarcasm. Here's what SQ should have said "Due to the latest incident affecting MH17, SQ has now redirected all routes to avoid the conflict stricken zone of Ukraine". This is how PR should be. Shame on such a big company like SQ with little to none PC tact.
Like · 6 · July 21 at 6:00pm

One notable accusation recurring in the negative posts is the term 'kiasu' to describe the 'typical Singaporean'. It is a local slang expression that signifies an attitude of 'not wanting to lose out', or 'wanting to get ahead of others', evoking a sense of self-importance. Singapore's reliance on people as a resource asset (because of the country's lack of natural resources) has led to the use of this local term to describe that competitive characteristic of the Singaporeans, generally regarded as a negative stereotype. These references feature in several FB comments as seen in Figure 3T.

Figure 3T: SIA's FB community uses 'kiasu' as an emotive trigger to lay blame

Salman Faris shame on a 5 star airline to act selfish at a time of disaster. do you still want to capitalize on a situation of this nature.
Like · Reply · 24 · July 18 at 7:34am

Yusuf Zahirsha What rubbish! I cannot understand why an international airline carrier would post such disgusting information.
Unethical.
Like · Reply · 22 · July 18 at 7:44am

Adam Lim You should hire better PR company, SIA! Show sympathy first, then inform and educate, gosh!
Like · Reply · 10 · July 18 at 12:34pm

Danny Tan I won't fly Singapore airline even if given free tickets for life with such arrogant & kiasu statement. Your statement here is indirectly blaming MAS on the tragedy. This is really inconsiderate & insensitive. Shame on you.
Like · Reply · 31 · July 19 at 5:08pm

'Eddie Corzova U did the right thing Danny!
Like · July 22 at 10:34am

Joe Boer The statement that "SQ AIRCRAFTS ARE NOT USING UKRAINE AIRSPACE" is dishonest. A deliberate attempt to mislead passengers that it has always avoided that area, hence a better airline than their neighbours
Like · Reply · 10 · July 19 at 7:19pm

Christian Fowler Not sure I want to fly with an airline such as Singapore Airlines when you don't even know your own flight routes!
Like · Reply · 86 · July 19 at 1:35am

Magdelene Lim too late....apology unacceptable!! You were lying n that is absolutely unacceptable!! You were using the same route and merely changed it to other routes after the shooting down of MH17!! This is so immoral and in hokkien "siah sueh".....shame on you SIA, SHAME ON YOU
Like · Reply · 1 · July 20 at 4:12pm

The use of local slang and highly negative responses to a perceived lack of empathy suggests that SM conversations tend to be more colloquial and emotive, presenting challenges to organisations that communicate within the medium. Such variation in the types of emotional content suggests that crisis-communicators need to gain a strong understanding of the motivating factors for emotional postings. Organisations increasingly need to understand the reasons behind posts and which response strategies will either inflame or diffuse an emotional situation in order to minimise the repercussions of increased sharing of negative emotions. As illustrated, a lack of customer service and poor communication on SM and across media channels, as in the case of Air NZ, can lead to anger, frustration and disappointment with the organisation, which are publicly expressed on SM platforms. Those who feel these strong emotions are also likely to turn to SM in order to seek recourse and force the organisation into responding. As such, it is imperative that organisations respond to emotional content, no matter how challenging it may be, and enter the debate to provide solutions before their audiences define the issue themselves, which could prove detrimental to reputation.

SM platforms mean that crisis-communicators are faced with a hyper-emotive community that could be hostile and has members that are much more likely to share emotional experiences and gain support from one another. Such challenges are unique to the SM environment and it is imperative that crisis-communicators create strategies to nullify negative emotional reactions. Findings indicate that the provision of timely information and solutions are amongst the core strategies that should be employed. When organisations respond to emotional content, they may be able to diffuse the situation and also ensure that the organisational voice and opinion is heard. Findings suggest that the airlines were ill-prepared to deal with emotional content. SM has increased the publicness of emotion and emotion-fuelled perceptions of organisations, heightening the impact that personal grievances may have on wider organisational reputation. Therefore, it is imperative that techniques are introduced to respond to emotional content to enable organisations to diffuse potentially damaging situations.

Impact of Prior Reputation and Crisis History

Findings highlight the validity of Coombs's (2004) claims that prior reputation and crisis history impact the current perception and reputation of an organisation. Although both airlines are national carriers for their respective countries, the nature of FB postings suggests connotations about the status of national carriers and prior reputations that differed somewhat between the two airlines. Both airlines are respected for their service culture although in SIA's case, there is a historical reference to strained political ties with Malaysia.

Air NZ is well respected internationally and domestically, having recently won the 2014 Airline Ratings Airline of the Year Award (*Airlineratings .com*, 2014). Air NZ is renowned for providing quality service and there is strong loyalty to the brand domestically. This loyalty creates a positive connotation around Air NZ's role as the national carrier, as shown in Figure 3U.

Figure 3U: Air NZ customers refer to their role as a National Carrier.

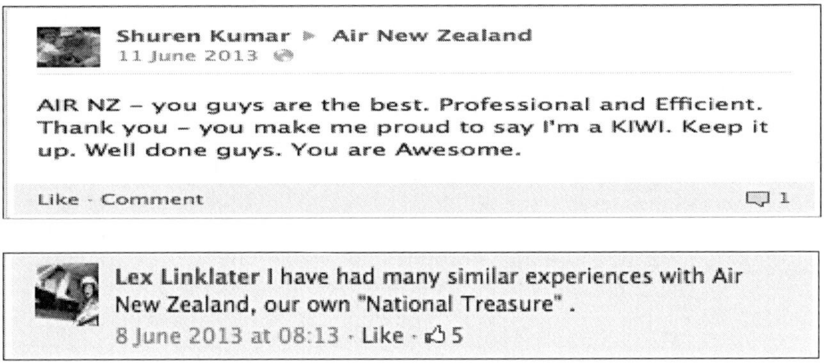

These positive connotations are further reinforced by positive comments made on Air NZ's FB page before the crisis situation, as shown in Figure 3V. These positive comments demonstrate the positive prior reputation that Air NZ held within their clientele.

Figure 3V: Air NZ customers share positive experiences prior to the crisis.

Figure 3W demonstrates how the positive prior reputation then impacts the views of Air NZ's actions during the crisis situation. It shows customers that were flying with Air NZ during the Antarctic Storm expressing gratitude towards the staff, despite significant delays and changes to schedule. The presence of positive feedback despite the crisis situation indicates that the positive prior reputation of Air NZ played a role in inviting positive feedback from customers during the storm.

Figure 3W: Air NZ clients post positive feedback of experiences during the Antarctic Storm.

Chris White ▸ Air New Zealand
20 June 2013

Thank you to the pilots and crew on Flight NZ8041 into Christchurch this afternoon. You all did a fabulous effort landing despite the extremely bad weather. On behalf of passengers, we applaude you.

Like · Comment 5 5

SIA also received a large number of comments in support of their post from those who argued that the airline was simply fulfilling an important information-providing role. These positive comments, shown in Figure 3X, indicate the importance of prior reputation, especially when contrasted with negative comments. Those who held the airline in positive regard tended to refer to its positive prior reputation in their responses.

Figure 3X: SIA's FB community defends the airline's status update.

Matthew Bramhall I think some of the comments on here are written by people that are both emotional and not thinking about the "bigger" picture. The language is appropriate and the statement is adequate for what has happened. Every western airline has reported already that they are now with immediate affect avoiding this air-corridor, including British Airways, Air France, Lufthansa and Virgin Atlantic etc. I am sure that many more will be following suit. The fact that an aircraft has been lost is terrible and a tragedy, and I'm sure that the team of SIA will have their colleagues thoughts in mind. Having flown with SIA on many ocasions there are countless staff from Malaysia working for this airline. People should remember that there are thousands of aircraft in the sky at any one time. There will be people that will be at boarding gates or about to leave shortly both in Singapore and from European destinations those passangers quite rightly would be worried about where flight will be going given the news that the aircraft was shot down.

Unlike · Reply · 216 · July 18 at 7:53am

> **Steve Tan** Hey SIA, you owe nobody an apology.
>
> So those who play the insensitive cards would rather them NOT say anything regarding the flight paths at all? Considering Singapore and Malaysia are side by side, it would be common that their flight paths would overlap as well, and customers would be concerned. Stating this, as many other airlines have, is not insensitive, it is informative.
>
> Like · 4 · July 22 at 6:55am

> **Marike Christi** Well, I have flown Singapore airlines many times to and from Amsterdam. They are terrific!
>
> Like · July 24 at 7:24pm

Comments like those shown in Figures 3W and 3X demonstrate the high positive opinion that such FB users have of SIA, suggesting that prior positive experience plays a significant role in prompting a defence of the airline. These independent voices of an active and involved public can help to create a more balanced view of the airline's service culture, lending a voice to an otherwise unrepresented participant on its own SM page.

While Air NZ and SIA enjoy a similar level of positive reputation with the public, the nature of their crisis situations differ in intensity and therefore yield different impacts to their respective reputations. For Air NZ, ideas of their prior reputation as depicted on their FB can be gleaned from their award-winning history and perceived greatness by proud citizens. In the case of SIA, Singaporeans and some identified as Malaysians indicated their preference for the airline based on past positive experience.

However, as prior reputation in the handling of Malaysian-Singapore issues was questionable, past incidents were cited to present a rather unethical version of SIA. Figure 3Z show remarks about the strained relationship between the two nations. SIA is depicted as being profit-driven in community relations, giving the impression of a negative prior reputation in some aspects of their business. Those who were angered or insulted by SIA's initial social media comment demanded action and shamed the airline into changing their statement and offering an apology. The Singaporean example also indicates how intercultural relationships may influence the prior reputation of the airline, with many Malaysians posting negative responses in reaction to SIA's status update.

Figure 3Y: SIA's FB community defends the airline's status update.

Took Bolton As I'm flying to Europe next month with SQ hearing this news got me worried whether SQ will fly on the same route. I'm relief now to be assured that they're not and thx SQ for letting us know. My thoughts are to the families of the passengers and the crews. RIP.
Like · Reply · 👍 1 · July 18 at 11:11am

Aspen Z Sanyu I hate getting involved in things like these. I really do. It'd be remiss of me, however, to not comment given the sheer level of idiocy and how ridiculous this has become. Singapore Airlines DOES NOT owe anyone an apology, especially not when many have deliberately taken an accusatory tone in response to a professional statement! I thought it was responsible of them to issue a statement reassuring their customers, given that they were merely 25km shy of an incident. Funny that some would think it's in poor taste/classless when surely they're the ones being disrespectful; a tragedy that has resulted in all those cruel casualties is hardly an appropriate avenue for promoting hate/personal resentment. Heaven forbid anyone should have peace of mind! Idiots... taking umbrage at innocuous remarks, says it all really.
Like · Reply · July 20 at 7:08am

Jimmy Arokia This is a total beatup by the stupid and ignorant Malaysians. As a Malaysian I am embarrassed by the lack of English comprehension. SIA merely advised their customers that they are not using Ukraine airspace not they have never used the Ukrainian airspace and not used to tout for business. If they have mentioned that they have not used then they are misleading but they did not. People get a life. The real perpetrators of this heinous crime of shooting down civilian airplane lies with the stupid Ukrainian separatists and you can see from the tv images that these people are essentially hillybillies with not a skkerick of humanity or understanding not to mess with the disaster zone or scene. Instead you see them parading around with children's toys and according to media report, it was alleged that most wallets and valuables have been spirited away. What ignorance and cruelty.
Like · Reply · 👍 1 · July 20 at 8:40pm

Gary Loh Gary SIA well done in your part, we respect your professionalism! I'm tired of the complaints, is it for the attention or is it for the better
Like · Reply · 👍 1 · July 20 at 11:53pm

Figure 3Z indicates that the perceived negative reputation of SIA may be influenced by Malaysian/Singaporean relations. Comments refer back to SIA's handling of previous tragedies and the relationship with Malaysia. The difference between the perceptions of Air NZ and SIA indicates that the status of a national carrier is not a sole contributor to prior reputation. The difference between the two indicates that prior reputation can be influenced by a number of factors, including regional relationship issues and prior handling of similar situations.

Figure 3Z: Singapore Airlines's customers refer to its prior reputation.

Mike Smyth I think SIA may wish to reconsider how it handles situations like this. SIA is coming across as very 'kiasu' when the greater imperative is surely to first show consideration, empathy and concern. Malaysians will not forget how quick SIA's first PR release with its tragic SQ006 crash highlighted that the pilot was Malaysian. What was and what is SIA trying to insinuate? The pursuit of profit should not result in loss of humanity.
Like · 14 · July 19 at 11:04am

Phooi Yan W This has nothing to do with Malaysia-Singapore relationship.
The posting clealy state that that they DO Not use the route.
Other airlines state that they are not using with immediate effect.
There is a very clear difference...How timely....
This give true meaning to adding salt to a wound...
Like · 4 · July 19 at 1:57pm · Edited

Kok Chwee Sim When something so tragic happens, airlines - even those who are competitors - should come together to show solidarity and seek safe skies to fly in. Between MAS and SIA, there is even more reasons for SIA to reach out to MAS and offer a hug and some kind words ... both came from the same origin as Malayan Airways, Malaysian Airways and Malaysia-Singapore Airlines.
Like · Reply · 9 · July 20 at 12:09am

Jessica Richardson SQ it is now all over the international press - you had a flight 25km away from MH17 at the time of the incident. The BUK missile system has a range of 42km. Not only were you in Ukrainian airspace you were potentially in range of the missile. It is time for you to put out a statement and apology. Unlike British Airways, Virgin, Turkish, Cathy Pacific, Air France, Qantas and all US airlines you made the decision to continue using Ukrainian airspace until MH17 went down. You have higher ticket prices than other carriers yet still used the shortest route over a war zone with known surface-to-air missile use. You have put your profits over the safety of your passengers and crew. My family and I are frequent flyers on the London-Singapore route and you have lost our custom for good. I used to be proud of Singapore's national carrier. Now I am ashamed.
Like · Reply · 71 · July 20 at 6:52am · Edited

Some FB comments, such as those in Figure 3Z, refer to SIA's past unsatisfactory performance, demanding answers to potential crisis situations; e.g. transparency in the use of future risky flight paths. These invitations to engage were met with a lack of response, showing an unwillingness on SIA's part to enter into dialogic communication on their SM page. By not entering the conversation, SIA leave their active FB users to collectively witness the growth of negative perceptions, which could come to define the organisational reputation. Because of the lack of SIA's representation and involvement in the crisis debate, the competing voices symbolise the airline's corporate culture of abandoning their public.

Figure 3AA: Unanswered questions on SIA's Facebook

Ahshad Shah If SIA is reall that concerned about the worries of its passengers, why not also give assurances that its planes are also not flying over the other war zones in Syria, Irag, Gaza, Israel, etc, just to name a few? Why not go all the way? Hypocrites!
Like · Reply · 1 · July 20 at 11:57am

Ivy Tan Why were you using Ukraine airspace before when so many airlines have taken a proper risk assessment to reroute. As a national carrier, you have not shown better risk analysis and foresight.
Like · Reply · 2 · July 20 at 1:35pm

Calvin Tham SQ, there are so many verified reports that you do infact use the very same.flight path of MH17, just that you flew at a higher altitude. Why dont you just be strong enough to admit that you flew? Admit that you made a grave PR error and get on. You apology was so insincere,"If we had offended ". So so insincere. CIVIL Airlibes all over the world offered condolences and support via social media, but instead.of offering support, you come out with a distasteful statement. Should have offered sympathies first if you want to make claims. Not tactful, no wonder you lost your best airline standing... bTW, I am a full fledge Singaporean, just do not like to pay exhorbitant rates for SQ.tickets and their service towards Fellow coubtrymen were never best!
Like · Reply · 2 · July 20 at 4:17pm

Vince Vince A few questions for Singapore Airlines. The airline knew about the danger of Ukraine airspace and had received notice not to fly the danger zone. Why the airline initially still flying the danger zone ? Shortest route ? Cut fuel cost ? As a consumer it's like we are paying for your service and you put us at risk until disaster happened and the airline makes a press release for not flying Ukraine airspace. It's like you are "slapping" yourself in the face. The company just exposed that the national carrier has no heart and were playing with consumers trust and destroying the SQ branding. I had long tried not to fly SQ partially because of the poor service rendered to Singaporeans. Now I see the company is running at the expense of consumers safety by cutting corners and I have to say its unethical.
Like · Reply · August 3 at 3:07pm · Edited

The impact that prior reputation may have on the perception of current crisis situations cannot be overstated in an SM environment. SM has digitised word of mouth systems, giving negative criticism and feedback higher 'shelf-lives' and wider audiences than ever before (Dellarocas, 2003). As SM increasingly becomes a platform to share experiences and gain information about an organisation, the presence of negative feedback could be potentially damaging to reputation. SM's accessibility has amplified the impacts of word of mouth, as people turn to these increasingly public platforms to lay complaints or give compliments. It is imperative that an organisation maintains and builds upon positive prior reputation in an SM environment, addressing complaints, engaging affected members of the public and handling criticisms in a way that resolves potential issues.

Conclusion

Analysis of the crisis communication strategies employed on FB by both Air NZ and SIA indicated that there is a need to change the current crisis-communication techniques for SM platforms and other such media forms. SM has created an unprecedented media environment in which the public voice is more powerful and more prevalent than ever before. The traditional strategies of apology, justification and diminishing risk (Coombs, 2007, & Benoit, 1995) are insufficient on a platform that seeks engagement with affected and active customers. Crisis-communicators must adopt new strategies and amend the old in order to continue to communicate effectively in an SM environment. Analysis of the crisis-communication techniques employed on FB by Air NZ and SIA has led to four key findings that can inform practical recommendations for the practice of SM crisis-communication. These findings are:

Firstly, organisations must communicate in a timely, accurate and concise manner, providing all information as it becomes available. Standardised answers need to be avoided and principles of dialogic communication should be implemented, favouring engagement and transparency.

Secondly, while emotional postings are challenging to airlines trying to maintain their reputation, avoidance of these posts leads to further frustration and anger towards the organisation, which in turn may cause further damage to reputation.

Thirdly, SM heightens the importance of prior reputation and crisis history and makes it necessary for organisations to participate in debate and counter negative feedback.

And finally, the analysis found that consumers become frustrated when information is released slowly; when standardised answers are used; when there is a lack of sincerity by the organisation; and when replies point the consumer to other channels for solving their queries and complaints. Organisations need to respond quickly and clearly, using SM to solve issues on the platform.

These findings give rise to five key practical recommendations for crisis communication strategies:

- Information provided must be clear, concise, timely and accurate.
- Crisis-communicators must have autonomy and the ability to engage with a 'human voice'.
- Organisations must engage with their public audience and respond to all feedback by providing solutions, even if the community challenges the organisation.
- Organisations must be honest and transparent in the information that they provide.
- Organisations must accept that using SM results in a loss of control over their media messages, but must continue to use the platform despite this.

SM is an unprecedented media environment, bringing its own sets of challenges and opportunities to those who work within crisis-communications. It is apparent that traditional approaches to crisis-communications from previous media environments cannot be applied directly to an SM environment without changes being made. SM communities demand interaction, openness and honesty. In such an environment, organisations will need to fully understand their role in a dialogic exchange and engage with their key customers in order to maintain a good reputation. Organisations need to deliver on promises, offer apologies when they have done something wrong and constantly offer explanations and provide information - in short, SM is moving organisations who prefer control towards dialogic communication. Traditional crisis-communications strategies still hold a place in an SM environment in terms of their relevance from the organisational and stakeholder perspectives. The message strategies of apology, justification and explanation have roots in Benoit's (1995) and Coombs's (2007) typologies and still have current relevance for applications in SM. However, these strategies should not be used in a prescriptive, standardised form. Messages should address issues raised directly and be honest and transparent. The rationale for application and the appropriate use of such messages must consider the dialogic needs of the SM environment if they are to be effective in addressing crisis in the context for which they are designed.

References

Airline Ratings. (2014) World's best airlines awarded by Airline Ratings. Retrieved March 20, 2014, from http://www.airlineratings.com/news/205/worlds-best-airlines-awarded-by-airlineratings%20Jan%2014.

Baxter, L.A., and Babbie, E. (2004) *The Basics of communication research.* Canada: Wadsworth.

Benoit, W.L. (1995) *Accounts, excuses and apologies: A theory of image restorations strategies.* Albany, NY: State University of New York.

Bhargava, D. (2010). The use of Internet in public relations and its impact on the practice: A New Zealand perspective. (Master's thesis, AUT University, Auckland, New Zealand). Retrieved from http://hdl.handle.net/10292/1052

Branthwaite, A., and Patterson, S. (2011). The power of qualitative research in the era of social media. *Qualitative Market Research: An International Journal*, 14:4, 430-440. Doi: 10.1108/13522751111163245.

Braun, V., and Clarke, V. (2006). Using thematic analysis in psychology. *Qualitative Research in Psychology*, 3, 77-101. Doi: 10.1191/1478088706qp063oa

Coombs, W.T. (2004). Impact of past crises on current crisis communication: Insights from situational crisis communication theory. *Journal of Business Communication*, 41, 265-288. Doi: 10.1177/0021943604265607

—. (2007). Protecting organisation reputations during a crisis: The development and application of Situational Crisis Communication Theory. *Corporate Reputation Review,* 10, 163-176.

Dellarocas, C. (2003). The digitization of word of mouth: Promise and challenges of online feedback mechanisms. *Management Science*, 49, 1407-1424.

Evans, K. (2011) Clearing the way for crisis communication. *Communication World,* 28, 34-37.

Facebook (2014). *Company Information: Facebook.* http://newsroom.fb.com/company-info/.Accessed 15th August 2014.

—. (June, 2014). *Investor relations: Facebook reports second quarter 2014 Results*. Retrieved from: http://files.shareholder.com/downloads/AMDA-NJ5DZ/3552719236x0x770468/310707b0-49ad-4fef-8044-dab9f32de911/FB_News_2014_7_23_Financial_Releases.pdf

Ihaka, J. (2013). Census 2013: Asians fast overtaking Maori population. *New Zealand Herald*. Retrieved http: http://www.nzherald.co.nz/news/print.cfm?objectid=11166485

James, B., and Asplund, J. (1 September, 2011). Social Media: The Three Big Myths. Gallup Business Journal. Retrieved from http: http://businessjournal.gallup.com/content/148694/Social-Media-Three-Big-Myths.aspx

Kent, M.L., and Taylor, M. (1998) Building dialogic relationships through the world wide web. *Public Relations Review*, 24(3), 321-334.

Kent, M.L., and Taylor, M. (2002) Toward a dialogic theory of public relations. *Public Relations Review*, 28, 21-37.

Kim, H.J., and Cameron, G.T. (2011). Emotions matter in crisis: the role of anger and sadness in the public's response to crisis news framing and corporate crisis response. *Communication Research*, 38, 826-855. Doi: 10.11777/0093655021038 5813.

Lindlof, T.R., and Taylor, B.C. (2011). *Qualitative communication research methods* (3rd ed.) Thousand Oaks, CA: Sage Publications.

Liu, B.F., Jin, Y., and Austin, L.L. (2013). The tendency to tell: Understanding publics' communicative responses to crisis information form and source. *Journal*

The Myth of Social Media (2014). *The Wall Street Journal*: Gallup Study. http://online.wsj.com/public/resources/documents/sac_report_11_socia lmedia_061114.pdf

Nabi, R.L. (2003). Exploring the framing effects of emotion: Do discrete emotions differentially influence information accessibility, information seeking and policy preference? *Communication Research*, 30, 224-247. Doi: 10.1177/0093650202250881.

Waters, R. D., Burnett, E., Lamm, A., and Lucas, J. (2009). Engaging stakeholders through social networking: How nonprofit organizations are using Facebook. *Public Relations Review*, 35, 102–106.

Waters, R. D., and Jamal, J. Y. (2011). Tweet, tweet, tweet: A content analysis of nonprofit organisations' Twitter updates. *Public Relations Review*, 37, 321– 324.

CHAPTER FOUR

THE ROLE OF INTERNET MEMES IN PUBLIC DISCOURSE: THE CASE OF THE PHILIPPINE PORK BARREL SCAM OF 2013

KAREN Y. VARONA

Overview

- Internet memes refer to 'units of popular culture that are circulated, imitated, and transformed by Internet users creating a shared cultural experience' (Shifman, 2013, p. 367). This paper explores the nature and content of internet memes on the 2013 pork barrel case and the role of these memes in public discourse in the Philippines.
- From Greek 'mimētpp' or 'imitator', the term 'memes' was first used by biologist Richard Dawkins in 1976 (Rintel, 2014) to refer to units of cultural information, which, like genes, their biological equivalent, are passed on from person to person by copying or imitation (Shifman, 2009/2011, p.1).
- The fast distribution of meme messages is attributed to the following characteristics: replicability, searchability, scalability, and persistence.
- In the case of the pork barrel issue, the majority of the memes came out in response to two significant events of the case: the disappearance of Napoles and eventual surrender in August 2013 and her controversial (non) testimony at the Senate hearing in November 2013. In addition, memes also came out in relation to current events involving entertainment/political figures, and to movies, television shows, music videos, video games, academy awards, beauty pageants, weather disturbances, bar examinations, and religious celebrations and holidays, among others.

Humour in Times of Crises

'Every joke is a tiny revolution.... Whatever destroys dignity, and brings down the mighty from their seats, preferably with a bump, is funny.'
—George Orwell (1968)

Figure 4A: King Kong meme

'Where was King Kong when we needed him?' the caption in the above meme reads. The photo showed the fictional gigantic ape superimposed on top of the still intact Twin Towers in New York City swatting at two approaching planes as if they were flies (Figure 4A). Kuipers (2002) noted the emergence of this new generation of 'copy-and-paste' photos on the internet after the September 11 terrorist attacks in the US. Circulated through emails or websites, most of the photos were 'clearly homemade' or 'not made by professionals' and were a combination of pictures and texts or other pictures (Kuipers, 2002). The jokes parodied, mimicked, and recycled material from mass media (e.g. advertisements, movies, television shows) and popular culture (Kuipers, 2002). The jokes were in the form of a collage (Giddens, 1991; Levi-Strauss, 1962, as cited in Kuipers, 2002) and quite flexible as varied elements could be combined and recombined to express varied messages. Kuipers (2002) noted: 'They paste the face of one person onto another's body, the slogan of one brand onto another picture. All the pictures collected are in some way composed of disparate elements. Even the simplest variety, adding a phrase to an existing picture, effectively creates a new picture with a new message.'

Rintel (2011/2013) likewise observed the spread of 'ghoulish humour' on the Internet in times of crises such as natural calamities, political upheavals and terrorist attacks. The death of Princess Diana (Davis, 1999, as cited in Kuipers, 2002), the Challenger disaster (Oring as cited in Kuipers, 2002), the US financial crisis, and the death of award-winning singer Amy Winehouse all produced widely-circulated disaster jokes (Rintel, 2011/2013).

Disaster jokes are folk productions characterized by timeliness and seriality (Rintell, 2011/2013). True to the nature of modern jokes, they are ever-changing, short-lived, and easily modified and shared (Wickberg, 1998, as cited in Kuipers, 2002). The most prevalent disaster jokes are image-based (or picture-based) internet memes (Rintel, 2011/2013), such as the King Kong meme shown in Figure 4A.

Internet Memes

Internet memes refer to 'units of popular culture that are circulated, imitated, and transformed by Internet users creating a shared cultural experience' (Shifman, 2013). Besides jokes, these also include songs, expressions, fashion styles, ways of doing, and even art, religion, and politics, which become 'viral' or spread 'rapidly and widely' (*Oxford Dictionary Online* [n.d.]) on the Internet (Shifman and Thelwall, 2009; Knobel and Lankshear, 2007).

Internet memes may come in the form of pictures, videos, animation, hashtags, websites, and others (Knobel and Lankshire, 2007; Rintel, 2011/2013). A well-known example of this in the Philippines is a viral video of inmates from the Cebu Provincial Detention and Rehabilitation Center dancing to Michael Jackson's *Thriller.* The video placed seventh in *Newsweek* magazine's 'Top Ten Memes of 2010' ('Memes', 2011).

From Greek 'mimētḗs' or 'imitator', the term 'memes' was first used by biologist Richard Dawkins in 1976 (Rintel, 2014) to refer to units of cultural information, which, like genes, their biological equivalent, are passed on from person to person by copying or imitation (Shifman, 2009/2011). This can be seen in how 'ideas, behaviours, and traditions' spread among a group of people or even an entire population (Heylighen,

1993). In fact, all cultural artefacts—images, books, poems, theories, religions, language, melodies, rumours—can be considered memes (Heylighen, 1993).

On the other hand, the term 'image-based Internet memes' or 'Internet memes' or simply, 'memes', refers to digitally manipulated photos that combine different visual elements, and/or photos of 'real' people in fictitious settings (Shifman, Coleman and Ward, 2007).

Similar to their gene counterpart, the process of 'variation, selection and retention', determines which memes will be successfully replicated, and which ones will not (Shifman, 2009/2011). Compared to earlier media forms, the Internet has the infrastructure to propagate memes globally (Shifman, 2009/2011). Boyd (as cited in Rintel, 2011/2013) identified the features of the Internet that facilitate the creation and dissemination of memes:

- *Replicability*: Digital objects are infinitely reproducible and exploitable across a range of platforms;
- *Searchability*: Finished versions of memes, as well as raw materials and templates, are easily found;
- *Scalability*: Digital objects are created for a particular audience but with the knowledge that they can spread to an unknowably large audience wherever the Internet is available; and,
- *Persistence*: Although individual digital objects may not last as long as analogue objects, they are infinitely transferable and storable in many locations.

Rintel (2011/2013) noted the 'huge' daily turnover of memes at such 'user-generated' content websites as *4chan*, *Reddit* and *Cheezburger Network*. Meme-making has also been simplified for practically everyone with the availability of engines providing raw materials and editing capabilities at such websites as *memegenerator.net*, *imgur*, and *Cheezburger (Rage Comic LOLBuilder)*. In Rintel's (2011/2013) words, the Internet has turned out to be the 'ultimate meme hothouse'.

Humour and the 2013 Pork Barrel Case in the Philippines

Often dubbed the 'mother of all scams', the controversial Php10-B Philippine Development Assistance Fund (PDAF) or pork barrel case first came out and stunned the public in the July 2013 issue of the country's leading broadsheet, the *Philippine Daily Inquirer (PDI).*

Based on an affidavit by whistleblower Benhur Luy, the *PDI* article detailed how Luy's former employer, businesswoman Janet Lim-Napoles, in collusion with some of the country's highest officials, had been pilfering billions of pesos of public funds through fraudulent projects and dubious non-government organisations (NGOs) since 2003 (*Timeline: On the trail of pork*, 02 Sept 2013).

Calls for transparency and accountability prompted the government to release an audit report, which revealed that for the years 2007 to 2009, some Php6 billion in pork barrel funds had been granted to questionable NGOs, including those linked to Napoles. The report also found that the supposed beneficiaries never received the funding or goods, and that the list of beneficiaries submitted by some NGOs contained names lifted from the lists of board exam passers published in newspapers or available online (Romulo, 7 November 2013).

The revelations sparked a series of protests in the Philippines against corruption and the pork barrel, notably the 'Million People March' on 26 August 2013, the first social-media-organised mass action in the country, which drew an estimated 75,000 people to historic Luneta Park in Manila, the capital city (*Timeline: On the trail of pork*, 2 September 2013).

To contain the crisis, the Philippine government began the process of suspending, and eventually abolishing, the pork barrel in August 2013. The Senate conducted hearings in the months that followed, which led to plunder complaints filed against Napoles and several other (mostly government) personalities, including three senators (Romulo, 7 November 2013).

In April 2015, exactly two years after the pork barrel case broke, Napoles was found guilty and sentenced to life imprisonment on charges of 'serious illegal detention' filed by her former aide turned whistleblower, Luy, and his family. As a backgrounder, the case began to unravel in April 2013 after authorities rescued Luy, who Napoles had forcibly detained in one of her luxury apartments for allegedly stealing her pork barrel money and contacts ('Janet Napoles gets life sentence for detaining Benhur Luy', 14 April 2015). Meanwhile, these events led to the arrests in late 2013 of Senators Jose Estrada, Ramon Revilla, Jr., and Juan Ponce Enrile.

Alongside news write-ups and commentaries, humorous materials on the pork barrel case circulated on the internet through social networking sites such as Facebook and Twitter, and through blogs and news websites, providing a 'cultural sideshow' (Shifman, Coleman & Ward, 2007). Among the most popular were image-based internet memes, which were also sometimes featured on primetime news television and mainstream newspapers.

Jokes (both face-to-face and mediated) and other pieces of popular culture (e.g. entertainment, fashion, food) are the basic elements of public discourse (Kuipers, 2002) making them essential to public life (Bourdieu, 1984, as cited in Milner, 2012). Through Internet memes, for example, 'the world is viewed', '[t]ruths are argued', and 'stances are taken' (Milner, 2012). Memes are an embodiment of free expression and public participation beyond the limitations of 'traditional media opinion-generation and distribution' (Brun, 2008, and Lessig, 2005, as cited in Rintel (2011/2013).

Internet memes are still generally understudied, but are gaining interest among researchers (Huntington, 2013). Scholars (Knoebel and Lankshire, 2007; Milner, 2012; Milner, 2011; Burgess, 2008) have found them to be significant in identity-formation, public discourse, and social commentary. In the Philippines, hardly any research has been done on internet memes, much less on their role in public discourse. This study is a step in that direction.

This chapter explores the nature and content of internet memes via a case study on the mid-2013 Pork Barrel scandal that dominated the news and public discourse in the Philippines for several months afterwards. Content analysis includes Internet memes on the pork barrel case from August 2013 until March 2014 located through the Google and Yahoo search engines. The seven-month period was chosen because the memes started coming out in August, in response to Napoles's disappearance after the Court issued a warrant for her arrest, and started petering out in March as the public grew weary of the long-running inquiry. Around 250 memes on or related to the 2013 pork barrel case were retrieved mostly from Facebook, in particular from pages dedicated to or often featuring Janet Lim Napoles, such as www.facebook.com/JanetLimNapulis; tl-ph.facebook.com/NapolesPH; and, Good Senyora Santibanez at www.facebook.com/GoodSenyoraSantibanez.

Other memes came from news websites (e.g. *Rappler, Interaksyon, International Business Times*), entertainment websites (e.g. *MYX music videos, Scoopboy*), blogs and Twitter. The proliferation of memes on Facebook is not surprising considering that the Philippine social network penetration rate was already at 95 per cent in 2011, earning for itself the moniker, 'Social Networking Capital of the World'; moreover, Facebook was found to be the most-visited website, surpassing even Google (*The Ten Nations Where Facebook Rules the Internet*, May 2011).

Postmodernism, Popular Culture, Humour and the Internet

Technological advances have not only made communication and transport faster, easier, and wider in scale, they have also redefined the concepts of time and space, making them 'less stable and comprehensible, and more confused and incoherent' (Harvey, 1989, as cited in Strinati, 1995). These 'confusions and distortions' are also evident in postmodernist popular culture — a 'culture sans frontiers, outside history' (Strinati, 1995). A classic example is the seminal 1980's American television crime series, *Miami Vice*, characterised by its use of collage, parody, genre stylisation, and elements from popular culture (Strinati, 1995).

Bakhtin (as cited in Reyes, 2005) described popular culture as 'carnivalesque' in that '[everything is] turned upside down', 'nothing is sacred', and 'nothing is what it appears to be'. Thus, meanings are hard to capture since they keep changing and keep slipping away. Moreover, critical theorists such as Stuart Hall (as cited in Reyes, 2005) see popular culture as a site of 'didactic struggle' — of 'containment and/or resistance', of 'affirmation and/or subversion', of 'refusal and capitulation'— between opposing forces.

Postmodernism on the internet is perhaps best embodied in its culture of 'produsage' (Brun, 2008, as cited in Rintel, 2011/2013) and remix (Lessig, 2005, as cited in Rintel, 2011/2013). Produsage refers to creating shared content in a networked and participatory environment, where collaborators are both users and producers at the same time ('Produsage', 2007). Thus, open-source software and user-generated social media sites, such as Wikipedia, are always evolving and never finished.

Moreover, new media technology and the internet have given rise to a 'remix culture', blurring the line between users and producers (O'Brien and Fitzgerald, 2006). Remixing, which involves 'modifying, bricolaging, splicing, reordering [and] superimposing original and other images, sounds, films, music, talk, is central to the success of internet memes' (Knobel and Lankshear, 2007). However, remixing has also raised ethical concerns on the use of copyrighted materials for cultural expression without consent (O'Brien and Fitzgerald, 2006). The copyright law provides exceptions for commentary, criticism and parody or satire, but determining whether remixed material constitutes any of these is a point of contention and still needs serious discussion (O'Brien and Fitzgerald, 2006).

Knobel and Lankshire (2007) observed that successful internet memes must have some or all of these elements:

1) Humour, ranging from the 'quirky and offbeat' and 'potty' to the satiric and outright sarcastic;
2) Intertextuality or 'cross-references to everyday and popular culture events, icons or phenomena'; and,
3) 'Anomalous juxtapositions of images' or peculiar combinations of photos and other visual elements.

In an early research, Kuipers (2002) also noted postmodernist tendencies in 'pictorial digital jokes' characterised by the collage of incongruous elements, which incorporate both reality and fantasy. Likewise, Shifman *et al.* (2007), in a study on digital humour, found that a primary feature of internet jokes was the unexpected combination of two incongruent components, in addition to what the authors called 'comic commodification of celebrities', wherein the images and/or sound bites of famous persons are manipulated to achieve a ridiculous effect (e.g. a bikinied Saddam Hussein consorting with Satan; prank calls using sound bites from Madonna). Shifman *et al.* (2007) further argued that people laugh at jokes because it makes them feel superior over others. On the other hand, Lynch and Raskin (2002 and 1985, as cited in Shifman *et al.* 2007) suggested that humour acts as a form of release for mental or nervous energy.

As Rintel (2011/2013) noted, internet memes come out in reaction to critical events. In the case of the pork barrel issue, the majority of the memes came out in response to two significant events during the case—Napoles's disappearance and eventual surrender in August 2013 and her controversial (non) testimony at the Senate hearing in November 2013. In addition, memes also came out in relation to current events involving entertainment and political figures within a playful context of movies, television shows, music videos, video games, academy awards, beauty pageants, weather disturbances, bar examinations, and religious celebrations and holidays, among others.

In terms of humour, the memes were mostly in the form of parodies and were generally more playful than aggressive or spiteful, depicting Napoles, her pork barrel scam cohorts and other high-profile politicians in all kinds of circumstances. The comments on the Facebook pages where most of the memes were posted were a different story, however, with comments ranging from jokingly tolerant to threatening and violent, but this will be discussed later.

True to the template established in previous studies (Burgess, 2008; Knobel and Lankshire, 2007; Shifman et al., 2007; Kuipers, 2002), the pork barrel memes were heavily intertextual, deriving humour from references to popular culture, especially the mass media. Also evident were outrageous combinations of images, or of images and texts; the irreverent use of celebrity images and/or quotes; and the frequent use of puns or wordplay. However, as humour is 'culture specific', the memes also featured 'symbols, stereotypes and codes' (Boskin, 1997, as cited in Shifman, Coleman and Ward, 2007) identifiable to the Philippine setting; as such, the memes that were created contained images of the peaceful 1986 EDSA-People Power Revolution that brought down the Marcos dictatorship; iconic characters/scenes from the movies of multi-award-winning Philippine actress Nora Aunor; Hollywood movies and all things American that resonate with the Philippine public; the faithful being anointed with ash in preparation for the Holy Week; and the local custom where the young and the not-so-young visit their godparents to ask for their Christmas gifts.

The most commonly-used references—usually in the form of superimposed images and/or wordplay—focused on popular or controversial movies, television shows, and/or personalities. For instance, quite a number of memes parodied Hollywood blockbusters, such as *The Hunger Games*. One meme entitled, *The Hungry Games: Catching Napoles* (Figure 4B), used the blurb 'Senate revolution begins with […] pork' and superimposed the face of Senator Miriam Defensor-Santiago on the body of the movie's heroine, Katniss Everdeen, shown aiming an arrow at Janet Napoles.

Figure 4B: Hunger Games poster starring Senator Miriam Santiago as Katniss aiming an arrow at Janet Napoles.

Another version, *The Plunder Games,* featured Napoles as Everdeen saluting her people goodbye prior to the Games and Senator Santiago, together with the people, saluting her back. Other parodies of Hollywood movies included *Thor, Gravity, Finding Nemo, Frozen, Transformers, Iron Man, The Conjuring, Pitch Perfect*, *Zombies*, and *Psycho*. There were also a few references to Philippine movie blockbusters such as *Amnesia Girl, When the Love is Gone, My Little Bossings,* and *Himala (Miracle).*

In contrast, references to television shows mostly focused on local or localized ones. One parody of the reality singing competition, *The Voice Philippines* (Figure 4C), used wordplay in its caption, *'Janet Napoles Kumanta na!'('Janet Napoles Sings!')*. '*Kumanta'* is rooted in the term, *kanta* (sing), which is also local slang for 'confesses'. The meme featured a 'singing' Napoles with Senator Santiago, Justice Secretary Leila de Lima, and pork barrel whistleblower Benhur Luy as her judges. Other memes parodied local or localised soap operas (e.g. *My Husband's Lover, Illegal Wife, Honesto*), game shows/game show segments (*Who Wants to Be a Millionaire, Willtime Bigtime*), noontime variety show segments (*Pinoy Henyo [Philippine Genius]*), nature-orientated shows (*Kap's Amazing Stories*) and even Korean dramas (*Meteor Garden*).

Figure 4C: The Voice.

Figure 4D: Flappy Bird

In addition, memes also referred to popular anime/manga and cartoon characters such as *Naruto,* the *Invoker*, and *Batman*, and to video games such as *Flappy Bird* (Figure 4D), *DOTA* and *Grand Theft Auto ('Grand Theft Senado' [Grand Theft Senate]).*

Besides movies and television shows, memes spoofed advertisements, advertising campaigns or advertised products. One meme reworked the Philippine government's *'It's more fun in the Philippines'* tourism campaign into *'No more fund in the Philippines'*. Other memes parodied a diverse assortment of products, including a facial cream (*Pond's Facial Cream*), epoxy (*Cord Marine Epoxy*), vitamins or herbal supplements (*Memo Plus Gold, Makahiya Herbal Capsule*), and fastfood chains *(Jollibee, McDonald's),* among others.

Memes also incorporated events, holidays and seasons as they came. One weather-themed meme featured a faux Twitter post from Typhoon Yolanda (referring to the local name of Typhoon Haiyan), which read, *'Si Napoles lang sinadya ko dito'* ('I came specifically for Napoles').

Other memes made use of timely pop culture news. Some memes drew on the notoriety of controversial American singer Miley Cyrus and portrayed Napoles twerking with an alleged senator cohort or superimposed her riding a wrecking ball. Another meme showed a scandalous image of Napoles inserted into the much-memed Oscar Awards group photo featuring Ellen DeGeneres and other Hollywood celebrities. Napoles has also been depicted as the reigning *Bb. Pilipinas* (Ms. Philippines), Ms. World, and Ms. Universe; as the proctor of Bar Exam corruption topnotchers; as *Forbes* magazine's top Philippine billionaire; as part of the official wedding picture of Great Britain's Prince William and Duchess Kate; and as Duchess Kate (with President Benigno Aquino III as Prince William), showing off a royal piglet to the world.

Figure 4E: Ash Wednesday

For Christmas, one meme showed an axe murderer hacking down a door and calling out to a cowering Napoles, *'Meri krismas ninang. Aginaldo*

ko?' (Merry Christmas, godmother. [Where's] my gift?). Meanwhile, Halloween memes depicted Napoles being hunted down by zombies or portrayed her as a zombie, while an Ash Wednesday meme (Figure 4E) showed her being anointed on the face with upside down crosses.

Finally, the memes also drew inspiration from popular expressions or terms such as *'selfie-selfie din pag may time'* (take a selfie when there's time); *'smile-smile din pag may crime'* (smile when there's crime); *'push mo yan'* (go for it); *'Napoles-zoned'* (a variation of friend-zoned or the 'let's just be friends' zone), and local political slogans such as Senator Enrile's *'Gusto ko happy ka' (I want you to be happy)* and former Senator Villar's *'Nakaligo ka na ba sa dagat ng basura?' (Have you ever bathed in a sea of garbage?)*

Thus, there is virtually no limit to the resources from which memes can draw their material. It is this, plus advances in digital and internet technology that allow memes to be easily replicated, modified, and/or passed on, that means pork barrel memes endured even during slow periods in the case.

Thematic Memes

Several themes emerged in the memes, mostly focused on the character of the people involved, in particular Janet Napoles and Senator Miriam Santiago, who was the senator who grilled Napoles during the Senate investigation. Napoles, as well as cohorts, was portrayed (1) as a shameless liar, (2) as a greedy thief, (3) as a criminal who should be jailed, and (4) as downright evil; while Senator Santiago was depicted as a judge, a defender of truth and justice, and as an adviser.

As mentioned, the most number of memes came out in reaction to Napoles' controversial testimony at the November 2013 Senate hearing and her limited repertoire of answers, mostly consisting of *'Hindi ko po alam'* (I don't know), *'Hindi ko po maalala'* (I can't remember), and 'I invoke my right against self-incrimination'. As a result, the dominant theme that emerged in the memes was that of Napoles (and her cohorts) as a shameless liar.

Figure 4F: Shameless Liar

Ranging from mere playfulness to outright sarcasm, the memes highlighted Napoles' refusal to tell the truth and the involvement of highly-placed government officials in the pork barrel case. On the more playful side, two nearly identical versions of *The Hunger Games* memes depicted a comical looking Senator Santiago as the character Effie Trinket, flamboyant chaperone to Everdeen (depicted as Napoles in the meme). In one version, Senator Santiago is holding a microphone to Napoles who exclaims, *'Di ko po alam!'*(I don't know!). In another (Figure 4F), Senator Santiago is asking Napoles, *'Sino-sino ba ang mga kasabwat mo? Sabihin mo na dahil baka ikaw pa ang ipapatay nila'* (Who are your accomplices? Speak up because they might have you killed); Napoles answers, 'I invoke my right *po*'. Other examples include at least two spoofs of the viral music video, *What Does the Fox Say?,* with one version showing the original artist and the other showing Senator Santiago asking that question and Napoles answering each time that she doesn't know (*'Di/Hindi ko po alam!').* In the latter, an angry and frustrated Senator Santiago exclaims, *'Heee! Punyeta!' (Heee! Damn it!)*

Among the more directly critical memes was a spoof of a poster of the Oscar-nominated movie *Gravity* (Figure 4G), which replaced actress Sandra Bullock's face with the face of Napoles and was captioned with 'I invoke my [right]'; the poster also featured another astronaut drifting away in the distance, this was labelled as Napoles's' alleged cohort Senator Enrile and captioned with his campaign slogan, *'Gusto ko happy ka'* (I want you to be happy). To play on the word 'gravity', the meme was titled, *GRABE TEH* (pronounced grabi-te and meaning, 'This is grave, sister'); this was followed by the subhead *Napakasinungaling Mo*; colloquially, the title and subhead translates to 'That's Just Too Much Sister, You're Such a Liar'.

Figure 4G: From the Sandra Bullock movie, Gravity

Figure 4H: Violent reaction, cursing Napoles

Another meme (Figure 4H) airs a more violent reaction to Napoles's claims of modest living despite being accused of pocketing billions of pesos from the pork barrel funds; it shows a smiling Napoles declaring, *'Hindi po kame mayaman. Sakto lang sa buhay'*(We're not rich. We just have a modest life), and a still image of a brawl from a popular local film featuring multi-awarded Philippine actress Nora Aunor captioned, *'T*ngina! Awatin nyo ako!'* (Whore mother! Stop me!).

Other memes ridiculed the attempts of alleged cohorts Senators Jinggoy Estrada and Ramon Revilla, Jr. to deny their involvement in the case through their privilege speeches. One meme, making fun of Senator Estrada's claim that whistleblower Ruby Tuason only brought him 'sandwiches' and not millions in pork barrel kickbacks, featured a burger with thick wads of money as filling. Another meme, mocking Senator Revilla's grievances over being accused and claim that he stands for truth and honour, captioned his photo with *KAP's Amazing Stories: 'Amazing story talaga'* (A truly amazing story), a pun on Revilla's nature-oriented television show of the same title.

Figure 4I: More Fun in the Philippines

No less sarcastic are wheelchair memes; these focused on the issue of how prominent personalities facing non-bailable charges, such as former president, Gloria Macapagal Arroyo (GMA), and former chief justice, Renato Corona, often found excuses for confinement in a hospital instead of in jail. One such meme had veteran Philippine actor Bembol Roco in the role of a psychic; the actor had his hand on his bald head, captioned with what translates to: 'I can sense something. Napoles will get caught. There will be a Senate Inquiry. She will get sick. She will be taken to St. Luke's Hospital.'

Another type of wheelchair meme was a fake ad for wheelchairs; it showcased 'customers' GMA and Corona, then featured one empty unit labelled 'reserved [for] Janet Napoles'. Still another version is a spoof of the 'It's more fun in the Philippines' tourism campaign (Figure 4I) where former GMA, Corona and Napoles are speeding away in their wheelchair with Senator Santiago in hot pursuit.

Other memes in the Philippine language mocked Napoles by prescribing medication to cure forgetfulness and shamelessness, such as:

- A memory-enhancing herbal supplement: *Memo Plus Gold. Don't you know the answer anymore?*
- A shame-inducing herbal capsule from the *makahiya* (shy) plant: *Makahiya Herbal Capsule. For shameless and thick-skinned people*; and,
- A facial cream for thick-faced people (see Figure 4J): *Napoles Facial Cream. For a face hard like no other.*

Figure 4J: Napoles Facial cream for hardened faces

The more vicious memes portrayed Napoles as a sex object or a rape victim; these were in response to her apparent lack of shame. Memes had

Napoles caught in two sex-scandals with local celebrities, twerking or riding a wrecking ball naked or near-naked, consorting with or marrying a local folk singer almost four times her age, seducing Santa Claus, posing in her bedroom or against the rocks scantily clad, or claiming to be another rape victim of a local television show host.

Another dominant theme is that of Napoles, as well as her cohorts, as a greedy thief. Memes used pigs and crocodiles, which are symbols of greed and avarice along with repeated references to plunder and thievery, money, and the extravagant lifestyle. The pig and the crocodile have long been used as classic symbols for greed (Ferber, 2007) or covetousness and gluttony (Soupac, 1993). Quite a number of pork barrel memes featured Napoles in porcine or reptilian form.

With her August 2013 disappearance, one meme speculated about her possible disguises and whereabouts by depicting her in post-plastic surgery form as *The Muppet Show's* Miss Piggy; there were other memes that depicted her as a real pig; as a pig or crocodile captured in the flood, such as the meme in Figure 4K, which headlines 'Flash Report! Janet Lim Napoles caught!'; and, as a prized pick for *lechon* (roasted pig) with the caption, 'You're next, Janet Napoles'.

Figure 4K: Napoles as a trapped pig

In a meme that combined the pig symbol with a pun on the tourism campaign, the faces of Napoles and seven of her alleged cohorts in the Senate were superimposed onto the bodies of pigs with a caption that read 'No more fund in the Philippines'; another meme had Napoles as a giant pig with five of her Senator cohorts riding on her back. Still another meme portrayed legislators as crocodiles basking in the sun with one asking, 'what will they do now that the pork barrel has been abolished'; while, another replies with jaws wide open, *'E di nganganga'*—a pun on the word *nganganga,* which literally means open-mouthed but is also slang for being left high and dry. In addition, after her surrender, a number of mugshot memes showed Napoles as Ms. Piggy or as having pig ears and a snout superimposed on her face.

Plunder and thievery were also recurring themes in the memes. For instance, the blockbuster movie *Thor: God of Thunder* was lampooned into *SenaThor: God of Plunder* (Figure 4L) and had Senator Jinggoy Estrada as Thor, with Napoles and Senators Revilla and Juan Ponce Enrile in supporting roles. The head of Thor's hammer was also replaced with a wooden barrel, a direct allusion to the pork barrel case.

Figure 4L: SenaTHOR: god of Plunder

Another plunder-themed meme, *Grand Theft Senado* [Grand Theft Senate] is a spoof of the popular video game, *Grand Theft Auto*. The meme portrays the pork barrel trio of Senators Estrada, Revilla and Enrile and six other incumbent senators as thieves.

Yet another meme showed people knee-deep in floodwater, lining up for rations; it had a caption that translates to 'It's better to be robbed than to be flooded like this! My goodness!', to which Napoles replies with 'I like that comment!'

There were a lot of memes that played on the words plunder, thief, and steal, such as *Plunder Games and God of Plunder*.

Figure 4M: Praying to mammon

The topic of money and pictures of cash also appeared repeatedly in the memes. There were memes that depicted Napoles in a bathtub filled with money, lying or sitting on a bed of cash, and on her haunches reaching out to a mountain of money. Meanwhile, the PDAF/pork barrel trio of Estrada, Revilla and Enrile were shown praying to an altar of money (Figure 4M). There were also memes in the form of a 10-Billion Peso bill with the image of Napoles and the trio; there was also a meme that mocked up a pay slip showing a salary deduction labelled '[for] Janet Napoles'. Moreover, memes criticized the extravagant lifestyle of Napoles's daughter, Jeane, by showing her in designer clothes, in a limousine, at her lavish birthday party, or hobnobbing with the rich and famous. One meme in Filipino featured her on a billboard thanking diligent taxpayers for her luxurious lifestyle saying, 'because of your money I was able to follow my whims', while another showed her in a photograph with singing sensation Justin Bieber and a caption that said, 'Fruit of the pork barrel'.

Another meme spoofed the controversial bar incident involving popular local actress, Anne Curtis, and her drunken pronouncement, 'I can buy you, your friends and this club,' to which Jeane was depicted as retorting, *'Yan lang? Mommy pakibili nga si Anne Curtis'* (That's it? Mommy, please buy Anne Curtis).

A significant number of memes portrayed Napoles as a criminal who should be in jail, mainly due to the proliferation of her mugshot memes in August, as well as memes showing or wishing her and her cohorts in jail.

Figure 4N: Demonised Napoles

Mostly playful, there was an assortment of mugshot memes; one branded Napoles 'Queen of [the] pork barrel'; another warned against following her example, *'Huwag akong tularan'* [Don't follow my example] (Figure 4N); another had her endorsing all sorts of things including a local showbiz couple (KathNiel Forever) and a local basketball team ('Good luck, Ginebra'); another alluded to the social media fad of gathering a number of 'likes' with its caption reading 'Just 50 likes and I'll kill myself. Promise'; another had her revealing her diet, 'I want pork'; other mugshot memes had her saying 'Go for it' for a variety of situations.

There were also a number of memes that depicted Napoles and her cohorts as prison inmates: one that used the dancing inmates of the Cebu Provincial Detention and Rehabilitation Center in the Philippines with the caption 'Senate Dance Club: It's more fun in the Philippines' (Figure 4O); another had the pork barrel trio in striped prison uniforms captioned with prison monikers, '*Pogi*' (Handsome) for Senator Revilla, '*Tanda*' (Old) for Senator Enrile, and 'Sexy' for Senator Estrada; another meme had Senator Enrile captioned with a modified campaign slogan '*Gusto ko HULI KA!*' (I want you to get CAUGHT!); and finally, there was a meme that showed a luxurious bedroom superimposed with prison bars as Napoles's prison cell, which was a criticism of the special treatment given to prominent personalities facing charges.

Figure 4O: Another tourism ad spoof

Perhaps influenced by Filipino religiosity, the dimension of good and evil also emerged in the memes. In particular, some memes portrayed Napoles (and cohorts) as evil by superimposing horns and upside down crosses, and by depicting her as a demonic being.

Figure 4P: *The Conjuring* movie spoof

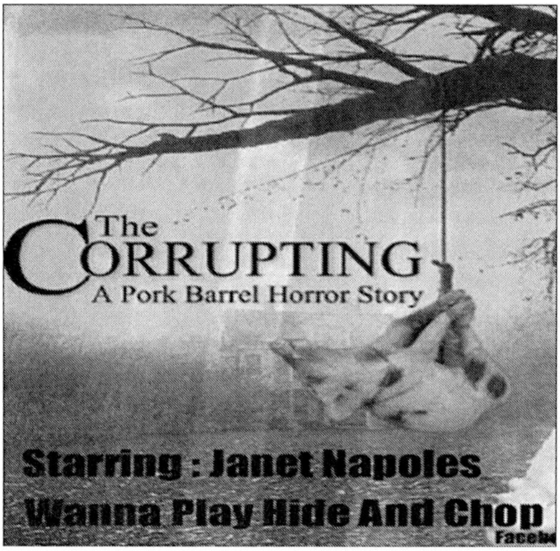

Napoles was shown with horns in a meme portraying her as the evil queen Maleficent and in one of the mugshot memes where she held up a sign that said *Huwag akong Tularan* (Do not follow my lead) (see Figure 4N); the pork barrel trio had cast shadows with horns in the 'Altar of Money' meme (see Figure 4M). In the Ash Wednesday meme (see Figure 4E), a priest was anointing Napoles with upside down crosses, signifying evil. Other memes portrayed her as an evil spirit or as the victim of an evil spirit like in a lampoon of the horror movie *The Conjuring* (Figure 4P), where she loses in a game artfully called 'hide and chop' (a pun on hide and seek). Napoles was also depicted as a witch being burned at the stake and as someone being hunted down by zombies (Figure 4Q). The zombie meme also alluded to the 1986 People Power Revolution, the historic rally that led to the downfall of corrupt dictator Ferdinand Marcos; the meme featured zombies calling on the people to go to EDSA, the site of the 1986 revolution, and join them in the hunt for the corrupt officials in government.

Figure 4Q: The Walking dead

Besides Napoles, another dominant figure in the memes was Senator Miriam Defensor Santiago, who was portrayed as an adviser, a judge, and a defender of truth and justice.

In the two *The Hunger Games* memes previously mentioned, Senator Santiago took on the role of Trinket, chaperone to the main character. In the Games, part of Trinket's duties was to inform the tributes (players) about pre-Game routines and how to conduct themselves to gain sponsors. In real life, the senator dispensed advice and explained legalities to Napoles, in effect, guiding her through the process. One of the memes even featured a direct quote from the Senator, 'Who are your accomplices? Speak up because they might have you killed.'

The memes also portrayed Senator Santiago nee Defensor as a judge and defender of truth and justice. One meme reworked *Thor* into *Miriam DefenThor* and featured the senator as the hammer-wielding Norse god with the senate in the background; it was an image suggestive of a judge banging her gavel in court.

The senator was also depicted as a judge in two meme versions of *The Voice Philippines*—*'Janet Napoles Kumanta Na'*, and *'Kilalanin ang mga Hurado'* ('Janet Napoles Sings' and 'Get to know the Judges')—where Napoles was a contestant. In another meme, Senator Santiago was portrayed as someone searching for truth and justice; the meme starts with

Santiago asking Napoles, *'Naniniwala ka ba sa sinasabi ng Bible na the truth will set you free?'* (Do you believe in the Biblical saying that the truth will set you free?), Napoles then replies. *'Hindi po. Baka the truth will send me to prison'* (No. The truth will probably send me to prison). Two memes mentioned earlier focused on showing the senator's efforts in catching the perpetrators, thereby serving truth and justice (i.e. pursuing Napoles, GMA and Corona in 'Wheelchair riding: More fun in the Philippines', and aiming an arrow at Napoles in *Hungry Games: Catching Napoles*).

Figure 4R: Spoofing classic Filipino film, *Himala* (Miracle)

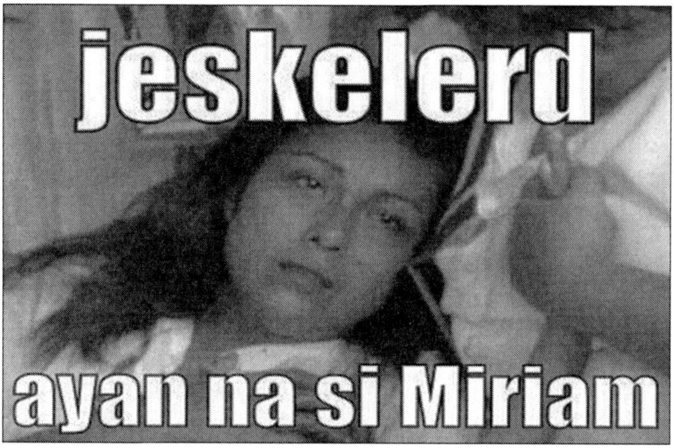

In addition, Senator Santiago was depicted as a figure to be feared, especially by those opposing truth and justice. A day after Napoles's testimony, one meme featured a scene from the classic Filipino film, *Himala (Miracle)* (Figure 4R), where the main character, Elsa, is seen clutching her chest and appearing faint, and the caption read, *'Jeskelerd, ayan na si Miriam'* (Oh my God, here comes Miriam).

However, it is also worth noting that while Senator Santiago was cast in heroic roles, she ultimately comes across as a ridiculous figure. This points back to the idea of Shifman *et al.*'s (2007) concept the comic commodification of celebrities, wherein people find humour in seeing the rich and famous in ridiculous situations. This idea is illustrated in the ingenious, satirical, and often irreverent representations of Napoles, her alleged cohorts, and even Senator Santiago in these pork barrel memes. In this respect, the internet, where the memes were created and circulated, is, to use Bakhtin's (2005) term, truly 'carnivalesque'. In this world, there is no established order, everyone is fair game, and the user is king—or queen.

Memes in Public Discourse

Overall, the 2013 pork barrel memes served as a venue for the public to participate in public discourse; they allowed people to express their opinions and take sides, and resist or even undermine the existing social order.

Primarily playful and humorous, the memes showed the propensity of Filipinos to find humour in dire situations. Beyond being a source of laughter, however, the memes became a means for people to express their opinions and take a stand on the issue of corruption. As discussed earlier, the memes portrayed Napoles and cohorts as shameless liars, greedy thieves, criminals who deserved to be in jail, and downright evil. It might even be argued that seemingly nonsensical memes such as the *Mona Poles* (*Monalisa*), *Frozen* (an animated movie) and beauty pageant (*Ms. Universe, Ms. World, Ms. Philippines*) memes were indirect commentaries on the case. That is, by making a laughing stock of Napoles and cohorts, it could be said that the memes were cutting them down to size.

Moreover, the comments on the memes on Facebook allowed people to vent their anger, primarily towards Napoles. Some of the reactions were quite aggressive and wished her ill: 'She should be slaughtered, not hanged'; 'Let's go kill her'; 'Die already, damn you, Janet!!'; 'Fry her!'; 'You'd make a delicious stewed fish'; 'If I become a doctor, and your doctor, I'll give you lethal injection right away. Damn you'; and, 'May your soul go to hell, sister Janet.'

Others called her names and swore at her. Some even used curse words or referred to ideas that were quite offensive: 'Son of a b*tch, return what you stole you follower of SATAN!!!'; 'Damn you, thiefffffffff!'; 'Stupid! I'll shoot you in the face'; *'F*ck you!';* 'Give her SH*T!'

Other comments were likewise critical but milder in tone compared to previous ones: 'You should rot in jail'; 'Pity you, the people of the Philippines against you. You have no allies, even the priest you gave money to and even the statue of [Jesus] the Nazarene brought to your house for prayers. A simple life, Janet, is sweeter, especially if you work hard for the money you spend'; and, 'You really are mother and daughter. Both swindlers!'

Moreover, by making the memes their own, people found a way to resist or even undermine the system. Whether producers, remixers, 'likers', 'forwarders', or 'commenters', people could freely criticize and ridicule the rich and powerful through the memes, thereby—in George Orwell's (1968) words—'[bringing] down the mighty from their seats' and '[upsetting] the established order.' Also important, the memes allowed alternative voices to be heard, voices usually crowded out or muted in the mainstream media that panders to the interests of the rich and powerful.

In fact, the Internet, the embodiment of participatory media for its potential to foster dynamic poly-vocal citizenship, is seen as the answer to exclusionary mass media (Castells, 2009, as cited in Milner 2013). Through the internet, marginalised sectors are able to access information and participate in public discourse just like everybody else (Milner 2013). Rintel (2011/2013) argued that the concern of future researchers should not be whether internet memes and other popular culture artefacts should be considered reasoned discourse, but rather 'what their place is in 21st century civil society'. Internet memes can be considered a form of civic action since they enable people to take an 'evaluative public position' (Rintel, 2011/2013).

Moreover, it should be emphasised that pop culture and pop humour do not cheapen but rather enrich public discourse by offering alternative ways of understanding (van Zoonen, 2005). Thus, just as music mashups (a combination of vocal and instrumental tracks of different songs) can be a form of media criticism (Atton, 2004, as cited in Milner, 2013), creating or sharing memes can be 'a political act or a performance of citizenship' (Baym & Shah, 2011, as cited in Milner, 2013).

Finally, on the importance of internet memes to the public sphere, van Zoonen (2005) perhaps phrased it best: 'Popular culture does have its flaws, but it needs to be acknowledged as a relevant resource for political citizenship: a source that produces comprehension and respect for popular political voices and that allows for more people to perform as citizens.'

References

Journals/Books/Internet Sources

Burgess, J. (2008). *Vernacular Creativity and New Media.* Doctoral dissertation, Queensland University of Technology, Brisbane, Australia). Retrieved from http://eprints.qut.edu.au/16378.

Ferber, Michael (2007). *Dictionary of Literary Symbols.* Retrieved from http://www. googlebooks.com.

Heylighen, F. (1996). Evolution of memes on the network: from chain letters to global brain. *Ars Electronica Catalogue*, Ingrid Fischer (ed.), Vienna/New York: Springer. Retrieved from http://pespmc1.vub.ac.be/Papers/Memesis.html.

Huntington, Heidi (2013) Internet memes as a form of visual rhetoric. *Selected Papers of Internet Research* 14.0, 2013: Denver, USA. Retrieved from www.spir.aoir.org.

Irvine, Martin (2005). Mikhail Bakhtin: Main Theories. *Dialogism, Polyphony, Heteroglossia, Open Interpretation: A Student's Guide.* Retrieved from http://www9.georgetown.edu/faculty.

Janet Napoles gets life sentence for detaining Benhur Luy. (14 April 2015). Retrieved April 2015, from http://www.rappler.com/nation/89857.

Knobel, Michele and Lankshear, Colin (2007). A New Literacies Sampler. *NewLiteracies and Digital Epistemologies 29.* Retrieved from www.peterlang.com.

Kuipers, Giselinde (2002). Media culture and internet disaster jokes: bin Laden and the attack on the World Trade Center. *European Journal of Cultural Studies* 2002 5: 450. Retrieved from http://ecs.sagepub.com/content/5/4/450.

Milner, Ryan (2011). The world made meme: discourse and identity in participatory media. (Dissertation) University of Kansas. Retrieved from https://kuscholarworks.ku.edu/.

Milner, Ryan (2013). Pop polyvocality: Internet memes, public participation, and the Occupy Wall Street movement. *International Journal of Communication* 7 (2013), 2357-2390. Retrieved from http://ijoc.org/index.php/ijoc/article.

O'Brien, Damian and Fitzgerald, Brian (2006). Mashups, remixes and copyright law. *Internet Law Bulletin* 9(2): pp. 17-19. Retrieved from https://eprints.qut.edu.au/secure/00004239/01.

Orwell, George (1968). Funny but not vulgar. *The Collected Essays, Journalism and Letters of George Orwell.* Harcourt Brace. CA: Retrieved fromwww.orwell.ru/library/.

Produsage: a working definition. (2007). Retrieved from www.produsage.org/produsage.

Reyes, Soledad (2005). *Reading Popular Culture.* Quezon City: Ateneo de Manila University.

Rintel, Sean (2011/2013). Crisis memes: the importance of templatability to internet culture and freedom of expression. *Australasian Journal of Popular Culture 2(2)*. Retrieved from http://www.intellectbooks.co.uk/journals.

Romulo, Michaela (07 November 2013). Timeline: Janet Lim-Napoles from scandal to surrender. Retrieved April 2015, from <http://www.rappler.com>.

Shifman, Limor (2013). Memes in a digital world. *Journal of Computer-Mediated Communication* 18 (3): pp. 362-377. Retrieved from <www.onlinelibrary.wiley.com/doi/10.1111/jcc4.12013/pdf>.

Shifman, Limor & Thelwall, Mike (2009). Assessing Global Diffusion with Web Memetics: The Spread and Evolution of a Popular Joke. *Journal of the American Society for Information Science and Technology*. Vol. 60, No. 12: 2567-2576. Retrieved from www.scit.wlv.ac.uk.

Shifman, Limor, Coleman, Stephen & Ward, Stephen (2007). Only joking? Online humour in the 2005 UK General Election. *Information, Communication and Society10* (4): pp. 465-487. Retrieved from http://www.informaworld.com/smpp.

Shifman, Limor (2009/2011). Anatomy of a YouTube Meme. New Media and Society. Vol. 14, no. 2: 187-203. Retrieved from nms.sagepub.com/content.

Shupak, Nili (1993). *Where can wisdom be found? The Sage's Language in the Bible and in Ancient Egyptian Literature.* Retrieved from www.jstor.org/stable/27909591.

Strinati, Dominic (1995). *An Introduction to Theories of Popular Culture.* London: Routledge.

The Explainer: What are memes? (13 January 2014). *The Conversation* [online newsletter]. Retrieved from <theconversation.com>.

The Ten Nations Where Facebook Rules the Internet. (May 2011). Retrieved from www.247wallst.com.

Timeline: On the trail of pork. (02 Sept 2013). Retrieved April 2015, from http://www.interaksyon.com.

Van Zoonen, Lizbeth (2005). Entertaining the Citizen. *When Politics and Popular Culture Converge*. Rowman and Littlefield Publishers, Lanham. Retrieved from googlebooks.com.ph.

Viral [Def. 2] (n.d.). Oxford Dictionary Online. Retrieved from

www.oxforddictionaries.com.
Zitron, Ed (April 26, 2011). The Future of Media is Visually Charged. *Forbes.com*. Retrieved from http://www.forbes.com/sites/edzitron/2011/04/26/visually/.

Internet Memes

Altar of money (November 2013). Retrieved from https://www.facebook.com/NapolesPH.
Ash Wednesday (March 2013). Retrieved from https://www.facebook.com/JanetLimNapulis.
'Breaking Newst! Janet Lim Napoles, nahuli na!' (September 2013). Retrieved from http://www.spot.ph.
Flappy Bird (November 2013). Retrieved from https://www.facebook.com/JanetLimNapulis.
Grabe Teh (November 2013). Retrieved from https://www.facebook.com/JanetLimNapulis.
Himala (*'Jeskelerd'*) (November 2013). Retrieved from https://www.facebook.com/NapolesPH.
'Huwag akong tularan' (August 2013). Retrieved from https://storify.com/interaksyon.com.
'Hindi po kame mayaman' (November 2013). Retrieved from https://www.facebook.com/JanetLimNapulis.
Kingkong (n.d.) Retrieved from http://www.strangecosmos.com/images/content/2259.
Miriam DefenThor (November 2013). Retrieved from https://www.facebook.com/NapolesPH.
Mona Poles (March 2013). Retrieved from https://www.facebook.com/JanetLimNapulis.
Napoles Facial Cream (November 2013). Retrieved from http://www.myxph.com/features.
Seducing Santa (December 2013). Retrieved from https://www.facebook.com/JanetLimNapulis.
Senate Dance Club (August 2013). Retrieved from https://www.facebook.com/pages/Ikwento-Mo-Kay-Delio.
SenaThor: God of Plunder (November 2013). Retrieved from http://www.myxph.com/features/6801/pork-barrel-memes-patok-sa-internet/.
The Corrupting (November 2013). Retrieved from https://www.facebook.com/NapolesPH.

The Hunger Games (*'Sino-sino ba kasabwat'*) (November 2013). Retrieved from https://www.facebook.com/JanetLimNapulis.
The Hungry Games: Catching Napoles (November 2013). Retrieved from https://www.facebook.com/SenyoraOfficial.
The Plunder Games (December 2013). Retrieved from https://www.facebook.com/JanetLimNapulis.
The Voice Philippines (September 2013). Retrieved from https://www.facebook.com/SenyoraOfficial.
'Wheelchair Riding. It's more fun in the Philippines'. (August 2013). Retrieved from https://www.facebook.com/NapolesPH.
Yolanda twitter post (November 2013). Retrieved from https://www.facebook.com/JanetLimNapulis.
Zombies (*'EDSA Tayo'*) (November 2013). Retrieved from https://www.facebook.com/NapolesPH.

CHAPTER FIVE

INVESTIGATING MALAYSIAN YOUTH'S SOCIAL MEDIA PRACTICE FOR CRIME PREVENTION

JAMILAH AHMAD AND NURZALI ISMAIL

Overview

- The rising crime rate in Malaysia is often associated with youth. This is due to the fact that each year there is an increase in criminal cases involving youth. They indulge in different kinds of criminal activities including gang crime, sex-related offences and drug abuse.
- One way to overcome the youth's involvement in crime is by engaging them in crime prevention efforts. This can be performed by using social media as Malaysian youth are identified as avid users of the medium.
- Social media is used by today's youth for different purposes, such as communication, entertainment, sharing of information, overcoming loneliness, developing new relationships and maintaining existing ones.
- Based on the Knowledge, Attitude and Practice model (KAP), this chapter discusses the potential of social media in assisting justice authorities to prevent crime.

The Phenomenon of Crime and the Youth

In Malaysia, crime is often associated with youth. They are identified as the most vulnerable to involvement in high-risk behaviours including those that are related to self-injuries, violence, suicide, substance abuse and sexual offences that may eventually lead to crime (de Guzman & Pohlmeier, 2014). Malaysian youth participation in crime is evident in the increasing number of offences reported against them (Cheng, 2014; Shah, 2013; Utusan, 2011). For instance, in 2011 there were 1,947 crime cases reported involving youth. While in 2013 the statistics revealed a staggering increase in youth-related crime cases, with 7,816 cases reported (Jaaffar, 2014). According to the Royal Malaysia Police, the number of crime cases involving youth in 2013 alone marked a 57% increase from 2012 (Jaaffar, 2014). These alarming statistics indicate a high rate of delinquency among Malaysian youth, an issue that has long bothered the nation (Kassim, 2005).

According to Mohammad and Azman (2012), lifestyle is one of the main factors that lead to Malaysian youth involvement in crime. This includes individuals who youths befriend; the level of parental supervision that they receive; and, the kinds of activities in which they engage (Mohammad & Azman, 2012). In a separate study conducted in the United Kingdom to explore youth lifestyle, risk and crime, Armstrong, Hine, Hacking, Armaos, Jones, Klessinger and France (2005) identified four crucial domains to explain youths' behaviour. These are: a) family, b) school, c) community, and d) peer. Each of these domains contains risk and protective factors that may influence the youth's behaviour and their participation or non-participation in crime (Armstrong et al., 2005).

As involvement in crime closely relates to the youth's own lifestyle or routine, it is important that they participate in positive activities together with family, friends and other members of the community (de Guzman & Pohlmeier, 2014). Participating in positive activities help youths avoid risky behaviour (de Guzman & Pohlmeier, 2014). Thus, beyond the perception of youth as minors who are always at risk and require protection, it is crucial that they are encouraged to be positive and contribute to their communities (Zeldin, 2004). This can be in the form of active engagement in positive development groups and organisations (Zeldin, 2004). It is through such engagement that youths have the opportunity to connect with adults, and participate in crime-prevention programmes and decision-making processes (Zeldin, 2004).

It is important to note, however, that Zeldin's (2004) proposal to engage youths in crime prevention efforts with other members of the community is easier said than done. As reported by the Economic Planning Unit of Malaysia's Prime Minister's Department, the state of community engagement to prevent crime in the country is generally still at a low level (EPU, 2015). This is due to the public perception that crime prevention should be the sole responsibility of the government and its agencies (EPU, 2015).

This chapter suggests that the renewed effort to improve the existing state of community engagement for crime prevention should strongly consider the utilisation of social media. This is due to the fact that Malaysia, like other ASEAN nations, has a huge number of social media users (Graham & Stephens, 2012; Stats, 2015). In preventing crime, social media can be utilised as a platform to engage and strengthen the relationship between different stakeholders, to increase awareness and to share information related to crime (UN, 2015). This platform is very effective, particularly in engaging youth, who are identified as the highest users of social media in Malaysia (Mahadi, 2013). While there is no doubt that usage of social media among the youth in Malaysia is high, it remains unclear if they utilise the platform for crime prevention. This leads to the overarching question, which this study attempted to answer: Are the Malaysian youth using social media for crime prevention? In order to answer this question, we investigated the youth's knowledge, attitude and practice with regard to their use of social media for crime prevention. The following research questions were asked: How are the youth using social media? What is the youth's level of knowledge, attitude and practice of social media for crime prevention? What is the relationship between the youth's knowledge, attitude and practice of social media for crime prevention?

The Youth's Social Media Use

Recent statistics show that Malaysia is ranked among the highest users of social media in the Asia Pacific region (Go-globe, 2015). This is influenced by the increased percentage of internet penetration in the country (Muniandy & Muniandy, 2013). As of the first quarter of 2015, the internet penetration rate in Malaysia is 70.4% (MCMC, 2015). According to Go-globe (2015), social media penetration in Malaysia is 53%, and it is sixth highest in the Asia Pacific region. In terms of time spent on social media, Malaysians spend an average of 3.3 hours on social media each day and it is third highest in the region (Go-globe, 2015).

Youths, aged 13 to 34, make up 80.3% of social media users in Malaysia (Mahadi, 2013). According to Mahadi (2013), the highest users of social media in Malaysia are youths aged 18-24 (34.5%), followed by those in the 25-34 (29.5%) and 13-17 (16.3%) age groups. The usage of social media networking sites such as Facebook and Twitter have become essential to the Malaysian youth's everyday life (Subramaniam, 2014). This is elaborated by Ismail (2014), who indicates that the youth in Malaysia use social media on a frequent basis to serve different functions, such as communication and socialisation, education, information-seeking and entertainment.

Mun, Li and Fernandez (2011) identify peer-to-peer communication as the main reason why Malaysian youths use social media. According to Mun *et al.* (2011), social networking sites like Facebook and Twitter provide ideal opportunities for the youth to communicate, socialise and connect with their peers. More importantly, social media provides an avenue for the youth to network and participate in on-line communities based on shared interest (Boyd & Ellison, 2008; Mun *et al.*, 2011). According to Shewmaker (2012):

> Social networking sites and the use of wireless communication programs allow real-time conversations with someone from a distance. This provides the opportunity to continue relationships that in the past would have been too distant and to build new relationships with friends from around the world. This open line of communication builds new understandings and collaborations for young people from very different cultures. They can build worldwide coalitions around everything from special interests and hobbies to activism activities.

Not only are the youths able to communicate, connect and collaborate with social media, but it also gives them the opportunity to share their work or content creation like images, videos and writing with one another (Mesch, 2009; Shewmaker, 2012). This indicates how social media is able to fulfil the youth's needs for relationship development and at the same time present them with a unique opportunity to become active media participants (Mesch, 2009).

In addition to communication, connection, collaboration and content creation, Malaysian youths also use social media for information-seeking and educational purposes (Hamat, Embi, & Hassan, 2012; Yin, Agostinho, Harper, & Chicaro, 2014). In their study about Malaysian university students' usage of social media, Hamat *et al.* (2012) indicate that majority of the respondents use social media for social learning purposes. The communicative and collaborative features of social media allow students to interact, work together and learn from one another (Hamat *et al.*, 2012).

Similarly, the findings of Yin *et al.* (2014) also show that besides social activities, many of the respondents are utilising social media to engage in learning. Students use social media sites including Facebook and Wikipedia, and media sharing tools such as YouTube and Dropbox, to support their learning (Yin *et al.*, 2014).

Entertainment is another important function of social media. It can help the growth of a particular social media site through increased user engagement (Weide, Ireland, and Kevorkian, 2011). In their explanation of entertainment through social media, Weide *et al.* (2011) elaborated:

> Social entertainment is the blending of entertainment content with social media functionality such as forums, reviews, ratings, and sharing and location options. The blending of entertainment and social experiences is not new, and most sites offering entertainment content incorporate various social experiences to increase user engagement with a particular site, piece of content, brand, or other entity. A key feature of social entertainment is conversation between users. This, in addition to the posting of new content as it becomes available, creates a real-time experience that is fundamental to a dynamic on-line social environment.

Among the entertainment practices in which youth in Malaysia frequently engage are downloading music and video files and playing on-line games (Baboo, Pandian, Prasad, and Rao, 2013). Malaysian youths engage in these entertainment practices to fill their free time, as well as to overcome loneliness and stress (Baboo et al., 2013; Ismail, 2014).

Based on the discussions presented in this section, it is evident that the youth make up a huge percentage of social media users in Malaysia (Mahadi, 2013). For the youth, social media is essential in their everyday lives (Subramaniam, 2014). It is through their usage of social media that Malaysian youths participate in several important community activities, including communication, socialisation, networking, collaboration, creation and sharing of media content, information-seeking, learning and entertainment (Baboo *et al.*, 2013; Hamat *et al.*, 2012; Mun et al., 2011; Yin *et al.*, 2014).

Preventing Crime with Social Media

Social media use for communication, networking, engagement and sharing of information and media content makes it an ideal platform to help prevent crime (UN, 2015). Social media can play three vital roles for crime prevention and investigation; it serves as a medium to conduct social investigations and uncover criminal activity and it is a means of engaging the community (SAS, 2015a). One way the authorities can carry out social investigation is by investigating a suspect's activity on social media, to look out for important clues and information (SAS, 2015a). In addition, the authorities can use social media to perform surveillance and to discover potential criminal activity that may harm the community (SAS, 2015a). More importantly, the authorities can use social media to engage the community by building a relationship with them so that they work together to combat crime (Denef, Kaptein, Bayerl, and Ramirez, 2012; LexisNexis, 2014; SAS, 2015a).

Social media can serve both positive and negative functions, depending on how it is used (Blomberg, 2012; SAS, 2015b). Besides its usage for crime prevention and public safety, social media can also be used to propagate crime (Blomberg, 2012). The use of social media for crime-related activities is explained by Blomberg:

> Accessible to millions of people both as consumers and, increasingly, as contributors, social networking and media websites provide a means of contact and communication between groups, some of which may have a serious impact on public safety. These sites can be used to influence opinion and to motivate either targeted groups or public opinion at large. Their potential extends into coordinating actions – including organised and opportunistic crime, political upheaval, and terrorist activity…Authorities need to anticipate the use of social media to foment unrest and incidents, especially around major events – concerts and sporting events, major political or economic summits, and elections. (2012)

Besides using social media to propagate crime, the platform is often used to spread incorrect information, including rumours, misleading facts and slander that could threaten public safety and harmony (Muniandy & Muniandy, 2013; Wok, Idid, and Misman, 2012). For instance, during the recent disasters involving Malaysia Airlines flights MH370 and MH17, as well as the landslides in Cameron Highland and severe floods in the state of Kelantan, it was found that many Malaysians were keen to share incorrect information related to these incidents (Mustafa, 2014). Not only can incorrect information disseminated through social media confuse the public, it can also cause unnecessary panic and complicate crisis-management and rescue efforts (Mustafa, 2014).

In order to avoid the propagation of criminal activities and the dissemination of incorrect information on social media, it is important for the authorities to make use of the medium as a means to engage the community, and to work together with them to prevent crime (Denef *et al.*, 2012). According to Denef *et al.* (2012), considering that media consumption, particularly among the youth, has shifted from traditional to new media, and its capability to mobilise people either in a good or in a bad way, the authorities should take this opportunity to actively interact and collaborate with them on social media to ensure improved public safety. Social media enables the authorities to share information and knowledge on crime and public safety with the youth, to respond to their queries and to encourage them to participate in community policing through the on-line sphere (Denef *et al.*, 2012).

Realising the importance of social media, Royal Malaysia Police launched its own official Facebook page in 2010, Twitter in 2011 and YouTube in 2012, with the aim of improving communication with the public, disseminating important information and increasing public awareness pertaining to crime (RMP, 2011). As of 2015, the Royal Malaysia Police has over 1.5 million likes on its Facebook page, 138,000 followers on Twitter and 5,729 subscribers on YouTube. According to the Police Chief, social media enables the Royal Malaysia Police to reach the public quickly and to inform and educate them on issues related to crime (Isa, 2015). Recently, the Terengganu State Police adopted the WhatsApp mobile application as one of its initiatives to combat crime (Sinar, 2015). According to the Terengganu Police, every district, school and mosque in the state have their own WhatsApp group (Sinar, 2015). The main aim is to improve efficiency, connect with the public, and enable them to lodge reports pertaining to crime in a timely manner (Sinar, 2015).

While the Malaysian authorities' efforts to engage the public, particularly the youth, to combat crime through social media is evident, it is unknown if such efforts are effective and successful. Is the public using social media to assist the authorities to prevent crime? It is only through careful investigation that we are able to gauge their knowledge, attitude and practice pertaining to this matter.

Knowledge, Attitude and Practice

This section discusses, in detail, the methodology of this study, including the respondents and procedure and the survey questionnaire adapted based on the knowledge, attitude and practice (KAP) model.

A total of 500 respondents took part in the survey that was conducted as part of the main research project entitled, *The Usage of Social Media in Assisting the Authority to Combat Crime in Malaysia*. The respondents for this survey were randomly selected based on the criteria that they must be between the ages of 15 and 30 and are users of social media. The respondents volunteered to participate in the study and they were aware of their right to quit at any time during the survey. Their confidentiality was also assured. As for the respondents under the age of 18, they were required to get the permission of their parents before participating in the survey. Permission was sought using a parental consent form. The respondents took a maximum of 15 minutes to complete the survey.

The survey was conducted in two different regions: (a) the East coast region of Malaysia that comprises three states, namely Pahang, Terengganu and Kelantan, and (b) the Southern region that covers Negeri Sembilan, Malacca and Johor. In each region, 250 respondents were selected to answer the survey. Among the locations in which the survey was conducted were higher educational institutions, schools, and other public places. The data collection procedure was completed within a one-month period.

The origin of the KAP survey model can be traced back to the 1950s when it was first employed to measure people's understanding, position and behaviour towards family planning (Launiala, 2009). Since then, the KAP survey has been successfully employed in different disciplines including in communication (UNICEF, 2015), education (Goutille, 2009), health (Kaliyaperumal, 2004), child protection and community development (Holman, 2012; IIDS, 2006), agriculture (Khoram, Shariat, Azar, Moharamnejad, and Mahjub, 2006) and the environment (Akpinar-Elci and Roberts, 2011; Besar, Hassan, Bolong, and Abdullah, 2013; Ehrampoush & Moghadam, 2005; Emanuel, 2010; GIZ, 2013). The KAP survey can also be adopted in studies that are youth-related (Ahmad, Noor, and Ismail, 2015; Ipsos, 2013). According to Kaliyaperumal (2004):

> 'KAP' study measures the Knowledge, Attitude and Practices of a community. It serves as an educational diagnosis of the community...KAP Study tells us what people know about certain things, how they feel and also how they behave. The three topics that a KAP study measures are knowledge, attitude and practice.

In a KAP survey, it is assumed that knowledge shapes attitude, and that both knowledge and attitude are fundamental to practice (IIDS, 2006).

Based on this assumption, it can be noted that knowledge, attitude and practice are interrelated (IIDS, 2006).

With regards to this study, a KAP survey was carried out to investigate the youth's social media practice for crime prevention. The questionnaire was divided into three main parts: a) Knowledge – six open-ended questions and 25 scale items were asked to gauge respondents' understanding of social media and crime; b) Attitude – 11 scale items were included focusing on respondents' attitude; and, c) Practice – 21 scale items were asked to understand their practice. All scale items under Knowledge, Attitude and Practice were measured using a five-point Likert scale. Prior to the actual survey, a pilot study was carried out involving 60 participants with the main aim of evaluating the research instrument. Answers for the open-ended questions under Knowledge were coded and grouped accordingly into themes. The internal consistency for all scale items under Knowledge, Attitude and Practice based on Cronbach's alpha were recorded at 0.832, 0.852 and 0.800 respectively.

This section presents the findings of the study based on the data collected from the survey. The findings are arranged according to sequence beginning with respondents' characteristics, usage of social media, knowledge, attitude and practice and the relationship between the three interrelated KAP components with regards to their use of social media for crime prevention.

Respondents' characteristics

Out of the 500 respondents who took part in the survey, 35.6% were male and 64.4% were female. In terms of age, 20.6% were in the 15-19 age group, 69.8% in the 20-24 age group and the remaining 9.6% in the 25-30 age group. When asked about their academic level, 26.6% were at school certificate level, 24.4% at diploma level, 44.2% at bachelor's level and another 4.8% at postgraduate level. We summarised the respondents' characteristics in Table 5A below.

Table 5A. Respondents' Characteristics

Variables	Frequency (N)	Percentage (%)
Gender:	178	35.6
a. Male	322	64.4
b. Female		
Age:		
a. 15-19	103	20.6
b. 20-24	349	69.8
c. 25-30	48	9.6
Academic level:		
a. School certificate	133	26.6
b. Diploma	122	24.4
c. Bachelor's degree	221	44.2
d. Postgraduate degree	24	4.8

The Youth's usage of social media

Descriptive statistics were used to analyse respondents' usage of social media. This includes information pertaining to the frequency and duration of social media usage, the sites that the respondents frequently visit and the number of friends that they have on social network. The findings show that 67.4% of the respondents use social media 16-30 times a month, 14% use it every day, 11.6% use the platform 6-15 times a month and the remaining 7% indicated that they only use it 1-5 times a month. A percentage of 38.4% informed that they spend between 1-4 hours each time they use social media, 28.4% use it for more than 30 minutes but less than an hour, 17.8% use it for 5-10 hours, 9% reported that they use it for more than 10 hours and the remaining 6.4% use it for less than 30 minutes each time. In terms of the social media sites that the respondents frequently use, many of them indicated that they use more than one social media site on a frequent basis. The findings show that the most-used social media site is Facebook with 79.2%, followed by Instagram 58.4%, WhatsApp 46%, WeChat 36.2%, Twitter 26.4%, YouTube 16.4%, blog 1.6% and others 11.2%. When asked about the number of friends that they have on social media, 37.8% informed that they have between 101-500 friends, 23.8% indicate 501-1000 friends, 19.6% below 100 friends and the remaining 18.8% have more than 1001 friends. The findings are summarised in Table 5B.

Table 5B. Social Media Usage

Variables	Frequency (N)	Percentage (%)
Frequency of usage:		
a. 1-5 times a month	35	7.0
b. 6-15 times a month	58	11.6
c. 16-30 times a month	337	67.4
d. Every day	70	14.0
Duration of usage:		
a. Less than 30 minutes	32	6.4
b. More than 30 minutes	142	28.4
c. 1-4 hours	192	38.4
d. 5-10 hours	89	17.8
e. More than 10 hours	45	9.0
Most-used social media sites:		
a. Facebook	396	79.2
b. Instagram	292	58.4
c. WhatsApp	230	46.0
d. WeChat	181	36.2
e. Twitter	132	26.4
f. YouTube	82	16.4
g. Blog	8	1.6
h. Others	56	11.2
Friends on social media:		
a. Less than 100	98	19.6
b. 101-500	189	37.8
c. 501-1000	119	23.8
d. 1001 and more	94	18.8

The Youth's level of Knowledge, Attitude and Practice of social media for crime prevention

Descriptive statistics were employed to examine respondents' knowledge, attitude and practice with regard to their use of social media and crime prevention. The findings reveal that, in general, the respondents are aware of what constitutes a crime. When asked what crime meant, 51.8% of the respondents answered that it is an act that is against the law. Another 48.2% of the respondents accept that crime is an act that is negative and irresponsible and it may cause harm to others. They identified murder, robbery, rape, bullying, gang activities, vandalism, drug abuse, illegal street racing, on-line fraud and breach of trust as acts of crime. 91.6% of the respondents agree that the youth contribute to the increase in crime in Malaysia. According to the respondents, among the factors that lead youths to crime are a lack of religious and/or moral awareness, a lack of family love and affection, poor law enforcement, negative peer influence, a lack of knowledge, poverty, and the harmful effect of media (see Table 5C).

Table 5C. Knowledge of social media and crime

No.	Item	Strongly Disagree & Disagree (%)	Not Sure (%)	Strongly Agree & Agree (%)
1	Crime is an issue that is taken seriously by the authorities.	8.8	16.8	74.8
2	Crime is an act prohibited by religion.	6.2	7.4	86.4
3	Crime cases are increasing each year.	3.0	11.8	85.2
4	Crime cases mostly involve youth.	6.8	14.6	78.6
5	Crime can threaten the safety of the country.	1.4	6.0	92.6
6	Crime can hamper the development of the country.	4.8	8.2	87
7	Crime can create anxiety.	1.6	8.6	89.8
8	Crime can have a negative impact on people's lives.	1.2	7.4	91.4
9	Crime threatens the economy.	3.4	13.8	82.8
10		1.8	6.8	91.4
11	Crime negatively impacts national harmony.	14.4	31.6	54

12	Crime can be dealt with using social media. Social media can be used:			
a.	For entertainment	8	22	70
b.	To manipulate	49.4	14.2	36.4
c.	To deliver information	4.2	8.8	87
d.	To incite hatred	54.4	11	34.6
e.	To get information	7.6	7.0	85.4
f.	To disseminate false news	54.2	10.2	35.6
g.	To persuade	27.6	27.4	45
h.	To imitate negative behaviour	57	8.6	34.4
i.	To educate	7.8	11.6	80.6
j.	To invade others' privacy	55	10.8	34.2
k.	To learn	7.0	10.6	82.4
l.	To access porn sites	58.8	11.4	29.8
m.	To build relationships	3.4	13.2	83.4
n.	To share information	2.6	10.4	87

In addition to the open-ended questions, an additional 25 scale questions were asked to understand further the youth's knowledge of social media and crime. The findings reveal that the mean score for knowledge was M=3.74, which indicates that the respondents' understanding pertaining to social media and crime is moderately high. A good number of respondents (85.2%) agree that crime cases are rising each year in Malaysia. When probed on the impact of crime, the respondents believe that it can threaten public safety (92.6%), national harmony (91.4%) and the country's development (87%). When asked about their knowledge of social media, the respondents think that the platform can be effectively used to deliver information (87%), share information (87%), get information (85.4%), build friendships (83.4%), learn (82.4%), educate (80.6%) and entertain (70%). However, when enquired about the role of social media to combat crime, only 54% of the respondents believe that it can be utilised for crime prevention. The findings are summarised in Table 5D.

Table 5D. Attitude of social media and crime

No.	Item	Strongly Disagree & Disagree (%)	Not Sure (%)	Strongly Agree & Agree (%)
1	Crime is an important topic discussed by members of the community.	6.6	22	71.4
2	Crime is a shared responsibility of the authority and the public.	3.2	7.8	89
3	Crime needs to be dealt with urgently.	0.6	6.4	93
4	Crime needs to be dealt with using different methods.	1.6	6.6	91.8
5	In dealing with crime, I am:			
	a. Very interested in assisting the authorities	3	29.6	67.4
	b. Willing to contribute and assist	2.2	25.6	72.2
	c. Ready to assist whenever needed	2.6	29.2	68.2
6	I can use social media to prevent crime because:			
	a. It is the medium I trust	16.4	45.6	38
	b. It is easy to use	1.8	22.6	75.6
	c. It is an effective medium	7.8	35.2	57
	d. It allows me to disseminate information swiftly	3.6	19.2	77.6

Similar to knowledge, the respondents' attitude was also moderately high. The mean score for attitude was M=3.97. A strong majority (89%) agree that crime prevention is a shared responsibility of the authorities and the public. They believe that the issue needs to be dealt with urgently (93%), using different methods and strategies (91.8%). On the other hand, a lower percentage (67.4%) of respondents showed interest in assisting authorities in combating crime. In terms of the respondents' attitude towards social media, only 38% of the respondents think that it can be a trusted platform to prevent crime even though a high 77.6% of the respondents think that information can be disseminated swiftly through social media, only 57% believe that it is an effective platform for crime prevention (see Table 5E).

Table 5E. Practice of social media and crime

No.	Item	Strongly Disagree & Disagree (%)	Not Sure (%)	Strongly Agree & Agree (%)
1	To avoid being involved in crime, I:			
	a. Avoid negative activities	2.8	6.4	90.8
	b. Acquire religious knowledge	2.2	6.0	91.8
	c. Avoid being with negative individuals	8.4	10.8	80.8
	d. Engage in useful activities	1.0	5.8	93.2
	e. Listen to parents' advice	0.4	4.8	94.8
	f. Make sure I'm with friends who have a positive attitude	2.4	10.8	86.8
2	Social media is the medium I use the most.	5.6	24	70.4
3	I frequently use social media:			
	a. For entertainment	21.6	15.6	62.8
	b. To manipulate	79.6	14.4	6.0
	c. To deliver information	20.6	12.8	66.6
	d. To incite hatred	81.4	10	8.6
	e. To get information	15.8	5.6	78.6
	f. To disseminate false news	82.2	9.8	8.0
	g. To persuade			
	h. To imitate negative behaviour	55.2	23.8	21
	i. To educate			
	j. To invade others' privacy	80.8	11.2	8.0
	k. To learn			
	l. To access porn sites	18.8	17.2	64
	m. To build relationships	78.8	11.4	9.8
	n. To share information	14.2	8.6	77.2
		81.8	10.8	7.4
		12	9.4	78.6
		11.2	6.6	82.2

In comparison to knowledge and attitude, the mean score for practice was slightly lower at M=3.27. When asked on how to avoid committing crime, a vast majority of the respondents agree that they should avoid engaging in negative/high-risk activities (90.8%) and being with problematic individuals (80.8%), acquire religious knowledge (91.8%), listen to parents' advice (94.8%) and engage in useful activities (93.2%). In terms of their social media practice, 70.4% of the respondents agree that social media is the medium that they use the most. When asked about their purposes for using social media, the respondents indicate that they use it to share information (82.2%), build friendships (78.6%), learn (77.2%), educate (64%) and for entertainment (62.8%). Even though majority of the respondents ascertained that they do not engage in negative practices on social media, it is important to acknowledge that there are still those who frequently use the medium to invade others' privacy (9.8%), incite hatred (8.6%), disseminate inaccurate news and rumours (8%), access porn sites (7.4%) and manipulate others (6%). The findings are summarised in Table 5E.

The relationship between the youth's knowledge, attitude and practice of social media for crime prevention

Correlation coefficient was employed to analyse the relationship between youth's knowledge, attitude and practice of social media and crime prevention. The findings in Table 6 show that there were significant positive relationships involving all three variables. The strengths of the relationships however, vary from weak to moderate. The relationship between knowledge and attitude was r=.510, n=500, p=<0.01; knowledge and practice r=.517, n=500, p=<0.01; attitude and practice r=.380, n=500, p=<0.01.

Table 5F. Correlation Test between Knowledge, Attitude and Practice

		Knowledge	Attitude	Practice
Knowledge	Pearson Correlation	1	.510**	.517**
	Sig. (2-tailed)		.000	.000
	N	500	500	500
Attitude	Pearson Correlation	.510**	1	.380**
	Sig. (2-tailed)	.000		.000
	N	500	500	500
Practice	Pearson Correlation	.517**	.380**	1
	Sig. (2-tailed)	.000	.000	
	N	500	500	500

Note. **Correlation is significant at 0.01 level (2-tailed)

It is evident that Malaysian youths are avid users of social media. This is shown in their frequency of usage and the duration of time they spend on social media. This finding is similar to Mahadi (2013) and Subramaniam (2014) who indicate that Malaysian youths are frequent users of social media and they regard the medium as important in their everyday lives. Facebook remains as the most frequently used social media site, followed by Instagram, WhatsApp, WeChat and Twitter. The fragmented and decentralised behaviour of the youth has turned social media into niche clusters of different sites, such as for instant messaging, news monitoring and photo sharing (Holliday, 2014). This, coupled with the youth's demand for privacy, have in fact transformed instant messaging applications such as WhatsApp and WeChat into the new breed of social media (Holliday, 2014).

In terms of the number of friends that they have, the findings of this study show that about 46% of the respondents have more than 500 friends on social media. According to Tong, Heide and Langwell (2008), the number of friends that the youth have on social media gives a certain impression of themselves. Some believe that having a huge number of friends on social media would make them more attractive (Tong et al., 2008). Hence, in order to make themselves look attractive, youths may be persuaded to randomly add 'friends' including strangers on their social network (Ismail, 2014).

Based on the findings of this study, it can be noted that the youth in general have a moderate knowledge of social media for crime prevention. The youth are aware of what constitutes a crime, factors leading to crime and the negative implications of crime to the individual, the society and the country. They are also aware of the potential of social media for swift information dissemination. Despite its potential as a medium for information-sharing, including those that are crime related, only 54% of the respondents of this study think that social media can be effectively employed for crime prevention. This finding in particular signifies that youths need to be better informed about the crucial role of social media in combating crime. As Fairbairn, Bivens and Dawson (2013) suggested, social media should be utilised as a crime prevention tool, due to its nature that provides opportunities for youth engagement and innovation.

Similar to knowledge, the youth show a moderate attitude towards social media for crime prevention. A huge percentage (89%) of the respondents agree that crime prevention should involve not only the authorities but also the public at large. However, the youth's willingness to assist the authorities in combating crime can be improved further. This is to ensure that the Malaysian government's aspiration to improve the public's participation in crime prevention efforts can be achieved (EPU, 2015). While the youth who participated in this study generally believe that crime prevention should take into consideration different means and strategies, only 57% of them consider social media as a viable tool to prevent crime. This is probably due to a lack of trust. In their explanation, Kim and Ahmad (2013) elaborated that the youth's willingness to participate in a particular social media community is very much dependent on their level of trust.

In relation to practice, the youth in general believe that, in order to avoid committing crime, they should acquire religious and moral knowledge, listen to parents' advice and engage in useful activities. In terms of their social media usage, the youth use the medium mainly to share information and build relationships. This finding is similar to Mesch (2009), Mun et al. (2011), Shewmaker (2012) who indicate that building and maintaining relationships and sharing information are the main reasons why the youth use social media. Even though a vast majority of youths who participated in this study ascertained that they do not engage in illegal and immoral behaviour on social media, it is important to note that there are still a small minority who frequently use the medium to access porn sites, incite hatred, and spread inaccurate news and information.

Based on the findings, we have found that relationships exist between knowledge, attitude and practice. This finding reaffirms the presumption that knowledge influences attitude and both knowledge and attitude are determinants for practice (IIDS, 2006). In relation to the youth's use of social media for crime prevention, it is important to continue to educate them on the potential of social media and to encourage them to utilise the medium as an effective means to combat crime. As proposed by Wolff, McDevitt, and Stark (2011), social media is the youth's main source of information; hence, it is important to communicate with them using the medium and to develop an effective crime prevention strategy with it. The key to success is to be able to engage the youth's participation in the crime prevention programme (Wolff et al., 2011). This however, is not easy to achieve, considering the liberatal nature of young people. They regard an on-line space that is built for them as being too formal, rigid and irrelevant (Brandtzæg, Haugstveit, Lüders, & Følstad, 2015). Thus, in order to engage their participation through social media, it is necessary to provide them with a space that is non-institutional and less formal (Brandtzæg et al., 2015).

This study investigated the youth's knowledge, attitude and practice of social media for crime prevention. The findings show that, Malaysian youth in general possess moderate knowledge, attitude and practice with regard to their use of social media for crime prevention. The relationships that exist between knowledge, attitude and practice highlight the needs for improved knowledge in crime prevention in order to have a better practice. Hence, it is important to continue to educate the youth on the potential of social media and to encourage them to utilise the medium for crime prevention. It is also important to take into consideration the youth's liberal nature. Thus, in attempting to engage the youth's participation, authorities need to provide an on-line space that is non-institutional, less formal and not rigid.

References

Ahmad, J., Noor, S. M., & Ismail, N. (2015). Investigating students' environmental knowledge, attitude, practice and communication. *Asian social science, 11*(16), 1911-2025.

Akpinar-Elci, M., & Roberts, D. A. (2011). The knowledge, attitude and practice on land degradation and sustainable land management in Grenada: Technical report and reccomendations. Grenada: Ministry of Agriculture, Grenada.

Armstrong, D., Hine, J., Hacking, S., Armaos, R., Jones, R., Klessinger, N., & France, A. (2005). Children, risk and crime: The on track youth lifestyles surveys: Home Office Research, Development and Statistics Directorate.

Baboo, S. B., Pandian, A., Prasad, N. V., & Rao, A. (2013). Young people and new media in Malaysia: An analysis of social uses and practices. *Journal of arts, science & commerce, 4*(2), 50-56.

Besar, T. A., Hassan, M. S., Bolong, J., & Abdullah, R. (2013). Exploring the levels of knowledge, attitudes and environment-friendly practices among young civil servants in Malaysia. *Pertanika journals of social science & humanities, 21*, 21-38.

Blomberg, J. (2012). Fighting crime through social media and social network analysis: SAS Institute.

Boyd, D. M., & Ellison, N. B. (2008). Social network Sites: Definition, history, and scholarship. *Journal of computer-mediated communication, 13*, 210-230.

Brandtzæg, P. B., Haugstveit, I. M., Lüders, M., & Følstad, A. (2015, May 26-29). *Participation barriers to youth civic engagement in social media* Paper presented at the Ninth International AAAI Conference on Web and Social Media, Oxford, UK.

Cheng, N. (2014, April 10). Teenage crime on the rise. *The Star*.

de Guzman, M. R. T., & Pohlmeier, L. A. (2014). High-risk behaviours in youth. *Extensions*.

Denef, S., Kaptein, N., Bayerl, P. S., & Ramirez, L. (2012). Best practice in police social media adaptation *COMPOSITE Project*: European Commission.

Ehrampoush, M. H., & Moghadam, M. H. (2005). Survey of knowledge, attitude and practice of Yazd University of Medical Sciences students about solid wastes disposal and recycling *Iranian journal of environmental health science and engineering, 2*(2), 26-30.

Emanuel, E. (2010). Wastewater management in the wider Carribean region: Knowledge, attitudes and practice (KAP) study. Carribean: Carribean Regional Fund for Wastewater Management.

EPU. (2015). *Kertas strategi 7: Mewujudkan persekitaran hidup lebih selamat dan terjamin*. Putrajaya: Economic Planning Unit, Prime Minister's Department.

Fairbairn, J., Bivens, R., & Dawson, M. (2013). Sexual violence and social media: Building a framework for prevention Ottawa: Crime Prevention Ottawa.

GIZ. (2013). Knowledge-attitudes-practices on environmental awareness: From interviews and discussions in Vientiane, Khammouane, Houaphanh and Sayaboury: Deutsche Gesellschaft Fur Internationale Zusammenarbeit (GIZ) GmbH.

Go-globe. (2015). Social media usage in Asia Pacific - statistics and trends. Retrieved June 8, 2015, from http://www.go-globe.com/blog/social-media-asia/

Goutille, F. (2009). *Knowledge, attitudes and practices for risk education: how to implement KAP surveys*: Handicap International.

Graham, M., & Stephens, M. (2012). A geography of twitter. Retrieved Sept. 19, 2012, from http://www.oii.ox.ac.uk/vis/?id=4fe09570

Hamat, A., Embi, M. A., & Hassan, H. A. (2012). The use of social networking sites among Malaysian university students *International education studies, 5*(3), 56-66.

Holliday, K. (2014). Why chat apps are the next 'breed' of social networks. *CNBC.* Retrieved June 26, 2015, from http://www.cnbc.com/id/101517922

Holman, A. (2012). *Knowledge, attitude and practice surveys in child protection: A step-by-step guide for child protection programmes to the design and implementaion of KAP survey methods*: The Child Protection Initiative, Save the Children.

IIDS. (2006). Knowledge, attitude and practice (KAP) survey under the community-based alternative schooling project (CASP) in Kathmandu district. Kathmandu, Nepal: Institute for Integrated Development Studies (IIDS)

Ipsos. (2013). KAP survey – knowledge, attitudes and practices survey on youth employment and participation. Montenegro: Ipsos Strategic Marketing.

Isa, S. Z. M. (2015, March 25). Polis, masyarakat berpisah tiada. *Sinar Harian*.

Ismail, N. (2014). *Young people's use of new media through communities of practice.* (PhD), Monash University, Australia.

Jaaffar, J. (2014, April 5). Peningkatan kes jenayah juvana membimbangkan. *Berita Harian*.

Kaliyaperumal, K. (2004). Guideline for conducting a knowledge, attitude and practice (KAP) study. *AECS illumination, 4*(1), 7-9.

Kassim, A. B. (2005). *Juveniles on remand: Trends and practices in Malaysia*. Paper presented at the 129th International Senior Seminar on Crime Prevention, Tokyo, Japan.

Khoram, M. R., Shariat, M., Azar, A., Moharamnejad, N., & Mahjub, H. (2006). Survey on knowledge, attitude and practice on sustainable agriculture among rural farmers in Hamadan province, Iran. *Sarhad journal of agriculture, 22*(4).

Kim, Y. A., & Ahmad, M. A. (2013). Trust, distrust and lack of confidence of users in online social media-sharing communities. *Knowledge-based systems, 37*, 438-450.

Launiala, A. (2009). How much can a KAP survey tell us about people's knowledge, attitudes and practices? Some observations from medical anthropology research on malaria in pregnancy in Malawi. *Anthropology matters journal, 11*(1), 1-13.

LexisNexis. (2014). Social media use in law enforcement: Crime prevention and investigative activities continue to drive usage: LexisNexis Risk Solution.

Mahadi, N. (2013, June 16, 2013). 13.3 million Malaysians are facebook users. *The Borneo Post*.

MCMC. (2015). *Communications & multimedia pocket book of statistics Q1 2015*. Cyberjaya: Malaysian Communications and Multimedia Commission

Mesch, G. S. (2009). The internet and youth culture. *The hedgehog review, 11*(1), 50-60.

Mohammad, M. T., & Azman, A. (2012). The lifestyle of young offenders before rehabilitation. *International proceedings of economics development and research, 56*(3), 11-16.

Mun, W. F., Li, L. M., & Fernandez, P. R. (2011). Social life connects the world: Malaysian youth's usage behaviour of social network sites. *International journal of arts & sciences, 4*(3), 157-178.

Muniandy, L., & Muniandy, B. (2013). The impact of social media in social and political aspects in Malaysia: An overview. *International journal of humanities and social science, 3*(11), 71-76.

Mustafa, A. F. (2014, Dec 31). Berita palsu, fitnah memudaratkan. *Berita harian.*

RMP. (2011). Ulang tahun pertama Facebook PDRM - terima kasih atas sokongan anda! Retrieved June 24, 2015, from http://www.rmp.gov.my/news-detail/2014/06/11/ulang-tahun-pertama-facebook-pdrm---terima-kasih-atas-sokongan-anda!

SAS. (2015a). Three best practices for using social media for crime prevention and criminal investigations. Retrieved June 19, 2015, from http://www.sas.com/en_us/insights/articles/risk-fraud/three-best-practices-for-using-social-media-for-crime-prevention.html

—. (2015b). Using social media to tackle crime. Retrieved June 19, 2015, from http://www.sas.com/en_za/insights/articles/risk-fraud/using-social-media.html

Shah, M. F. (2013, October 29). Youth crimes up to 538 cases for the first half of the year. *The Star.*

Shewmaker, J. (2012). Youth and social media. Retrieved June 17, 2015, from http://socialmediaweek.org/newyork/2012/02/15/youth-and-social-media/

Sinar. (2015, Jan 31). Guna WhatsApp banteras jenayah. *Sinar Harian.*

Stats, I. W. (2015). Internet world stats. Retrieved Mar 10, 2015, from http://www.internetworldstats.com/stats3.htm

Subramaniam, B. (2014, Jan 5 2014). On the social media circuit. *The star.*

Tong, S. T., Heide, B. V. D., & Langwell, L. (2008). Too much of a good thing? The relationship between number of friends and interpersonal impressions on facebook. *Journal of computer-mediated communication, 13*, 531-549.

UN. (2015). *The role of the public in strengthening crime prevention and criminal justice.* Paper presented at the 13th United Nations Congress on Crime Prevention and Criminal Justice, Doha.

UNICEF. (2015). Communication for Development (C4D). Retrieved June 25, 2015, from http://www.unicef.org/cbsc/index_65178.html

Utusan. (2011, July 18). Jenayah libatkan remaja, pelajar sekolah semakin meningkat. *Utusan Malaysia*.

Weide, K., Ireland, G., & Kevorkian, S. (2011). Social entertainment 2.0: What is it, and why is it important? Framingham, MA: International Data Corporation.

Wok, S., Idid, S. A., & Misman, N. (2012). Social media use for information-sharing activities among youth in Malaysia. *Journalism and mass communication, 2*(11), 1029-1047.

Wolff, R., McDevitt, J., & Stark, J. (2011). Using social media to prevent gang violence and engage youth. Boston, MA: Executive Office of Public Safety and Security (EOPSS) Office of Grants and Research.

Yin, J. L. S., Agostinho, S., Harper, B., & Chicaro, J. F. (2014). The engagement of social media technologies by undergraduate informatics students for academic purpose in Malaysia. *Journal of information communication and ethics in society, 12*(3), 177-194.

Zeldin, S. (2004). Preventing youth violence through the promotion of community engagement and membership. *Journal of community psychology, 32*(5), 623-641.

CHAPTER SIX

BUILDING A DIGITAL COUNTERPUBLIC: CIVIC AFFORDANCES OF TWITTER UNDER THAI AUTHORITARIAN GOVERNANCE

CHANON ADSANATHAM

Overview

- The usage of social media in Southeast Asia—specifically Thailand—for political activism has not received any attention in cross-cultural rhetorical studies. As a result, even though the study of mass communication had taken a transnational and multimodal turn, our understanding of global digital rhetoric remains biased towards the West.
- This chapter examines the use of Twitter in Thailand during the Red Shirt Movement in May 2014, wherein the Thai military suspended the constitution, removed the government, and instituted martial law, citing national 'stability' and 'peace' as justifications. The coup censored the media, banned public assembly, and outlawed criticism of the military. However, Thai citizens who were against the coup, better known as the 'Red Shirt Movement', took to Twitter to protest the military and demand democracy.
- The study draws upon Michel de Certeau's concept of tactic, Michael Warner's theory of counterpublics, Gunther Kress's notion of synesthesia, and Joel Penney and Caroline Dadas's study of hashtag activism.

Real Coup, Virtual Revolt

In May 2014, Thailand, a country normally ruled by a constitutional democracy, became a military-run nation when army leaders seized power from the government, suspended the constitution, and declared martial law. Political infighting over a controversial amnesty bill to grant former Prime Minister Thaksin Shinawatra immunity against corruption charges had divided the country, leading to protests that shut down public universities and downtown businesses. To 'return happiness to the people', the military abolished the elected government on 22 May 2014, instituting a thirteenth coup in Thai history (National News Bureau, 2014). A junta, led by General Prayuth Chan-o-Cha, has since been governing the nation. Calling itself the National Council for Peace and Order (NCPO), the junta has outlawed any political gesture, rally, or message that might disturb national stability. It also temporarily shut down television stations, radio programs, and websites seen as a threat to peace. Most notably, citizens reported that at one time, the NCPO blocked Facebook and Line (a popular chat program) to circumvent political mobilization and dissent, but Twitter, a microblog with a 140-character limit, was not impacted. Thai civilians who disapprove of the coup have been using it as a subversive platform against the junta; it has become a productive space for civic action in a politically restrictive time.[1]

This chapter examines the ways in which Thai civilians employed Twitter to subvert the NCPO, drawing upon interviews with twenty avid political tweeters, survey responses from 100 active users, and analysis of their tweets.

Civilians' tweets represent rhetorical[2] compositions that aim to fulfil five broad purposes: updating and learning political happenings; expressing commentary and emotions; satirising the junta; offering political analysis and insights; and, rallying morale and resistance. Each of these aims has deeper, multi-layered significances; hence, they must not be taken at face value. They provide a means toward achieving multiple political goals, and as a whole, they enable citizens to challenge authoritarianism and censorship to empower electronic civil disobedience—making it possible to sustain civic actions and morale under a precarious political condition. Ultimately, through their political tweets, civilians have created an alternative networked public space to build a digital counterpublic toward democratic hopes, despite continual political uncertainty in Thailand.

---

[1] Thanks to the cheaper cost of mobile phones and increasing internet penetration rate in Southeast Asia, there has been a 700% increase in web and social media usage in the region over the past decade (Accenture 2012).

[2] Rhetorical here is the adjective form of the word rhetoric, which I define as the purposeful use of semiotic resources to achieve a communicative purpose.

The Limitations of Social Media Research in Asian Context

In recent years, Twitter has been used for political activism, democracy building, and social justice worldwide. It has become a technology and space for facilitating mobilisation, updating information, circulating second-hand information, presenting opinions, forming connections, initiating conversations, soliciting global attention, advocating awareness, enticing actions, and seeking assistance (Varnali and Gorgulu, 2015; Penney and Dadas, 2013; Lindgren, 2013; Neumayer and Valtysson, 2013; Lim, 2012). These functions of Twitter represent the ten typologies of social media usage in a wide range of civic contexts. To date, researchers have studied the significances of the typologies in nine major settings: the Moldovan uprising to contest the election results in Chisinau (Munteanu and Mungiu-Pipidi, 2009), the Occupy Wall Street Movement to rectify wealth distribution in America (Penney and Dadas, 2013), the nationalist demonstration to defeat fascism in Germany (Neumayer and Valtysson, 2013), the Egyptian Revolution to overthrow the corrupt president (Johnson et al., 2013), the Occupy Gezi demonstration to preserve a historic park in Turkey (Varnali and Gorgulu, 2015), the Libyan uprising to oust the government of Libya (Lindgren, 2013), the Green Revolution to challenge the election results in Iran (Burns and Eltham, 2009), the Indignados Movement to reform the European economy (Theocharis et al., 2014), and the Black Lives Matter campaign to fight racial injustice in the United States (Conley, 2014). Evidently, Twitter has become a transnational platform for political demonstration and reform, and this has led to lively scholarly debates about its efficacy and limitations.

Malcolm Gladwell (2010) argues that social media is a poor platform for activism because to be effective, a movement requires a tightly organized hierarchy and strong ties among members who are willing to engage in high-risk actions. However, Gladwell contends that Twitter fosters loose, decentralized networks of people with weak ties, making it an ineffective means for mobilizing change. He claims that it has led to 'slacktivism'— the convenient act of showing support for a cause by signing or clicking a website instead of taking actions offline to actualise change. Similarly, Evgeny Morozov (2009) posits that the hype over the 'Twitter Revolution', the belief that the microblog was influential to restoring democracy in the Middle East, is a myth. He argues that the majority of people tweeting about political happenings in that region were not local citizens but rather, Westerners living outside of the Middle East.

Therefore, the claim that Twitter sparked a revolution is a flawed one, Morozov contends. It stemmed from a poor understanding of the local context. Further, he adds that social media has created a new danger; it makes it easier for the authorities to monitor citizens' political moves, aggrandising governmental power in an unprecedented manner.

On the other hand, sociologist Dhiraj Murthy (2013) maintains that Twitter can be a viable platform for social change. He counters that Gladwell has set up a false binary between strong and weak ties, forcing a false dilemma between the two. For Murthy, a combination of weak and strong ties is desirable for activism, and he believes Twitter can strengthen both ties by enabling on-line/off-line connections and activities. Protesters can now meet each other on-line and/or offline, allowing for multiple ways to build rapport, morale, and actions. Murthy's argument is supported by Ginger Johnson, Brant Tudor and Hasan Nuseibeh's (2013) study of the use of Twitter in the Egyptian Revolution. They discovered that although 'social networks do not inspire political revolutions any more than they incarnate freedom', they can 'effectively provide the most effective means to date for organizing protesters in nations with oppressed peoples and repressed freedom of speech' (Johnson et al., 2013). For this reason, Johnson and her collaborators caution against dismissing the microblog as politically unimportant or ineffectual. Although Twitter has some of the drawbacks that Morozov posits, the site has enriched potentials for civic actions in ways that were not previously possible (McCaughey, 2014). Intervening in the slacktivism debate, Martha McCaughey (2014) cautions against asking a yes/no question about whether or not social media fosters activism. Instead, she urges us to look at how it enables new methods of protest: 'Web 2.0 has facilitated the creation and spread of content, changing social-movement activism and organising.... We therefore can no longer simply ask whether or not Web 2.0 impacts protesting or people's likelihood to end up in a face-to-face protest.... Social media impacts social and political change by presenting new ways to make change and new ways to protest'.

Yet, the debates and understanding of Twitter's political functions are not cross-culturally diverse. The majority of scholarship focuses on the West or the Middle East, skewing our insights to these two regions. Additionally, researchers have primarily focused on examining the connection between on-line action and offline protests (Theocharis, et al. 2015; Varnali and Gorgulu, 2015; Salem, 2015; Tufekci and Wilson, 2012). Indeed, many studies are conducted under democratic presumptions and in settings where there is freedom of speech and assembly (Theocharis, et al. 2015; Varnali and Gorgulu, 2015; Salem, 2015; Neumayer and Valtysson, 2013; Penney and Dadas, 2013). As culture, political condition and communicative norms differ from one nation to another, we need to evaluate to what extent existing typologies, paradigms, and in particular, 'slacktivism' can be extrapolated to other places, specifically to a *coup d'état* setting such as Thailand. Still needed, then, is a more diverse, localised understanding of the uses of Twitter across political/cultural contexts. Cross-cultural rhetoric scholars (Mao, 2014; Sun, 2012; Lu, 2004) have long been urging communication and writing researchers to develop richer knowledge of textual and technological practices across cultures—to expand our comprehension of rhetoric and writing beyond Eurocentric models. Toward those ends, this essay remedies the diversity gap in current Twitter scholarship. Through investigating how Thai civilians are tweeting to subvert the junta and analysing the multi-layered rhetorical functions of their texts, this chapter broadens our knowledge about the political affordances and limitations of social media beyond Western and Middle Eastern paradigms—fostering more heteroglossic insights about the power of digital communication for civic actions.

The Multi-layered Rhetorical Functions of Thai Civilians' Tweets

The chapter examines how Thai civilians are tweeting to subvert the junta and in the process, create dissent to propel the hope for democracy. Interviews, survey findings, and analyses of civilians' tweets showed that tweets aim to accomplish five broad aims: inform and learn political developments; convey political editorials; ridicule the junta; offer analysis of current events; and rally morale and resistance. Although these aims represent specific motivations for tweeting, they are not mutually exclusive but complement and reinforce one another. A tweet to alert that the junta has shut down Facebook, for instance, can also serve as a critique of censorship. Thus, instead of seeing each aim as discrete, we should conceptualise them as interconnected toward the ultimate goal of rectifying democracy. Below is an analysis of the Thai citizens' aims in an attempt to elucidate their multi-layered functions, drawing upon civilians' perspectives to offer emic insights.

Fostering an Informed Citizenship

To be informed and to inform others regarding socio-political events was the top reason why many Thai civilians, who disapprove of the coup, used Twitter. They tweeted to update developments in two ways: reporting information they learned first-hand or retweeted information others composed—articles, videos, images, messages, etc. Some civilians like to append hashtags (#) to their tweets to categorizs the subject matter and sometimes to clarify context. For example, when the junta shut down a television station's homepage, citizens tweeted a screenshot of the site, which displayed the following note: 'This website was shut down through the NCPO's order', adding hashtags #censorship and #Thaicoup to the tweet. When the junta closed a busy Bangkok highway junction to enforce curfew, civilians took pictures of the empty road and tweeted it to alert other drivers, along with the following message: 'On the highway, very empty.' Approximately half of the tweets to inform developments – a total of 526 – are retweets or re-circulated information posted by others. The other half consisted of updates that civilians composed on their own.

Initially, what drove Thai citizens to turn to Twitter for updates were the junta's censorship of the media. On 22 May 2014 the NCPO shut down news websites, television programs, and radio stations and ordered news producers to attend an imperative meeting to learn a new guideline: Do not report content that can hinder national stability. Unable to rely on traditional media for updates, the civilians interviewed for this study decided to turn to social media for happenings. People began sharing what they knew and posting what they saw on the streets. The design of Twitter made it easy for them to swiftly write and disseminate information. Joel Penney and Caroline Dadas (2013) observed: 'The specific architecture of Twitter has been noted by scholars for its particular emphasis on rapid textual exchange among a multitude of actors and publics.... The brevity of Twitter message—limited to only 140 characters—almost seems to be purposefully designed for quick circulation'. Thai civilians have recognized this affordance and have capitalised upon it to turn the microblog into an alternative news channel. Through tweeting political developments, they have created a less filtered outlet for sharing news, eluding state censorship. While the junta has been able to regulate mainstream media, they are less successful in controlling the updates civilians compose on social network. As a result, some citizens have come to see the microblog as a more reliable source for current events.

Jade,[3] a prominent tweeter of political happenings, claims that the Thai media cannot be fully trusted because they are closely monitored by the state. Hence, they often do not report details in a thorough, candid manner, making it difficult for people to fully grasp what is happening. Jade is particularly concerned that television and radio stations are now becoming a propaganda channel for the state. His concern is not unfounded if we consider the structure of the Thai broadcast industry. In her research on Thai media ownership, Pirongrong Ramasoota Rananand (2003) discovered that the government owns seventeen television and 523 radio stations nationwide, leading her to conclude that the Thai broadcasting industry is 'business-cum-politics' Consequently, stations are not always willing to air contentious issues that might threaten state authority; they have to practice self-censorship to avoid being fined or worse, shut down.

Thus, some Thai citizens think that the information posted on social media is more candid; it has not been filtered to appease authority. As Jade relates: '[Tweets] can allow people to have more *critical awareness*. At the very least, they help us know more truthful and correct information because sometimes televised media doesn't report the truth that reflects the real situation. So tweets allow me to know more and evaluate how much faith and trust I can put into the government.' Jade's remark about 'critical awareness' and 'evaluation' here is significant. It suggests that reading and posting informative tweets is not merely a means to disseminate and receive updates. They allow him and others to gain awareness that can lead to informed citizenship—suggesting that Twitter offers a productive, informative platform for cultivating their political acumen.

Similarly, Jib, who primarily uses Twitter as a news source, indicates that what attracted her to Twitter is the brevity and speed at which happenings can be posted and shared by both local and international communities. This, she sees, is an affordance not available through traditional media. Specifically, she believes sharing and learning disparate sociopolitical happenings from domestic and international sources on social media can enable some transparency and accountability in the government because she thinks when things are constantly censored and the public becomes uninformed, corruption and abuse of power can occur more easily. For Jib, then, disseminating and reading a wide range of information on Twitter—what other people and international media tweeted—provide an 'alert' and 'education' to sharpen her political insights. Specifically, she sees Twitter as a good platform for raising public awareness to circumvent her from

[3] Pseudonyms are used in this article to protect the Tweeters.

becoming politically blinded because of the junta's supreme authority: 'Since censorship has been heavy, we need a new platform for accessing information.... Twitter provides an alternative media....What it can do is create public awareness. This can deter problematic governmental actions.' Thus, Jib is not tweeting current happenings to merely update events. She is doing so to hinder governmental abuse of power, as currently there are no checks and balances in place. In sum, in the Thai context, what appears as a 140-character message to inform political developments plays more complex functions beyond what is evident at first glance.

Convey Commentary or Emotions to Create Political Identification and Opposition

Additionally, civilians tweet to express political comments and emotions. Twitter provides a safer platform for them to broadcast their thoughts to a large audience, allowing them to have a public 'soapbox'.[4] Their commentaries can be classified into ten types:

1. Critical observation: 'Suthep's look doesn't show confidence.'
2. Praise: 'Student protesters are our brave new hope.'
3. Ridiculing a political condition or figure: 'Hello, Thailand, a nation ruled by soldiers, once more.' 'This is North Korea $#@!.'
4. Outburst: 'Can we end this? You #@$.'
5. Statement of feeling or condition: 'So sick of soldiers.' 'So happy, no soldier in my neighborhood.'
6. Lament: 'Thais never learn from history.'
7. Impolite attack: '$#@ Prayuth.' '$#! the soldier.'
8. Defending a figure or cause: 'They say Yingluck [former prime minister] cheats. Show me the corruption evidence.' 'Don't you agree with Pavin [a political critic]?'
9. Critiquing an initiative or action: 'The government's [peace keeping] meeting is merely a show.'
10. Declaring political stance: 'I won't accept dictatorship because I love democracy built upon voting rights.'

Commentary tweets are often retweeted, suggesting that they tend to strike other civilians' interest. The ones that politely ridicule the government are more frequently shared, while those resembling an outburst or an impolite attack are usually not.

---

[4] Soapbox is slang for a platform where one can stand to talk about public issues.

Civilians reported that they tweet political commentaries against the junta not merely to vent—but to speak out against authority during repressive times. Despite strict censorship, they want to be able to 'present perspectives about political happenings to others, to add opinionated voices to the mix', and they see Twitter as a desirable platform to achieve those aims. It is simple to use and provides a less risky method for broadcasting candid thoughts to the public on-line. Unlike the once popular Thai web boards, which often require personal data such as one's full name and governmental identification card numbers, tweeters can remain anonymous through using a fictive handle and image for their account. Furthermore, the fact that Twitter is an American corporation makes it difficult for the Thai government to confiscate data or the server, something they had done in the past to Thai websites. For added security, some civilians now use a virtual private network (VPN) when they tweet. In doing so, they hope that they can sway public opinion through frequently presenting their commentaries on political issues. As Boon, who likes to tweet his political opinion, elaborates: 'When we don't agree with current values or manner of things in our country, we should assert our views, ones that are the opposite—and do so very frequently so that we might be able to sway public opinion. I aim to alter public attitude through the frequent commentaries I put out. They might change the thoughts of my followers, perhaps starting with a few. Then multiply from there.' Boon's remark indicates that his tweets aim to induce common ground through persistent, frequent delivery of his political comments. In this sense, they function to achieve what Kenneth Burke (1950) calls identification. According to Burke, persuasion is only possible when an audience comes to identify with the rhetoric through symbolic action (the use of language): 'As for the relation between 'identification' and 'persuasion': we might well keep in mind that a speaker persuades an audience by the use of stylistic identifications; his act of persuasion…[is] for the purpose of causing the audience to identify with the speaker's interests' Accordingly, commentary tweets represent civilians' symbolic action to induce similar viewpoints through a snowball effect.[5] As such, they also function as persuasive discourses – and not merely expressive or cathartic prose.

In addition, through their commentaries, civilians are appropriating social media into a public podium for countering the coup. According to Chai, an avid political tweeter since 2007, because the junta has outlawed political

[5] A snowball effect is an expression representing a process that initially starts out small but picks up momentum and becomes larger as an item or activity develops.

rallies, social media is one of the remaining platforms that allows an average citizen to critique the government and deliver her voice in public. He relates: 'The government has banned so many actions….Famous political figures have been given a gag order…[but] those of us who are a nobody [not a public figure] can turn to social media to voice our opinion…. It's the main platform for speaking out now. It's the only remaining space that can empower people, no matter who you are.' Likewise, Su, an academic commentary tweeter of Thai culture and politics, notes: 'Civilians have been severely silenced and shut down; therefore, they need [a place] to engage in dissent…. When you speak to people in public about their political opinion, they are not as verbal because they can't be, but when they come on-line, they discuss more, share more, comment more; they offer more and more thoughts.' In regularly tweeting their commentaries, civilians are able to virtually build a domain of dissent; they have created an alternative public space for civic contestation.

Their tweets exemplify what Bibak Rahimi (2011) calls 'inventive ways of practicing politics by shaping spaces of contestation', i.e., through composing dissenting commentaries, civilians transform Twitter into a 'decentred space of political communication', where 'diverse voices of marginalised status…are expressed and communicated, producing distinctive spaces of alternative utterances to realign the dominant public spheres' . Though this space does not immediately remove the junta, it keeps opposition alive under constrained freedom of speech and assembly.

Satirize the Coup to Reduce Political Apathy, Publicize Concerns, and Protect Oneself

Closely related to commentary tweets are satire messages about the junta. Often, such a message is multimodal, combining images and texts. The greater availability of camera and graphic applications now makes it easier for people to create image-rich communication. Multimodal satiric discourses address a wide range of issues, from governmental initiatives, to coup supporters, to General Prayuth, to censorship, to the military's violence against citizens. In this section, I will focus on two satirical tweets that were widely shared and present perspectives from the tweeters to enrich our understanding of their functions.

The first most frequently-circulated satire image, shared 853 times, was posted by tweeter Wan; it is a photograph of a young soldier fully suited in an army uniform with a protective helmet walking down the centre aisle of a train, gripping a large black machine gun. He appears to be patrolling the passengers. Two seated female travellers, one on the left side and another on the right, stare at him with a shocking, fearful, uncomfortable look. Most of the passengers have all been seated in an orderly fashion. The picture is tweeted with the following caption: 'This photograph is called *Feeling Comforted, Thanks to the Thai Army*.'

In this satirical visual-textual rhetoric, Wan employs sarcasm as a key strategy to mock the growing military power in Thailand. The women's faces contradict the caption, showing aversion and agitation, qualities opposite of comfort. The soldier appears to have inconvenienced Thai citizens. In particular, the female ethos here is significant. Women and children are perceived as 'vulnerable figures' in traditional Thai society. Their fearful countenance implies that the military is harming the weaker, more defenceless people; they are making them feel insecure and tense. Furthermore, the setting of the picture is strategic. Framed against a calm, orderly background in which passengers are sitting in an orderly manner, the soldier's imposing presence makes him appear as a disruptive figure in a peaceful setting. This reinforces Wan's larger message that the military has intruded upon citizens' lives, threatened their peaceful existence, and created a public disturbance—a theme that frequently recurs throughout his tweets.

Wan explains that in tweeting this image (and other satirical ones), he is trying to attract a politically moderate audience to recognise the NCPO's danger and nuisance to Thai society. However, he worries that if his post is too harsh or aggressive, his audience, those who are politically withdrawn, might lose interest or worse, 'unfollow' him on Twitter. Thus, he uses humorous messages with images and witty captions as a strategy to add 'flavour and variations' to his point to entice interest: 'Anything that's always the same old—when people tweet only one kind of message [e.g. text]—is dull. Their numbers of followers won't increase. I've seen accounts losing followers, but if you add colourful varieties into your tweets, then they become more compelling.' Additionally, Wan relates that he employs humour as a way to lighten the intensity of his point. He believes that politics has become a stressful subject for Thais because of continuous fatal political fighting over the years; hence, some of his followers have tuned out from political issues to avoid becoming overwhelmed with negativity. By tweeting satirical messages, such as the soldier's picture, Wan hopes to inform them about his political concern, critique the government, raise alarm, and induce laughter at the same time.

In short, his satiric tweets exemplify a rhetorical discourse for covertly raising political awareness and propelling civic interest to curb political apathy without arousing undesirable pathos.

Furthermore, civilians tweet satiric images and texts to simultaneously criticise and publicise their political concern in a less risky manner. Gong, a photographer/artist and active tweeter with more than 9,000 followers, reveals that he uses satire to share a bothersome civic issue so that it will not be swept under by other trending news on-line and become forgotten from public memory. Specifically, he sees humour as a safer way to criticise the government: 'Some people post lots of direct critiques of the government. I don't do that. I make satirical images…because it's an indirect, diplomatic way to present my censure. There are many political topics that we can't openly discuss, so by making them humorous, it's less risky.' When pressed, Gong can pass his tweet off as a joke. To create his satire, Gong would first decipher which political issue is most alarming at the moment. Then he looks for images and comments that others have made about that concern and uses Photoshop to integrate them into a coherent design. For instance, when the junta outlawed a symbolic gesture for anti-coup solidarity, the raising of three fingers (index, middle and fourth), Gong took a picture of Sombat Boon-ngam-anong, a famous civilian protester, enacting the gesture, positioned it next to another image of Sombat holding up only his middle finger, and superimposed the following quotation above the images: 'Don't outlaw the three fingers salute because those who disagree with the edict will continue to do it, and if the gesture gets reduced to just one finger, it'll be a bigger deal. Speaking from the heart.' Gong has employed remix[6] as a method to invent his ridicule. Through this strategy, he is able to create what seems like a witty message to publicise a serious concern about censorship, while perhaps inducing laughter at the same time. The power of remix to motivate political action has been well recognised in digital writing studies. Abby Dubisar and Jason Palmeri (2010) argue that political remixes represent 'an important form of civic action' toward activist rhetoric, emphasising: 'Despite the fact that many of the political remixes…are often quite humorous and/or irreverent in nature, they also can have a substantial influence on how [political] candidates and issues are viewed. In this sense, the digital political remix is an important form of citizen action…[and] one way in which young people participate in public civic discourse' . Gong's remixed satiric tweet is a case in point.

---

[6] A remix is a piece of media made from assembling disparate materials created by others to produce a new creative object.

Offer Political Analysis and Insights to Motivate Reflection toward Change

Besides satirising the government, civilians also tweet to analyse political happenings. While subjective and reflective of the composer's stance, analysis tweets move away from resembling a critique, satire, or emotional outcry toward a more reflective, deliberative message that offers an insight. For instance, consider the content and tone of the following messages: 'If the [overthrown] government doesn't agree with martial law, it's allowed to petition the king for a veto'; 'what will the NCPO do next? One way to find out is to look at previous meeting tapes of officials'; 'the military announced the outcome of today's reconciliation meeting with dissenters: Go home and come back to chat again tomorrow. This means no party has been willing to compromise, so all members need to go home and rethink their stance.' Notice how these tweets are not confrontational or mocking in tone, but they aim to provide informative, thought-provoking information. Interjections and impolite diction are absent. Depending upon the complexity of the subject, analytical tweets can require more than 140 characters to compose, but civilians have creatively worked around this constraint in several ways. Some are tweeting their message in a series, one after another, and they use the numeric notation '1 of *x*' to signify continuity. Others are linking their Twitter account to Facebook, which allows writers to post up to 63,206 characters in their status update field. Civilians would compose their analysis message there and then paste the URL of their Facebook message as a tweet, redirecting their audience to Facebook to read their complete thought. This creates a cross media flow and cross-platform composition. In their study of Twitter usage, Christina Neumayer and Bjarki Valtysson (2013) discovered that protesters are creative about how to work around the limitations of a given interface. They often connect and circulate their message across platforms, from one technology to another, such as from Facebook to Twitter; hence, their post is not confined to one channel but is 'picked up by other media as cross-media coverage flow in which temporalities of on-line media such as Twitter are hybridized' . This enables more exposure and enlarges the audience of a message. Tweets that offer political analysis are often retweeted, indicating that readers find them to be worthy of sharing with their social network followers.

Civilians who tweet political analyses indicate that they do so because they want to motivate contemplation toward political interests and ultimately, reform. Vee, a medical scientist who likes to analyse political happenings, explains: 'My goal in tweeting is to advocate democracy…. To do this, I use analysis as my main strategy. I see myself as more of a political analyst. I like to analyse complicated issues, ones that people may not understand, but I might. I'll give my insights and use them as a weapon to aid my political fight—to disseminate my [political] thoughts.' Vee adds that he sees analysis as a useful genre because if done well, it can promote critical thinking, leading to more progressive views and actions. In fact, he thinks confrontational and emotional tweets that are polemical in tone are ineffective for inducing change: They turn off citizens, particularly those who are politically moderate and those who hold an opposite view. Specifically, Vee believes contentious discourse increases resistance and flaming counterattack, which hinders productive exchange. He believes that offering political analysis and insights, on the other hand, presents a less confrontational, less threatening approach to motivate political reflection toward progressive actions. His practice echoes the tenets of Rogerian rhetoric. According to Carl Rogers (1951), it is often difficult to induce change through traditional argumentation methods because they are often agonistic. An arguer attempts to defeat her opponent by making counterarguments to refute the opposite claims. Both interlocutors become wrestlers in a challenge to dominate one another, which leads to high emotions that increase resistance or 'mental blocks' toward the willingness to change. What is more effective, Rogers suggests, is a discourse that is less adversarial or combative—one that aims to reduce 'defensive distortions', 'the insecurities', and 'the defensive exaggeration' toward deep listening that drives an openness to change. Offering political analysis to yield contemplation and insights appears to be Vee's strategy towards decreasing potential resistance.

In like manner, Zo indicates that he tweets political analyses to entice people to care more about politics. Because most of his Twitter followers are not politically motivated, he does not write messages that are overtly critical of the junta to prevent turning away his readers. Indeed, he avoids overloading his followers with politics by limiting his tweets on the subject to 40%; mixing them with personal topics such as food and sports. In particular, he restrains himself from posting harsh critiques, as he related: 'I won't cuss out or condemn politicians because I don't know how many of my followers can handle political issues, but I hope my [analytical] messages will gradually spark political thoughts and interests. I can't predict what my tweet will do, but I hope it motivates people. They might not have known what's happening politically, but now they can become aware and reflective.' Zo adds that since Twitter enables all messages to be shared, he is particularly concerned about how his tweet might be altered in ways that run counter to his intention: to entice political reflection that leads to civic reform. This motivates him to carefully consider the tone of his texts. He sees composing more 'politically neutral' tweets in the form of an analysis as a good, conservative strategy to circumvent disagreement from people who might retweet this post—particularly, those holding the opposite stance. If his message gets retweeted, it can appear non-threatening to both pro and anti-coup supporters. Zo appears to be heeding what Jim Ridolfo and Danielle DeVoss (2009) call rhetorical velocity: the strategic consideration of how one's text might be re-circulated and/or re-composed by a third party in digital realms. As re-circulation can alter and create new meanings to a message (Gries, 2013; Queen, 2009), writers should no longer tweet without considering its potential for reuses and misuses. Given that digital messages can be shared across platforms, writers must think beyond their immediate audience to wider contexts, as Zo is doing.

In sum, tweets offering political analysis exemplify rhetorical texts that aim to recruit political engagement through inviting political reflection; they are enticement/solicitation discourses in a deliberative tone. Altogether, they indicate that Twitter has become an important space for Thai civilians to share their political insights and, in the process, impel civic concerns and interest, another important step toward rectifying democracy.

Rally against the Government to Foster Morale and Garner International Support

Lastly, civilians are utilising Twitter to mobilise electronic rallies and demonstrations against the junta. While social media has often been seen as a tool to coordinate protests offline (Theocharis, et al. 2015; Salem, 2015; Lindgren; 2013; Tufekci and Wilson, 2012), this is not its main function in Thailand, since public assembly was outlawed in May 2014.[7] Since then, civilians have turned to social media as a space for rallying against the NCPO. In this regard, they have made three key moves:

First, citizens invented various Thai and English hashtags to denounce the coup and appended them to their tweets: #nocoup, #ripthailand,

[7]Civilians used Twitter to announce rally places early on, but this was short-lived, since public assembly is illegal.

#ripthaidemocracy, #anticoup, #bringbackourdemocracy, #dontwantcoup, #perishdictators, #fightmamafight. And they called upon one another to use these hashtags in their post. For example, in the early days of the coup, Jesda tweeted the following message: 'Share so the rest of the world can know == Victory Monument #nocoup #thaicoup #antithaicoup #freedomthailand #prayforthailand.' Additionally, when a vocal TV personality, Leena Jung, publically criticised the coup for shutting down her station, Boon coined the hashtag #fightmamafight and urged his followers to 'join in masses to give support to Leena' by tweeting the tag. Furthermore, now instead of tweeting a complete sentence to rally against the coup, some civilians use a series of hashtags to string together a tweet: '#nocoup #anticoup #thaicoup #freedom #thailand'. In doing so, they have re-appropriated hashtags into a new form of syntax and style.

Hashtags are no longer merely used to organise information, but they are functioning as a passionate call, shout, and pledge, things we typically witness at a traditional rally. We might see their constant, repetitive, widespread use to resemble an ongoing rally cry, which becomes 'louder' as more people (re)display the tags.

Boon, who invented several of the rally hashtags, explains that he sees them as a good device to 'attract people to speak out on a pressing topic' so that there can be more public voices noticing and discussing civic concerns. Because hashtags can be easily searched, shared, and aggregated on Twitter and the wider web, he thinks they can help raise awareness about a pressing issue. As a tag becomes more widely used across social media, it can turn into a 'trending' topic, meaning that it gets widely mentioned by a large number of tweeters in their posts. This helps generate publicity in ways that are difficult to achieve in a traditional platform (e.g. print media). In this sense, hashtag functions as a marketing tool to 'rally' tweeters to notice and discuss a political issue; it aims to generate momentum or 'buzz' on-line.

In addition, using hashtags allows politically likeminded civilians to feel some sense of comfort and connection to one another in a time when they can no longer legally gather in public. Hashtags provide a 'social marker' for people to identify with one another without having to physically meet (Neumayer and Valtysson, 2013). Seeing what issues are being discussed through tags helps civilians realize that there are other likeminded people who are talking about similar causes, and this enables them to retain a degree of hope in politically depressing and segregated times. As Teerada, an avid political tweeter since 2010, reveals: 'It'll be difficult [to change the current political situation]. It won't be easy, but seeing what's being tweeted provides a sense of relief. At the very least, you see that there are likeminded people. Right now, we're in a condition where we can't do anything, but at least, we can be comforted that there are others like us. There's a group of us on-line.' In this sense, tweeting and using hashtags help sustain a sense of morale among silenced citizens. Civilians can feel connected and become a part of a group by using and spreading anti-coup tag symbols.

Originally, hashtags were invented for aggregating topics on Twitter to allow for easy searches; however, Thai civilians have expanded their functions, transforming them into a rally gesture, expressive syntax, attention-getter, and morale booster. This indicates that hashtags have become rhetorical signifiers that go beyond being a meta-communicative label for classifying information. They now resemble what Alice Daer, Rebecca Hoffman and Seth Goodman (2015) call 'communicative genres': 'dynamic, interactive functions of designed software being appropriated by users for tacit, recurring purposes of meaning-making within and across social technologies' . Through Thai civilians' creative appropriations, hashtags are now a polysemic text for subverting the junta.

Aside from hashtags, civilians also use Twitter to contact international organisations, diplomats, and journalists. When martial law was first announced on 20 May 2014, some Thai people tweeted pictures of soldiers acting violently toward defiant citizens to international humanitarian organisations and news networks such as the Human Rights Watch, CNN and the BBC to spread global awareness about political abuse and solicit repudiation. They also tweeted images of their missing family members and friends, whom they believed were abducted or murdered by the army, to the United Nations as a plea for help. Most notably, since the Thai military is controlling all branches of government with no checks and balances in place, some civilians have come to believe that no local institution can effectively counter the junta. Hence, they tweeted esteemed foreign diplomats such as the American ambassador to Thailand for intervention: 'Dear @KristieKenney Please help @chaturon.[8] Please protect Democracy. Best regards, Thais.' Moreover, civilians also wrote to international organisations to share their side of the story to challenge the junta's report about local happenings. Sunisa relates: 'Recently,

[8] Chaturon Chaisang, former Minister of Education, is an outspoken critic of the coup.

democracy lovers tweeted pictures and messages to the American embassy, the UN, the BCC, and CNN because they want outsiders' assistance in *spreading the truth* about what's happening—facts that are not coming from the report of the NCPO, but from the people, and in addition, they want to seek help in terms of justice.' Thus, Twitter is not just an alternative media space for civilians but a counter media platform to negate state officials' representation of 'truths'. It is unclear whether tweets to international organisations made any difference, but through continuously contacting authorities in mass volume on Twitter, civilians are working to rally the global community to join in their fight against the junta. They have extended their efforts and mission beyond the Thai border, transcending local authorities and geographical confines.

Finally, civilians have created graphic symbols to protest their silencing and to affirm unity. The first frequently tweeted graphic is a thick, solid, black horizontal line used to cover up the words of a tweet. It resembles viscous duct tape utilised in construction, so in employing the black line, civilians are signifying that their freedom of expression and thoughts have been sealed and that the junta has silenced their speech, as if someone has taped their mouth shut. In addition, protesters reconstructed their outlawed anti-coup solidarity gesture—the raising of three fingers—by typing three lowercase L letters back-to-back: 'lll'. They frequently tweet this symbol, appending it to their message. Some even made the 'lll' mark more permanent by making it a part of their Twitter handle. Through these moves, civilians are rhetorically using graphics to pledge solidarity and demonstrate defiance against the coup, and they are motivating others to follow suit. As the 'lll' symbol and horizontal line circulate throughout social network, they affirm and announce the tweeters' standpoint and condemnation against the junta, spreading and keeping the anti-coup spirit alive. Through their creative use of graphics, Thai citizens have been able to continue their political protests, without having to publically gather on the street.

Collectively, all of the digital protest moves—from using hashtags, to contacting the international community, to designing subversive graphics—are digital *tactics* that enable civilians to accomplish things typically done at a rally in a safer public space to elude censorship and arrest, voice their demand, advocate their creed, show solidarity, contradict authority, seek assistance, and maintain morale. According to Michel de Certeau (1992), tactics constitute a calculated action to re-appropriate the restrictions or encroachment from the authority into opportunities for a more favourable situation. It is the opposite of strategy, which he defines as authoritative moves circumscribed from above to limit citizens' actions. Tactics open up subversive agency against strategy. Thai civilians' digital rally actions are a case in point. Their digital protest moves exemplify creative compensation *tactics* against political oppression in a time of restricted freedom, thought, and assembly.

The Drawbacks of Twitter: From Character Limit to Surveillance

All in all, Twitter has been a productive rhetorical space for Thai civilians to achieve multiple civic aims: informing and updating political events, expressing commentaries, providing political analysis and insights, ridiculing the government, and demonstrating against the government. Yet, despite these functions, the site is not without drawbacks. First, the 140-character limit can be constraining.[9] It makes it difficult for civilians to compose sustained, lengthy discourse or engage in a deliberative dialogue to build a public sphere, an open egalitarian space where citizens of pluralistic polity can gather to speak from and across differences in a productive manner on issues of common concern (Harbermas, 1964; Sheridan et al., 2012). As previously noted, dialogic exchanges are difficult to carry out within a 140-character limit. Second, political tweets can draw flaming attacks from those holding an opposite view. Many interviewees mentioned that 'trolls', people who patrol the web to incite discord, have attacked them via tweets. The 140-character limit of Twitter, however, makes it hard for civilians to engage in a rational debate with their opponents. So, tweeters often resort to blocking their dissenters, which occludes the possibility for a dialogue to engage difference. Third, Twitter is subjected to surveillance by the government. The state can monitor every posted message and prosecute people. Specifically, a hashtag such as #nocoup allows for easy aggregation and tracking of protesters' momentum and developments (Neumayer and Valtysson, 2013), enabling the state to keep current with all anti-coup actions. Therefore, Thomas Poell (2015) and Morozov (2011) have cautioned against hailing social media as a magic platform for a democratic revolution. As technology exists within a system of power relations, it can become a panopticon (Foucault, 1977) to aggrandise state power (Neumayer and Valtysson, 2013). Lastly, Twitter is the second largest

---

[9] Interviewees did not report using a tweet extension program (e.g. TwitLonger), which allows them to compose beyond 140 characters.

social media site in Thailand. It comes in second after Facebook. As of January 2015, there are 4.5 million Thai Twitter users and 30 million Facebook accounts (Vichienwanitchkul, 2015). Even though Twitter has a large presence in urbanised Thailand, we need to recognise that its reach is limited compared to Facebook. We must also recognise that a digital divide still exists and that social media platforms accessed via the internet are not available to all citizens.[10]

Given the limitations above, we must not exalt Twitter as the ideal technology for Thai democracy-building. At the same time, however, we should not dismiss its importance and affordances. As demonstrated by the study, Twitter remains a viable, active platform for silenced citizens to assert political dissent, rally for change, and sustain hope for democracy under a repressive condition. According to Neumayer and Valtysson (2013), 'technologies can reproduce existing hierarchies and systems of power but [they] can be appropriated for subversive action to challenge power and lead to political change'. Or as one civilian puts it, 'Twitter is an important tool and weapon in our advocacy and fight for democracy.' As such, interviewees report that the numbers of political tweeters are continuously increasing, suggesting that the site will continue to be an important platform for Thai civic actions. Ultimately, the power and potentials of Twitter lie in careful, critical use and rhetorical awareness of its affordances and limitations—not abandonment.

Conclusion: The Emergence of a Digital Counterpublic

When the Thai military seized power and outlawed public demonstration, civilians did not buckle from the prohibition but capitalised upon the affordances of social media to carve out another public space for political action. Through their tweets, citizens have transformed Twitter into an alternative civic arena for subverting authoritarianism. They have enacted digital civil disobedience, one which is networked, open, and borderless. Through their on-line disobedience, the protesters have come to constitute a counterpublic: 'members of subordinated social groups [who] invent and circulate counterdiscourses, which in turn permit them to formulate oppositional interpretations of their identities, interest and needs' (Fraser, 1990). According to Nancy Fraser (1990), counterpublics emerge in response to political exclusions; they 'function as bases and training

[10] According to InternetLiveStats, Thailand has an internet growth rate of 8% per year. In 2014, it had 19,386,154 internet users in a population of 67,222,972.

grounds for agitational activities directed toward the wider [dominant] publics'. Specifically, they 'counter' by producing subversive discourse to foster a new social arrangement or structure, one that marks itself against the dominant sociopolitical/cultural horizon (Warner, 2002). In the Thai context, 'counterdiscourses' against the junta are created through texts composed and circulated on social networks through computers and mobile instruments. Civilians rely upon social media to accomplish their 'agitational activities' (Fraser, 1990). As such, they represent what we might call a digital counterpublic: a subordinate collective that capitalizes upon the affordances of networked technologies to invent rhetorical agitational discourses to contest the dominant power structure and, in the process, foster ways to rectify the sociopolitical system and reinvent social realities.

Seeing Thai civilian tweeters as a digital counterpublic complicates our understanding of 'slacktivsm' and typologies of social media usage. Considering the complex functions of Thai civilians' tweets—which are not without risk—we need to question the binary between 'slacktivism' and activism by heeding the political context in which the tweets are being composed. Freedom of speech and assembly are not an inherent transnational right. Given the restricted political freedom in Thailand, protests and activism now need to change form and *tactic* for practicality and safety; otherwise, civilians risk losing their freedom, ability to rally, or lives altogether. If we carefully analyse the complex, multi-layered functions of Thai civilians' tweets, we cannot dismiss their significance as merely 'slacktivism'. They are rhetorical discourses that aim to foster governmental accountability, checks and balances, critical political awareness, informed citizenship, international support, civic interest, democratic solidarity, and morale—all of which are foundational elements of a strong democracy. Yet, much Twitter research tends to focus on the extent to which social media helps enhance or coordinate offline protests. Recognising the multi-layered affordances of Thai civilians' tweets thus augments and deepens current understanding about the typologies of tweets by motivating us to not take them at face value. As this essay demonstrated, we need to look beyond what is at the surface of the typologies by analysing their deeper functions to grasp how they operate and most significantly, what they are overtly *and* covertly doing. In sum, as cross-cultural communication researchers, we need to ground our analysis of social media practices upon a careful understanding of sociocultural/political circumstances—gleaned from *listening* to and *respecting* the voices of local citizens, who have the highest stake in their social futures. Through doing so, we can develop a more localised, multidimensional understanding of the ever changing complexity of subversive political rhetorical strategies in what is now an increasingly technologically mediated, digitally interconnected, yet politically unpredictable transnational world.

References

Accenture. (2012). *Surfing Southeast Asia's powerful digital wave.* Retrieved 19 June 2015, from http://www.accenture.com/us-en/Pages/insight-surfing-southeast-asias-powerful-digital-wave.aspx.

Burke, K. (1950). From *a rhetoric of motives*. In. P. Bizzell & B. Herzberg. (Eds.), *The Rhetorical Tradition*. (pp. 1324-1340). Boston: Bedford/St. Martins.

Burns, A. & Eltham, B. (2009). Twitter free Iran: An evaluation of Twitter's role in public diplomacy and information operations in Iran's 2009 election crisis'. In Papandrea, F. & Armstrong, M. (Eds.). *Record of the communications policy & research forum*. (pp. 298-310). Sydney: Network Insight Institute.

Conover, M., et al. (2013). The digital evolution of Occupy Wall Street. *PLoS ONE,* 8.5: e64679. doi:10.1371/journal.pone.0064679.

Daer, A., Hoffman, R. & Goodman , S. (2014). The rhetorical functions of hashtags forms across social media applications. *Communication Design Quarterly*, 3.1, 12-16.

de Certeau, M. (1992). *Practices of Everyday Life*. (Rendall, S., Trans.) Oakland, CA: University of California Press.

Dubisar, A. M., & Palmeri, J. (2010). Palin/Pathos/Peter Griffin: Political video remix and composition pedagogy. *Computers & Composition*, 27(2), 77-93. doi:10.1016/j.compcom.2010.03.004.

Fraser, N. (1990). Rethinking the public sphere: A contribution to the critique of actually existing democracy, *Social Text* 25(26), 56-80.

Foucault, M. (1977). *Discipline and Punish*. (Sheridan, A. Trans.) New York: Vintage.

Gladwell, M. (2010). Small change: Why the revolution will not be tweeted. *New Yorker.* Retrieved from *http://www.newyorker.com/magazine/2010/10/04/small-change-malcolm-gladwell.*

Gries, L. E. (2013). Iconographic tracking: A digital research method for visual rhetoric and circulation studies. *Computers & Composition*, 30(4), 332-348. doi:10.1016/j.compcom.2013.10.006.

Harbermas, J, Lennox, S. & Lennox F. (1964/1974). The public sphere: An encyclopedia article. *New German Critique,* 3. 49-55.

Johnson, G.A, Tudor, B. & Nuseibeh, H. (2013). 140 Characters or less: How is the Twitter mediascape influencing the Egyptian revolution? *Middle East Journal of Culture and Communication*, 6, 126-148.

Lim, M. (2012). Clicks, Cabs, and Coffee Houses: Social Media and Oppositional Movements in Egypt, 2004-2011. *Journal Of Communication*, *62*(2), 231-248. doi:10.1111/j.1460-2466.2012.01628.x.

Lindgren, S. (2013). The potential and limitations of Twitter activism: Mapping the 2011 Libyan uprising. *TripleC,* 11.1, 207-220.

Lu, X. (2004). *Rhetoric of Chinese cultural revolution*. Columbia, SC: University of South Carolina Press.

Mao, L.M. (2014). *Comparative rhetoric*. New York: Routledge.

McCaughey, M. (2014). *Cyberactivism on the participatory web.* New York: Routledge.

Morozov, E. (2011). *The net delusion: The dark side of Internet freedom.* New York: Public Affairs.

Iran: Downside to the 'Twitter revolution'. (2009). *Dissent*. 56(3), 80-85.

Munteanu, I & Mungiu-Pippidi. (2009). Moldova's Twitter revolution. *Journal of Democracy*, *20*(3), 136-142.

Murthy, Dhiraj. (2013). *Twitter*. Cambridge: Polity.

National News Bureau of Thailand. (2015, June 19). Retrieved from http://thainews.prd.go.th/CenterWeb/News/SpecialNewsList?NT22_TmpID=TM57053102.

Neumayer, C & Valtysson, B. (2013). Tweet against Nazis? Twitter, power, and networked publics in anti-fascist protests. *Journal of Media and Communication Research*, 55, 3-20.

Penney, J., & Dadas, C. (2014). (Re)Tweeting in the service of protest: Digital composition and circulation in the Occupy Wall Street movement. *New Media & Society*, *16*(1), 74-90. doi:10.1177/1461444813479593.

Poell, T. (2015) Social media activism and state censorship. In D. Trottier & C. Fuchs. (Eds.), *Social media, politics and the state*. (pp. 189-205). London: Routledge.

Queen, M. (2008). Transnational feminist rhetorics in a digital world. *College English*, *70*(5), 471-489.

Rabimi, B. (2011). The agonistic social media: Cyberspace in the formation of dissent and consolidation of state power in postelection Iran. *Communication Review*, 14, 158-178.

Rananand, P.R. (2003). Internet and democracy in Thailand. In. Indrajit Banerje. (Ed.), *Rhetoric and reality: The Internet challenge for democracy in Asia*. (pp. 288-313). Singapore: Times Academic Press.

Ridolfo, J & DeVoss, D. Composing for recomposition: Rhetorical velocity and delivery. *Kairos,* 13.2. Retrieved from http://kairos.technorhetoric.net/13.2/topoi/ridolfo_devoss/.

Rogers, C. (1951). Communication: Its blocking and its facilitation. Retrieved from http://www.redwoods.edu/instruct/jjohnston/English1A/readings/rhetoricandthinking/communicationitsblockingitsfacilitation.htm.

Salem, S. (2105). Creating space for dissent: The role of social media in the 2011 Egyptian revolution. In D. Trottier & C. Fuchs. (Eds.), *Social media, politics and the state*. (pp. 171-188). London, Routledge.

Sheridan, D., Ridolfo, J. & Michel, A.J. (2012). *The Available Means of Persuasion*. Anderson, SC: Parlor.

Sun, H. (2012). *Cross-Cultural technology design.* Oxford: Oxford University Press.

Theocharis, Y., Lowe, W., van Deth, J. W., & García-Albacete, G. (2015). Using Twitter to mobilize protest action: online mobilization patterns and action repertoires in the Occupy Wall Street, Indignados, and Aganaktismenoi movements. *Information, Communication & Society, 18*(2), 202-220. doi:10.1080/1369118X.2014.948035.

Tufekci, Z., & Wilson, C. (2012). Social Media and the Decision to Participate in Political Protest: Observations From Tahrir Square. *Journal Of Communication, 62*(2), 363-379. doi:10.1111/j.1460-2466.2012.01629.x.

Varnali K, Gorgulu V. A social influence perspective on expressive political participation in Twitter: the case of #OccupyGezi. *Information, Communication & Society* [serial online]. January 2015;18(1):1-16. Available from: Academic Search Premier, Ipswich, MA. Accessed June 21, 2015.

Vichienwanitchkul, M. (2015, January 13). Online marketing in Thailand: the state of social media. *Syndacast.* Retrieved from http://syndacast.com/infographic-online-marketing-thailand-the-state-of-social-media/.

Warner, M. (2005). *Publics and Counterpublics.* New York: Zone Books.

CHAPTER SEVEN

ON-LINE DATING: EXPLORING THE DIGITAL WAYS OF FINDING LOVE IN INDONESIA

TONY CHALKLEY

Overview

- On-line dating has experienced significant growth in Asia as well, with the number of new web services growing exponentially. It would appear that the practice of using on-line dating to find love is now a global phenomenon.
- This chapter intertwines current research literature and data from conversations with university students in Australia and Indonesia in order to explore how the changing world of on-line dating is helping/hindering young people as they shape and develop identity, represent themselves in the virtual world and ultimately, how they might (or might not), find love online.
- Facebook has become the 'de facto' dating service, outside mainstream dating sites. But users still add a 'healthy degree of scepticism' to ensure their safety, security and emotional wellbeing whilst on-line.

Mediated Dating

Something had changed in the public perceptions around 'online dating'. Firstly, a rough consensus had formed (especially in the media) that now tells us that 'online dating' has become 'respectable' and, secondly, today's students—as opposed to students ten years ago—do not react with horror when discussing the internet as a place to find love.

This chapter is divided into three sections; the first section presents an introduction to what might be called 'moderated dating' – that is, using a media interface to seek company, love, lust and/or marriage. In this chapter, the definition of 'moderated dating' starts with a 'wife wanted' advertisement in a 150-year-old newspaper and ends with a 'kiss' or 'wink' on a modern day web site. The second part of this chapter examines the research literature in an effort to understand what factors might motivate people to engage in online dating; what are they looking for and is it something missing from their day-to-day life? How do they represent themselves, develop credibility and how do they evaluate the 'truthfulness' of others on the site? The third and final section will intertwine this research literature with stories told to me by students in Australia and Indonesia. In their stories, participants tell how they used 'respectable' sites like Facebook as a 'de facto' dating service, how some used mainstream dating sites to seek out partners that are considered socially 'unacceptable' by their families and friends and most importantly they told me how they use a 'healthy degree of scepticism' to ensure their safety, security and emotional wellbeing whilst on-line. The final section will also include an outline of how longstanding ethnographic techniques were used to collect and frame these data.

Using the media to find love seems to be a relatively new phenomenon, but this is not quite correct. For some people, it is difficult to understand how we reached a point in time when we can employ global positioning and mobile applications like 'Tinder' and 'Grindr' to instantly accept or reject a potential partner (one we have yet to meet). Certainly, this immediate and disembodied approach to finding love is relatively new, but the idea of using the media to find a partner is not. Foucault's theories around the genealogy of change are useful and insightful here; on-line dating has not suddenly appeared in our everyday lives as a powerful, modern phenomena, but instead, like a family history, its 'acceptability' and adoption has many twists and turns and similar to our family trees, some side branches die off and disappear (Faubion, 2002).

The appearance of on-line dating as part of conventional narratives in television and film has helped to normalise the use of technology as a way to seek love and the pervasiveness of online socialisation has also contributed to a change in how we perceive on-line dating today (Finkel *et al.*, 2012). The classified advertisement is no longer considered the most effective way to look for love (consider it a 'deceased' part of the 'dating family tree'), but these printed advertisements gave birth to what was to come – an acceptance that using the media to find love might just be 'ok'. Take these now redundant advertisements from newspapers published during the Civil War in the United States:

Figure 7A: Advertisements placed in the Newport Newspaper (Pennsylvania 1861-1865 - http://www.advertisingforlove.com/2009/10/ah-young-love.html)

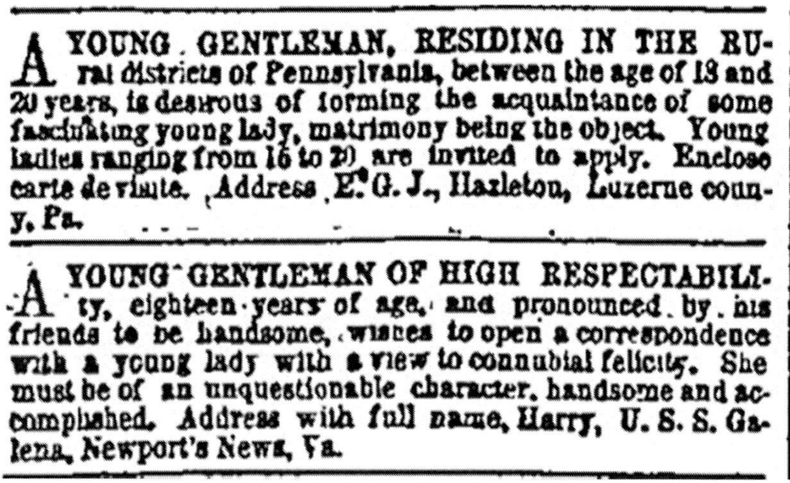
A YOUNG GENTLEMAN, RESIDING IN THE RU-ral districts of Pennsylvania, between the age of 18 and 20 years, is desirous of forming the acquaintance of some fascinating young lady, matrimony being the object. Young ladies ranging from 16 to 20 are invited to apply. Enclose carte de visite. Address E. G. J., Hazleton, Luzerne coun-ty, Pa.

A YOUNG GENTLEMAN OF HIGH RESPECTABILI-ty, eighteen years of age, and pronounced by his friends to be handsome, wishes to open a correspondence with a young lady with a view to connubial felicity. She must be of an unquestionable character, handsome and ac-complished. Address with full name, Harry, U. S. S. Ga-lena, Newport's News, Va.

The intentions and desires expressed in these advertisements (Figure 7A) seem humorous to the modern reader, but in reality, the goal of these expressions of interest was not so different to the internet postings we read today. For example, suitor number one told us very little about himself, but was quite clear about the requirements for his perfect partner and his intentions for her:

> *A young gentleman, residing in the rural districts of Pennsylvania, between the age of 18 and 20 years, is desirous of forming the acquaintance of some fascinating young lady, matrimony being the object. Young ladies ranging from 16 to 20 are invited to apply. Enclose carte de visite. Address E.G.J., Hazleton, Luzerne county, Pa.*

Likewise, suitor number two ('Harry') discloses little about himself, except to say that he was well-bred and perceived by his friend to be 'good looking':

> *A young gentleman of high respectability, eighteen years of age, and pronounced by his friends to be handsome, wishes to open a*

> *correspondence with a young lady with a view to connubial felicity. She must be of an unquestionable character, handsome, and accomplished. Address with full name, Harry, U.S.S. Galena, Newport's News, Va.*

Reading between the lines, it can be seen that both these advertisements have subtle messages in their subtext – for example, from his address it can be assumed that the first correspondent was a farmer (or son of a landowner) in one of the wealthiest districts of Pennsylvania; while, number two, 'Harry' was stationed on a Union Navy ship, so we might presume he is a sailor. The reason why 'Harry' used only his first name and yet demands the full name of his potential lovers is a mystery! To the modern reader, these 150-year-old 'love wanted' classifieds read as 'a little foreign', 'very formal' and 'humorous' even, but this chapter shows the reader that they were not so very different to the profile postings you find on 'RSVP' and many other dating websites. Paraphrasing Marshall McLuhan, 'whilst the medium might have dramatically changed, the message has not' (McLuhan, 1967).

Going On-line

The world of on-line dating is a different, unpredictable, and yet increasingly accepted, world. At some time in the past ten or so years, on-line dating had become progressively more popular and increasingly socially acceptable. Ten years ago, university students made shocked and horrified faces when this topic was mentioned, but today, the response is a little different. Scanning the most popular Australian dating websites revealed services such as 'Intelligent matching based on compatibility and partner preferences', some aim to 'connect, engage and entertain singles: making single life an exhilarating and complete experience.' and one new site promised to assist people who are 'looking for extra thrills and romance through discreet relationships, casual encounters and extra-marital affairs. Meet for romantic adventures with local married women or attached men'.

Facebook offers many opportunities to 'mine the data' of friends in order to find a date and now eBay has a tab for 'dating'! Why has on-line dating become popular? Back in 1995, when on-line dating was relatively new, Bradford Scharlott and William Christ found that online dating was becoming popular because it promised:

> '.... the ability to communicate with others without revealing details about one self enables the shy user to interact without fear of rejection.

> Moreover, as the questions about their personalities and fantasies reveal, (on-line) 'Matchmaker' enables these users to communicate in ways that in other contexts they might feel too socially inhibited to do.' (Scharlott and Christ, 1995. p.201).

The primary focus of this chapter is concerned with how members of on-line dating sites communicate; in particular, how do they behave/communicate in the on-line dating world? As far back as 1995, researchers were discovering that:

> 'The pattern of sending and receiving messages on [Matchmaker] suggests that, generally speaking, men and women on the system employ different communication strategies. Most men seem inclined to maximise the number of users they contact, presumably to increase their chances of finding someone interested in a physically intimate relationship; most women, by contrast, seem inclined to contact fewer men and then try to establish more sustained communications' (Scharlott and Christ, 1995, p.202).

This observation reads like a high school biology lesson in mammal reproduction; a 'successful male will have many matings'. Surely it's not that basic? This early research found that the way men and women communicate on dating websites was actually very complex. Women had different motivations and expectations to start with, women were more successful at meeting a partner (and sustaining a relationship), men disclosed less in their profiles and wrote less in their messages. Researchers found that women log in and reply more frequently, men tended to infrequently log in and would tend to bulk post their replies. Men tended to not initiate (or would abandon) conversations that didn't assist them in their 'quest', but women would occasionally contact other female members (the 'competition'), sharing their on-line experiences. Later in this chapter you will read how, nearly twenty years later, little had changed; university students tended to engage with dating sites in a very similar manner! (Scharlott and Christ, 1995)

So, what is different about this medium and why/how do people engage with it? Answering this question proved to be not a simple task. People's motivation for using dating websites was as varied as the number and types of sites available to them. Some sites seem to have a very obvious reason for participation; the web site 'Ashley Madison – life is too short, have an affair' found at <www.ashleymadison.com> is clearly a place for married people to seek out extramarital excitement (it is also a place single people go to for secret relationships and as one member stated on her public profile 'husband stealing'). The dating site 'You Must like Dogs'[1] has a number of levels of engagement, but fundamentally, the explicit/primary motivation to become a member, was that you must enjoy the companionship of canines (your own and that of a potential partner). When you examine more generic dating sites (such as 'RSVP' and 'Flirt') the explicit/primary motivation is to 'meet someone' but the secondary motivations were much more complex. What sort of 'someone' did they want and for what type of relationship? In their study into the use of the internet to meet potential partners, Couch and Liamputtong found that;

> 'The reasons participants gave for using on-line dating were varied, and included seeking a soul mate, seeking sex, looking for fun, relaxation, to ease boredom, or because it seemed an easy way to meet people'(Couch and Liamputtong, 2008).

These findings seemed logical, because these are the same reasons people go to nightclubs, join a book group, attend a party or sign up for a speed dating night at a local restaurant. Realizing the reasons people used on-line services is one part of understanding online dating, but, perhaps more interesting, is the motivators that lead people to search, click and sign up. Couch and Liamputtong again:

> 'For most of the participants, changing personal circumstances provided the impetus for using on-line dating. These included being very busy at work, most friends becoming partnered, having children …moving to a new city' (Couch and Liamputtong, 2008)

These findings resonated with the stories in this study. Students joined RSVP (and other sites) for reasons such as: breaking up with a boy/girlfriend; moving to a new location; work and study hours were not compatible with a social life; and when they found themselves surrounded by paired up couples. Whilst changes in personal circumstances appeared to be one of the principal drivers for involvement in on-line dating, other significant social changes are thought to have contributed to the rise of mediated match making: factors such as delayed marriage, the introduction of 'no fault' divorce, a growing acceptance of *de facto* relationships and many other social reforms have resulted in the promulgation of on-line dating into everyday life. The fact that we undertake an ever growing number of 'day to day' on-line activities also influences our opinions around digital matchmaking; we buy groceries on-line, play games online,

---

[1] (http://www.youmustlovedogsdating.com/, 2014)

socialise on the web and even do our banking online, so why wouldn't we look for love in the same manner?

Exploring First-hand Experiences

Over the years working as a university academic, I have taught, talked with and listened to thousands of student conversations. I have also asked them about how their relationships, quest for love and social lives have been affected by a life 'increasingly spent online'. The majority of discourse was about 'day to day' things such as struggling to find time to study, the challenge of understanding and applying theory, doing well in assessment and how students experienced the 'hurdles' of undertaking a degree. On the whole, fairly mundane stuff! Then something changed. Student stories started to include a new and different topic; they began discussing their problems with what I called 'the rise of the digital self and the (seeming) decline of the physical self'. Some students told me that, in spite of having hundreds of online 'friends', they rarely seem to meet potential partners in a social setting. This chapter shows how a sample of Deakin University and Universitas Indonesia students have used online matchmaking services to find love, in response to problems with diminished social/geographic opportunities.

In order to ensure the anonymity of participants, their stories are presented using a recognised ethnographic technique: as a series of vignettes constructed as composite identities (Schensul and LeComte, 1999). The process of creating composite identities takes the personal characteristics of the participants and merges them to form a series of amalgamated characters, each with a distinct voice and identity (Schensul and LeComte, 1999). In this research, the process of manufacturing composite profiles was relatively straightforward. By examining the characteristics of individual students in this study, a pattern emerged. There seemed to be some clearly identifiable typical (and atypical) behaviours, mutually held beliefs, shared ethical positions, common idioms, mutual understandings, similar family backgrounds and shared understandings about how some young people have begun to use online dating to find love (or at least, a relationship that might lead to love).

These stories were merged to form a sedimented account: a process where stories are brought to life through composite identities. Ethnographers have long used the concept of 'sedimentation' to illustrate how, like sand on a beach, meaning is produced in layers with socially constructed meanings layered over time. Cooper *et al.* argued that 'The geological metaphor of sedimentation allows us to consider a dialectical rather than a linear view of change. Case studies show how one archetype is layered on the other, rather than representing a distinct transformation where one archetype sweeps away the residues of the other'(Cooper *et al.*, 1996) In this case, one of the important layers of sediment was the research literature, providing an historical layer that allows the reader to contextualise what the students told me in their stories.

In this case, four composites seemed to be the best way to accurately and honestly represent the many sedimented stories gathered in this study (I have employed these composites in earlier research and found that this technique effectively 'brings to life' participant stories by encouraging the reader to more actively engage with the data). These composites are called 'Nisrina', 'Bree', 'Max' and 'Angga', names selected simply because they are common names and seem to appear very often in my conversations. Who are 'Nisrina', 'Bree', 'Max' and 'Angga'?

'Nisrina' is in her early 20's, comes from Jakarta, Indonesia. She has a number of 'close' male friends at the university, but also spends significant time 'talking' to her 'old' school friends, most of whom still live at home with their parents, but a few are studying abroad. She posts many photographs on 'normal' social pages and is an infrequent member of a dating site called 'muslima'. Mostly she just reads the profiles of others. She works at least four nights a week at a shop owned by a family friend and is a little stressed at the moment as she struggles to balance the commitments of work/study/life. She has no boyfriend at present, but wants one. She describes her parents as 'fairly cool Muslims' and doesn't feel any pressure to marry in a pre-arranged manner, but she knows that any potential boyfriend will be very closely scrutinised. A local boy has sent her an on-line 'kiss' and she thinks she might reply.

'Bree' is similar to Nisrina in that she is at an Australian university to study hard. 'Bree' is the first in her family to go to university and as she has only just turned 18, she feels like the youngest member in most of her classes and finds most male members annoying and lazy. She, too, has gathered a number of new, 'geographically co-located' friends, a number of which reappear as online friends. Due to the vast distance back to her family farm, she doesn't visit home very often, but usually gets a text/mms (most days) from her sisters. She has yet to find a part-time job and with no car, this is proving harder than she thought. Bree has joined 'RSVP'

and 'Flirt', but the initial rush of inappropriate contacts has 'put her off a bit'. Some of the men who sent her winks were more than 30 years her senior. Some profile pictures were images of male genitalia.

'Max' had a great time at high school, where he was considered 'sporty' and 'hot'– he is socially competent and seems to get on well with everyone. He lives on campus at the university and continues to play sport and go to the gym most days. He has had a number of 'girlfriends' but none of these relationships have endured. Early in the year, he and a male friend signed up for 'Tinder' and Max has proved to be very popular. He has been on many 'Tinder' dates and the vast majority of these have led to a one-off sexual encounter. At present he is having a break from 'Tinder' in order to focus on his university exams.

'Angga' is a third year student who has lived his whole life in Indonesia, mostly in Java. An active thespian, 'Angga' spends most of his non-study time involved in music or theatre. He also has a part-time job at a large HMV store. He lives at home and on the whole, he is happy: his mother does his domestic chores and his father keeps a close eye on his grades. 'Angga' has a Facebook page but mostly he chats on web forums for young gay men in Indonesia. In the last few weeks, he has started (tentatively) using an app very similar to 'Grindr' (a popular gay pickup site) to follow a number of men in his local area. He has no local boyfriend, but is involved in an online romance with a man in Europe. He believes that his family are unaware of his preferences and he intends to keep it this way.

Composites such as 'Nisrina', 'Bree', 'Max' and 'Angga' have long been a useful tool for ethnographers as they allow them to personalise the connection between important personal experiences and an area of knowledge. In this study, composites were used as they ensure participant confidentiality by conferring anonymity on a large number of people who have told their stories, by 'telescoping character traits and anecdotes drawn from a number of sources into a single representative sketch' (Zeller, 1995, p.167).

Composites are not without their limitations, and one of the challenges with the production and employment of composite narratives is the risk of stereotyping. This risk was addressed in this project by ensuring that the narratives of each and every participant were used or included. Where possible, the stories and accounts were drawn from the contributions by as many students as possible. As a result, these data contain a number of sometimes–contradictory positions and opinions that cannot be easily reconciled. This is an accurate representation of the data, students used contested narrative to produce meaning, and they were often divided, sometimes unified and occasionally ambiguous about how they perceived the world of online dating. This contested 'meaning making' is the principle focus for much narrative ethnography, and the stories from 'Nisrina', 'Bree', 'Max' and 'Angga' were no exception - their stories were framed in the social theoretical thinking espoused by Spradley in 1979 (and supported by the work of Dorr–Bremme some years later):

> 'The essential core of ethnography is this concern with the meaning of actions and events of the people we seek to understand … people make constant use of these complex meaning systems to organise their behaviour, to understand themselves and others and to make sense out of the world in which they live'. (Spradley, 1979. pp 66-67)

This is because;

> '... the goal of modern ethnography is to take a primary interest in how human groups routinely make sense of their world and act sensibly in it'. (Dorr-Bremme, 1985. p.66)

Having decided to use composites to ensure anonymity whilst telling stories that were, at times, personal and confronting (especially for those students who felt that their actions were certain to result in family disapproval), the next concern was how to best represent the content of these stories. Van Maanen suggests that there are three approaches to the representation of ethnographic stories: realist, confessional and impressionist (Van Maanen, 1995). The realist approach most closely follows positivist traditions, attempting to remove the author from the text, aiming to realistically tell the tale as 'truthfully' and 'scientifically' as possible. The second approach, confessional, is an approach where the author is revealed within the text by writing about emotional reactions and unexpected developments as part of their explanation. Van Maanen describes the third approach as impressionist; the author is the teller of a tale in dramatic form of episodes considered to be notable and significant.

Figure 7B. Small sample of current on-line dating sites.

Managing On-line Identities

Almost without exception, participants told how they 'rarely believe all they read' when it comes to digital communication, but this scepticism becomes particularly acute when they were using dating sites. Nisrina said that, initially she spent just a few minutes setting up her profile when she first joined and a little later returned to the site and 'value added' to her description;

> *'....as I looked at other profiles, I realised that there was a certain 'type' of profile picture, a particular way to talk about yourself and mostly, to get attention whilst giving little away. Most people had some 'hint of mystery' and 'promise of excitement' in their profiles. I actually described myself honestly and in plain language. My photo was not 'sex' enough and I wasn't playing the game like other girls.'*

'Bree', 'Max' and 'Angga' also admitted that they used a mixture of 'truth' and what they called 'semi-truth' to manipulate and promote their on-line profiles. They did this in order to ensure that they were highly 'visible' to their intended audience and to appeal to as many admirers as possible. This use of 'semi-truth' to construct identity was well established in the literature and seemed to be an everyday practice in the competitive world of online dating;

> 'A commonly accepted understanding of identity presumes that there are multiple aspects of the self which are expressed or made salient in different

> contexts….there are three domains of the self: the *actual self* (attributes an individual possesses), the *ideal* self (attributes an individual would ideally possess) and the *ought self* (attributes an individual ought to possess).' (Ellison *et al.*, 2006)

As a (secret) gay person living in a conservative country, 'Angga' said he was very aware of the tensions when moving between these three identities, he also told me how this movement between 'selves' was both 'liberating' and 'depressing':

> *'I love being able to get on-line and talk, flirt and share experiences. But! When I get off-line, I have to kill off part of my real identity and live a life that is a deception. This is hard'*

The female students in this study also claimed that the competitive nature of digital matchmaking made them feel like they should only present their 'ideal self' online; energetic, flirty, adventurous and sexy. Bree described her experience on-line:

> *' the photos are such a stress, I am not bad looking, but a quick look at the profile of others suggests that I need more make up, more pout, more skin and bigger breasts. To start with, I was honest about my study, fitness level, interests and achievements. But in order to get attention, it is cleavage, mindless posts and a username that suggests that you suffer from a form of nymphomania. This is not me in real life, why should I be like this in on-line?'*

But, not all students thought that the use of multiple identities was a problem, some participants appreciated the opportunity to engage in some shared deception (Ellison *et al.*, 2006). For example, Max:

> *'Well, of course you don't tell ridiculous lies, especially if there is a chance you will meet and hook up, like on tinder. I have used a good photo and dropped 3 kilos off my real weight and added 2cms to my real height. I played saxophone at high school, so pretend to still play and have a sax in my room. I also claim to go rock climbing as a hobby, not true. Girls love it, girls do it too, tell little lies that don't really matter'.*

The act of 'forgetting', 'not including' or 'over-stating' is not just the domain of online dating sites – we do this on social media sites, eBay, YouTube and even Snapchat. In 2001, a study found that 86% of participants felt that others misrepresented their physical appearance (Gibbs *et al.*, 2001) and this was found to be the case; a quarter of on-line dating participants reported misrepresenting some aspect of their identity, most commonly age (14%), marital status (10%) and appearance (10%). But, Max found that these misrepresentations were moderated by the likelihood of a physical meeting;

> 'Anticipation of face-to-face communication influences self-representation choices and self-disclosures because individuals will more closely monitor their disclosures as the probability of future face-to-face interaction increases' (Ellison *et al.*, 2006).

As a member of the 'Muslima' dating site, Nisrina was acutely aware of what she said, did and disclosed on the site. She was cognisant of the cultural contradiction she faced: the pressure to publicly involve her family in any potential relationships was offset against the fact that 'Muslima' offered her the chance to personally and privately pick from the five million registered members. As she used the 'sort by suburb' function, she hoped to ensure that she was only interacting with people nearby. The longer she used the site, the more she became only interested in people she might meet in person:

> *'I don't lie on-line, it is a waste of time. I wear a hijab in everyday life, I have one on in all my images* (some girls have private images that are more revealing). *I love to read, I work hard, I study hard, and I love my family. I want to marry a man who I have chosen, one who is my age, knows me and loves me for who I am. On-line dating is a mixed blessing for me – I can be brutally honest, this is liberating, but in an environment where Muslim girls have photos with a hijab and cleavage and list 'obedience and submission' as personal traits, I sometimes find it challenging to get attention.'*

Nisrina's experience of the tension of 'fighting for attention' whilst remaining (mostly) 'true to yourself and your beliefs' was a recurring story in the data and when asked 'why did she bother, why did she sign up?' Her answer was interesting:

> *'I signed up because a female friend in* [Javanese City] *had successfully used the site to find a boyfriend and then I also discovered that boy I sit next to in class was also a member, as was his brother. We sat down in Starbucks and he convinced me to do a basic sign up for a laugh'.*

This involvement triggered by familiarity seems to be a global phenomenon. In their 2103 study, Pew Research found that having a friend or associate who uses online dating greatly increased the likelihood of signing up:

> '42% of all Americans know an on-line dater, and 29% know someone who has used on-line dating to find a spouse or other long-term relationship. Familiarity with on-line dating through usage by friends or family members has increased dramatically since out last survey of on-line dating in 2005. Some 42% of Americans know someone who has used on-line dating.' (Duggan, 2013)

Like many of the findings in this chapter, this made sense. We tend to seek out the recommendations of others and, if possible, undertake similar activities. If most of our friends recommend we buy books from a particular on-line store, look for movie advice from a web review service and use services like spark notes to help with essays, why wouldn't we entertain the idea of joining a dating service on their list of recommendations?

The final, and possibly most significant, finding in this study concerns the idea of staying safe on-line. In both Australia and Indonesia, it seemed that not a week goes by without an 'online dating goes wrong' story appearing in the media. These stories usually take one of two forms: some are about lonely and vulnerable people being defrauded of significant sums of money; and, the other concerns (mainly) younger girls being lured into situations that result in sexual assault. All of the female participants in this study mentioned safety as a concern, as did the vast majority of male participants. Bree summed up the problems very well:

> *'In the real world you feel like you have control of the situation, if the event is going poorly, you go home and with a potential 'pick up' you see what you are getting. If they are a 'tool' you can tell. But, on-line it is harder to see through the smoke screen and spot the creeps. I have so many men that are, like, older than my father trying to hook up with me. One very pushy guy had his age as 21 but didn't seem to write like a 21-year-old bloke. I found his profile picture was an image ripped from google. I blocked him, but what if we had decided to meet up and he was a sexual predator? This worry is in the back of my mind with every interaction. I am also over "dickpics"* (a photograph of the sender's genitalia)'

Angga had similar, but different problems with staying safe as he transitioned from online interaction to face to face meetings:

> *'I have heard rumours of extremist anti-gay men getting on the site, organising a meeting then turning up with a gang to beat up their proposed date. The thought of this puts me off and makes me frightened to go to the next level. On-line seems fairly safe, but the interface with the*

real world is not. Sometimes I wonder 'what is the point of on-line dating if you can't go on a date?'

These were only two examples of issues with the safety, integrity and reliability of online dating services. Participants told of being approached for paid sex, of constant requests for explicit images of themselves, of persistent contact with people outside their interests/age/preferences and some even spoke of the sense of disconnection they felt after repeatedly using a 'hook-up for sex' application on their phone. A few also talked about the great friends they have made, the love affairs they have experienced and in some cases, realising a long-term partnership as a result of looking for love online. In summary, looking for love is tough. Looking for love on-line is even tougher than it seems.

References

Cooper, D., B. Hinings, R. Greeenwood, R and J. Brown (1996). Sedimentation and Transformation in Organizational Change: The Case of Canadian Law Firms *Organization Studies,* 17, 623 - 647.

Couch, D., and P. Liamputtong (2008). Online Dating and Mating: The Use of the Internet to Meet Sexual Partners. *Qualitative Health Research,* 18, 268 -279.

Dorr-Bremme, D. (1985). Ethnographic Evaluation: A Theory and Method. *Educational Evaluation and Policy Analysis,* 7, 56-83.

Duggan, M. (2013). Online Dating and Relationships. *In:* SMITH, A. (ed.) *American Life Series.* Pew Research Institute.

Ellison, N. and J. Gibbs (2006). Managing Impressions Online: Self-Presentation Process in the Online Dating Environment. *Journal of Computer-Mediated Communication,* 11, 415-441.

Faubion, J. D. (ed.) (2002). *Questions of Method - Power: Essential Works of Foucault 1954-1984,* London: Penguin.

Finkel, E., P. Eastwick, B. Karney, H. Reis and S. Sprecher (2012). Online Dating: A Critical Analysis From the Perspective of Psychological Science. *Psychological Science in the Public Interest,* 20, 1-64.

Gibbs, J., N. Ellison and R. Heino (2001). Self Presentation in online personals: The role of anticipated future interaction, self disclosure, and perceived success in Internet dating. *Communication Research,* 33, 1-26.

McLuhan, M. (1967). *Understanding Media: The Extensions of Man,* Canada, Spere Publications.

Scharlott, B. and W. Christ (1995). Overcoming relationship-initiation barriers: The impact of a computer-dating system on sex role, shyness, and appearance inhibitions *Computers in Human Behavior,* 11, 14.

Schensul, J. and M. Lecomte (1999). *Analyzing and interpreting ethnographic data,* Walnut Creek, AltaMira.

Spradley, J. (1979). *The Ethnographic Interview,* New York, Holt, Rinehart and Winston.

Van Maanen, J. (ed.) (1995). *Representation in Ethnography,* Thousand Oaks, California: Sage Publications.

Zeller, N. 1995. Narrative Strategies for Case Reports. *In:* HATCH, J. & WISNIEWSKI, R. (eds.) *Life History and Narrative.* First ed. London: The Falmer Press.

On-line Sources

<http://www.youmustlovedogsdating.com>2014. *Dating site for people who love canine companions* [Online]. Available: http://www.youmustlovedogsdating.com/.

<http://www.ashleymadison.com>2014. *Ashley Madison* [Online]. Available: http://www.ashleymadison.com [Accessed May 2014.

CHAPTER EIGHT

AMBIENT NEWS IN VIETNAM: OPPORTUNITIES, RISKS, AND INFLUENCES IN THE EMERGENT USE OF SOCIAL MEDIA

BRADLEY FREEMAN
AND HOANG THI KIM KHANH

Overview

- New technologies and digitalisation of media are impacting the global news media landscape even as the length of time that audience members will wait on the latest news item that is of interest to them is decreasing.
- Changes to media (and journalism) are occurring at the individual country level and among them is the active usage of social media in news delivery.
- Even countries like Vietnam, where media is not considered free and independent, media outlets and media workers are increasingly engaging with social media. These bring new opportunities, risks, and influences associated with social media and news.
- The news organisations in Vietnam have started to pay attention to the role and impact of social media on journalistic activities. It is for this reason that they are gradually interested in designing social media guidelines or policies and providing training courses for the use of social media for newsroom employees.

Digital news delivery

Around the world, the use of social media in gathering and disseminating news is growing. The length of time that audience members will wait on the latest news item that is of interest to them is decreasing. Twitter is often mentioned in this regard; audience members may retweet a piece of news, or they may add first-hand information or opinion to a story, becoming citizen journalists or commentators to a degree. Professional journalists and editors are also making use of the social media platforms. This chapter investigates the ways individual journalists and editors in Vietnam are utilising social media platforms to gather and disseminate information as well as connect with their audiences. Which social media sites are they using the most? To what degree are gatekeepers involved in this practice? What lessons can be learned concerning the emergent use of social media and its relation to traditional media in Vietnam?

The ways in which new and social media are altering the world's communication landscape are, without question, multitudinous. These changes, largely a result of expanding digital technologies and a maturing internet, are allowing and fostering new approaches to content-gathering, distribution and creation. The range of research topics for media scholars is expanding along with the innovative uses of the technologies and software. One of the areas now receiving greater attention in the literature is how the social media platforms are being used by media workers and outlets; for example, researchers are investigating how journalists, editors and netizens alike are using these platforms to gather and disseminate information, as well as to connect directly with audiences.

Digital communication tools are being used by average citizens to reach out around the world to many more people than was previously possible or likely – with relative ease, while professional media workers are using these new platforms to enhance their own routines, largely revolving around information retrieval and propagation. Traditional media outlets are in on the changes as well. Years ago, they developed home pages in the Web's 1.0 stage, and now they see the advantage to engage with audiences using the social Web 2.0 (O'Reilly, 2012). At the same time, governments and policy-makers are struggling to keep up with the changes –trying to figure out what all of this will ultimately mean for their societies. The degree to which the diffusion of new media (and, by default, social media) is occurring, or 'allowed' to occur, is not the same from one country to the next; neither from the perspective of media companies nor the governments. Speaking of the changes now affecting the newspaper industry, Brock wrote: 'In different societies these changes will work through in different ways and at varying speeds. But the overall direction is plain: old habits of thought and behaviour have to be remade for new conditions' (2013). In the age of globalisation, the 'speed' of technological adoption is fast, and the 'ways' are perhaps becoming less different from one place to the next; McLuhan's 'global village' is becoming more and more a reality – making these changes ripe for investigation.

It is difficult to generalise how research is proceeding when it comes to journalism practices and the internet. Literature on journalism and the internet (or Web 1.0), while having only surfaced in the past 15 years (Garrison, 2000; Pavlik, 2000), is starting to look dated to researchers, but this is not the same everywhere (Bastos, Lima &Moutinho, 2010). We must remember that the life and times of traditional media, and the move towards a converged space, are not occurring at the same pace throughout the globe. It is clear, however, in developed urban centres that Web 2.0 (the interactive and social web) has now attracted the attention of the media industries and media researchers. Even still, the vast majority of published studies tend to be based on the observations of Western scholars studying Western media (or the Global North). The assumptions made in one context do not always apply to another. To be fair, researchers are often writing within the contexts with which they are most familiar; their immediate target readership is thus most likely to be comprised of national colleagues and the perspective can be Janus-faced (i.e. it depends on one's relation to the subject matter as to how it is experienced). This is still okay, because we need the country-level descriptive information in order to build our knowledge base.

Reese (2001), and Willnat, Weaver and Choi (2013) are among a vanguard of scholars who recognize the deficiency in the literature and have called for more international perspectives in research on journalism practices as examples. The present study joins the call from these researchers to analyse and investigate the news products that are being created in the 21st century in different nations. We look at how Vietnamese journalists and editors are engaging each other and the audiences for news and information in their country via social media. In this case, we are interested in observing and explaining their use and interactions in the Web 2.0 environment using social media. Inevitably, in seeking global norms, there will be comparisons among and between the media workers of different countries, but first we must accurately understand the basics of the environments we are comparing. This chapter's research, descriptive by design, investigates how a select group of Vietnamese journalists and editors are utilising social media, specifically Facebook, in their work routines.

Two cases in Vietnam, the placement of a Chinese oil rig off the Vietnamese coast in 2014 (see Perlez, 2014), and tree conservation in Hanoi (see *If a tree falls*, 2015), gave indication that the interactions between news and social media (workers, audiences, and observers) are more than worthy of investigation in the country of Vietnam. Our survey did not specifically mention these cases or others, as our intent here was merely to observe and report on general attitudes and uses of social media by the media workers. We do recognize, however, that these stories (and others) represent ripe areas for further studies and investigations into the social media influences in the news process.

Given these stated areas of consideration, the study proposes three main questions to guide this chapter's path: How and in what ways are Vietnamese journalists utilising the various social media platforms to gather information and disseminate news? (Opportunities); How is the use of social media impacting the role of traditional journalism practices? (Risks); What lessons can be learned and practices shared concerning the emergent use of social media in the media landscape of Vietnam? (Influences).

Journalism Practices, and Ambient Journalism

Topics related to new and social media are among the most widely-studied in the mass communications literature of the past decade. A number of researchers have taken on the abundant and varied aspects related to this vast subject area. Studies dealing with journalism and new media and social software vary to a certain degree in terms of their methodology and theoretical approach.

In some ways, new and social media are synonymous; however, the study does not intend to conflate the two. New media usually refers more generally to the internet and certain applications of the World Wide Web, while social media are probably best described as a specific example of Web 2.0 applications, an outgrowth of Web 2.0 if you will, where interactive modes of communications became prominent – and users began to use the Net for greater two-way and multi-path message creation and distribution (see O'Reilly and Battelle, 2009). All of these various phenomena have led to numerous research avenues. In the case of social media, perhaps Lewis et al.(2012) said it best when noting that '[f]or communication researchers in particular, the dramatic growth of social network sites has provided an ocean of data that reflect the new media activities and artefacts: tweets, status updates, social recommendations, and more' . One area of research concern is how the social media in particular are enabling users and media workers to bring greater amounts of, and access to, news and information into the media marketplace both within individual countries and around the globe (Van Der Haak, Parks, & Castells, 2012).

In this regard, users, governments and media outlets are interested, and in some cases concerned, with the ways in which social media can play a role in the information gathering and dissemination processes.

Literature examining how media workers are utilising social media has grown considerably in the past five years. Many studies have highlighted the situation of Western journalists (Newman, 2009; Braun and Gillispie, 2011), their internet use and new technologies (Hermans, Verger, and d'Haenens, 2009), and specifically their use of Twitter (Ahmad, 2010; Artwick, 2013; Barnard, 2014; Bruns, 2012; Bruns and Burgess, 2012; Hermida, 2013; Noguera-Vivo, 2013; Russell, 2015). We are also seeing growth in international studies investigating social media activities of media workers in 'developing contexts' (Jordaan, 2013; Bosch, 2015). Donsbach (2010) wondered if there were universal aspects to all of this, asking 'whether human behaviour is unique in every new instant or instead follows universal laws, meaning that it repeats itself and can thus be predicted' . This question is ever more pertinent given the digitalisation growth of the media, and the increasingly multi-cultural and global nature of production and consumption of media products. Donsbach notes this by adding 'the question has been raised as to which developments in the media and in journalism are of a global nature and which are culturally specific' even as he concluded that 'there are a number of indications that something like a global journalist is emerging' .

What is known of how social media is affecting the practice of journalism globally is increasing. At the same time, it is acknowledged that exactly what it means for the overall news industry in any given country, or even globally, is still not entirely clear (Kwak, Lee, and Moon, 2010). On the one hand, use of the internet and social media allows for instantaneous distribution of news; on the other, it also allows for the immediate dissemination of opinions and conjecture. The internet and social media allow traditional media outlets to reach and connect with more people faster (and across borders), but the technology also allows one person to have agency in the process of information-gathering and dissemination as well (Broersma and Graham, 2013). Cooper (2006) refers to the use of social media in certain respects as representing 'the Fifth Estate'. While this may not be true everywhere yet, undoubtedly, the relationship between producers and users is changing rapidly, and on a global scale. In the traditional, basic model of mass communication, a one-way communication path was typical. Media practitioners were gatherers of information, gatekeepers, editors; these were then distributed via media outlets. The end product was constructed at the top and largely limited to a specific geography, whereas now there is greater global interactivity; and internationally available (social) media platforms mean that more 'producers' (Bird, 2011) are involved in the process.

The issue of journalism practice and how it has been affected by social media in Vietnam is clearly an important topic. Franklin (2012; 2014) identified several factors that are changing the landscape for journalism; of these we note one in particular: 'an expansive role for social media as sources and drivers of news' (2012). We are interested to discover the ways in which the social media have been employed and deployed and brought about change to the media and journalism practices. Specifically, this chapter joins the discussion by relating the experiences that are now occurring in the country of Vietnam. Vietnam represents an interesting site for an examination of this topic for many reasons. As with other countries, networked media content has historically seen regulation from a centralised group authority. The use of social networking sites, however, leads to greater 'networked individualisation' (Wellman and Haythornthwaite, 2002). Thus looking into how digital technologies and tools have led to social media growth and fostered greater contributions from both average users (Franklin, 2012, reported on the 'shifting audience requirements for news',) and professional journalists (and their media outlets), represents an important area of research. Our aim is to provide a look at how the Vietnamese media workers are using social media in this early stage of development (and to find out if policies on this existed and were being followed), and also to provide some insights with the experiences in Vietnam.

Ambient Journalism is a relatively recent concept in the academic literature, and there are not many studies that are utilising the nascent concept. Of those that do exist (Bruns, 2010; Hermida, 2010a; Hermida, 2010b), the definitions used indicate that this is a form of news absorption that is growing as more and more people adopt technologies that 'push' news and information their way. The concept is both active, for those who are reposting and retweeting, and passive for those whose eyeballs glance at the links and blurbs. We do not wish to draw an overemphasis to the term; we merely wish to state that the nature of news delivery and consumption is changing, and the terms ‘ambient journalism’ or ‘ambient news’ may end up being useful to employ in this discussion. The increasing use of technological hardware and social media software is creating the conditions for the growth of the ambient journalism environment. What this means for media workers and audiences remains to be seen, but that it is occurring is undoubtedly so.

Media Landscape of Vietnam

The country of Vietnam represents an interesting case study in journalistic social media norms and practices, although we cannot go so far as to say that it is wholly unique. The dangers and pressures that exist for Vietnamese journalists and editors are similar in many respects to those that exist for journalists and editors in other countries. Indeed, the influences on media content explicated by Shoemaker and Reese (2013) are as applicable in Vietnam as any other country; here we would point out the importance of the ’dominant ideology‘ and ’extra media‘ levels, historically driven by the government, and only recently by advertisers as well. The factors explained by Franklin (2012) that are radically changing the journalistic landscape are also relevant for Vietnam, specifically the ‘expansive role for social media as sources and drivers of news; dynamic changes in government media policy; as well as shifting audience requirements for news’. However, it is the precise mix of these factors and elements that makes Vietnam unique. As a communist country, direction and control continue to come down from the top, yet the implications of a market economy coupled with greater media choices and access to the Internet, and increasing numbers of younger Vietnamese seeking to contribute to a more diverse public dialogue (Gainsborough, 2010), has led to a unique environment and evolving media landscape. ‘The majority of urban middle-class youth read newspapers and magazines in print and on-line formats, seeking local and international news, sports and celebrity gossip’ (Earl, 2013, paraphrasing King, et al., 2008). It is in this environment that we observe one aspect to this growth; journalists' and editors' use of social media, to both document the processes and attempt to offer some preliminary explanations for them.

Media in Vietnam can be said to have started in the late 1950s with government-owned newspapers, then radio, and later television:

'Vietnam's mass media have always been subject to some form of government control' (Earl, 2013). Today, in the post-reform context (post-1990s), there is a private media sector divided between platforms and geography, and control is perhaps best described as strongly paternalistic. The platforms include the traditional media, most of which is still holding strong from earlier years (in terms of formats, audiences, and regulations), and the newer digital media, which is diffusing throughout the country due in part to the adoption of computers, smartphones and the mobile internet (around since 1997); 'On-line versions of popular newspapers first became available in June 1998' (Earl, 2013, paraphrasing Marr, 1998). The two prominent geographic centres of media production are located in the south in Ho Chi Minh (Saigon) and in the northern capitol city of Hanoi.

The Vietnamese media landscape is dynamic and has been undergoing significant changes in the past five years. Gainsborough wrote: 'urban Vietnamese are now able to access a far greater range of media sources, despite censorship, than they were ten to fifteen years ago, so the situation is not static' (2010). As in other countries, the government has had an interest in shifting financial responsibilities over to the media sectors for their operations. This has led also to less strict monitoring by government bodies following a so-called 'light touch' approach on regulation, and a greater reliance on co-regulation with industry (some would say self-censorship) and audiences in the media marketplace (similar to what some will know as the Singapore model). This situation was also fostered by the rapid adoption of the internet, which by and large has been difficult for all nation-states to control and regulate – both in terms of the technology and the content, although we have many cases where stricter control has been attempted, with varying degrees of success (Warf, 2013; Gill et al., 2015).

The widespread adoption of social media software occurred in Vietnam around the same time as it was diffusing throughout much of the world; perhaps only with a slight delay as some early innovator countries. Vietnam has a total population of roughly 93 million (Worldometers, 2014), with an internet penetration rate of around 45% (InternetWorld Stats, 2015). When it comes to reporting on social media use, it is difficult to know the exact numbers of users or percentages, chiefly because the numbers are rapidly changing. A local social platform known as 'Zing Me' had been popular up until 2012, when Facebook overtook it in terms of active users (McGrath, 2015). The number of Facebook users was quoted as around 26 million in late 2014 (Carter, 2014); and was represented as having a usage percentage of 22% in another source (Wearesocial.net,

2015). The number of mobile smartphones is growing – and this means more users are going on-line via their mobile phones. The Android operating system holds an edge over Apple's iOS on smartphones in Vietnam (Pearce, 2014); Apple fares much better in the growing tablet market (Appota, 2015). Figure 8A shows the level of internet penetration; again roughly 45 to 46% of the population (i.e., 43 of 93 million people) is regularly accessing the Internet with social media use, and specifically the use of Facebook and Twitter is also shown.

While Twitter has seemed to capture the most attention in the Western literature in terms of its use by media workers, it is Facebook which holds clear dominance in the Vietnamese media marketplace in this regard. Looking at the website rankings for Facebook versus Twitter for example, we can see that Facebook ranks as the third most popular website in Vietnam, whereas Twitter is at 53 (Alexa, 2015). More research is needed to ascertain why Facebook enjoys greater use, and to be fair, Twitter has seen good growth in Vietnam (it was ranked 148 in 2013). For now, we may only speculate as to why this is the case (an on-line blogger has several ideas on this topic, see Do, 2012, 2013, 2014). Facebook diffused before Twitter in the country.

Figure 8A. Internet Penetration and Social Media Use among Vietnam's Population.*

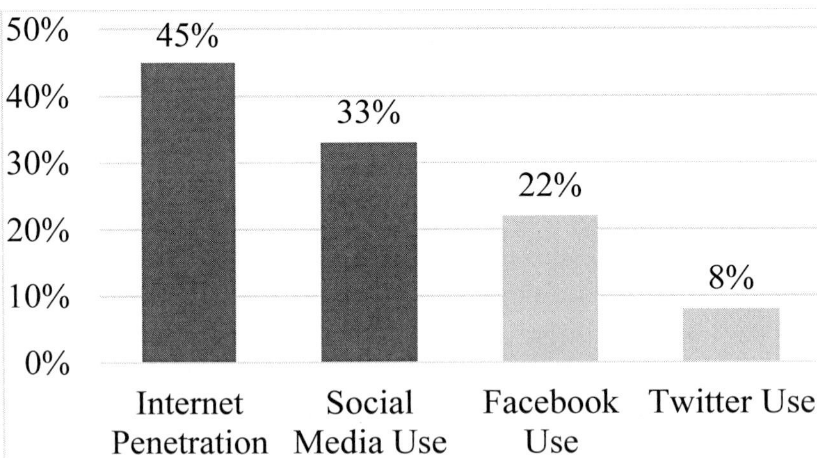

**Sources: Internet penetration* -Internet Live Stats, *2014; and Internet World Stats, 2015. Facebook use -Statista, 2015. Twitter use -Kemp, 2015.*

Another anecdotal reason may rest with the fact that prior to Facebook, many Vietnamese youths used Yahoo Blogs and perhaps they got in the habit of writing longer blog entries. Twitter restricts messages to a limited number of characters and is by and large, an open platform wherein anyone can see your tweets. (Although, it is possible to direct a tweet or send a private message without having a prior relation with the receiver). Facebook, on the other hand, requires some sort of connection in order to be able to see the private wall posts of the user (there is a greater two-step flow network effect at play). Thus, Facebook allows for greater possibilities for discussions among friends with a modicum of privacy if the user wishes it. As many are already connected with Facebook, they perhaps see Twitter as redundant. Another reason may be that Twitter's interface was not using the Vietnamese language until only recently. Finally, there was one report of difficulties in accessing Twitter in 2013 (Do, 2013); though officially this was never confirmed. For whatever reason, Twitter's popularity is lower in Vietnam than it is in other Southeast Asian countries and is generally not very popular. Clearly, this is an area worth further investigation – and it is perhaps one that may turn out not to be unique to Vietnam, but answered in some way by diffusion, uses and gratifications, or other related theories.

Ambient News in Vietnam

As our study centred principally around three research questions, we developed techniques to best get the specific information that would help us answer these questions. With the purpose of providing some pilot sketches about the status of ambient journalism in Vietnam, we were interested in the behaviours of journalists and news organisations in using social media, together with their perceptions and opinions about the roles and impacts of social media on their daily journalistic work and the journalistic profession.

Based on the survey instrument that Weaver and Willnat (2012) used for the book *The Global Journalist in the 21st Century*, we selected and modified the questions pertaining to social media, translating them to Vietnamese, so that it could be reasonably used for our study. The revised questionnaire included a total of 22 questions, divided into two main parts. The first five questions focused on the general information about the journalists themselves, such as the name of their news organisations, current positions, their experience, and the highest educational degree obtained. The second part included 17 questions on a number of issues, including whether the news organisation provided training for the use of social media; whether there existed a policy or set of official guidelines for the use of social media in the newsroom; the frequency, time spent on, and the main purposes as to why the journalists were using social media; and of course, how the respondents personally felt about social media's effects on the practice of journalism.

We delivered the questionnaire with no specific distribution design over a two-week period (from 24 May to 9 June), to over 220 addresses that had been collected and obtained from various resources, both on- and off-line. A total of 71 valid questionnaires were returned. As we encouraged redistribution of the survey, in a snowball fashion, we cannot accurately report a response rate; best guess, for what it's worth, would be around 35%. The respondents came from 44 different news organisations.

The response total of 71 replies, while seemingly low, reached and represented what we felt would be the minimum feasible number preferred in order to gain descriptive insights into what was happening among media workers in Vietnam. We recognise the limitation of this number from a quantitative standpoint; thus we do not suggest that the behaviours of those included in our study represent anything or anyone beyond the 71 who responded. That being said, we are confident that our respondents do provide valuable qualitative indications as to the types and kinds of social media uses, perceptions, and behaviours that the wider community of Vietnamese media workers are engaging in and share to a certain degree.

In total, 71 journalists responded and this number included 2 trainees, 5 part-timers, 30 full-time reporters, 18 editors, 2 vice heads of department, 5 department heads, 7 assignment editors, and 2 deputy editor-in-chiefs. Nineteen of the respondents were working in print media newsrooms, while 31 others indicated that they were working for on-line journals, 20 in television stations, and one reported as working in a radio station. Most of them have a degree or certification in journalism and only 9 respondents (at 12.68%) indicated that they had never taken any journalism courses. Their average years employed as a journalist is 6.8 years, with the more detailed numbers presented in Table 8A.

Table 8A: Demographic Background of Journalists

Characteristic	*Frequency*	*Percentage*
Employment		
Printed Newspaper	19	26.76
Radio	1	1.4
Television	20	28.17
On-line Newspaper	31	43.66
Years Employed as a Journalist		
Under 1 year	0	0
1- under 5 years	24	33.8
5- under 10 years	30	42.25
10 – under 15 years	10	14.08
Over 15 years	7	9.86
Position		
Editor in chief	0	0
Deputy editor in chief	2	2.82
Assignment editor	7	9.86
Department head	5	7.04
Vice head of department	2	2.82
Full time Reporter	30	42.25
Editor	18	25.35
Trainee	2	2.82
Part timer	5	7.04
Education		
Masters or higher	17	23.94
Bachelors	32	45.07
Degree from vocational school (college)	1	1.4
Certification in Journalism	12	16.9
Have never taken any journalism courses	9	12.68

N = 71; Results from Social Media Survey, June 2015.

The behaviours of news organisations

Designing the social media guidelines or policy for newsroom employees

Social media has had strong impacts on journalism. To use it effectively, the appearance of a policy or official guidelines for the use of social media in the newsrooms is becoming increasingly necessary and popular. Among the 71 media workers who participated in the survey, 15 confirmed that their offices do indeed have a policy for their staff members who intend to use social media platforms in reporting or producing stories. The respondents came from 12 different news organisations, including 3 TV stations, 4 print newspapers, and 5 on-line journals. The 12 organisations with social media policies thus represent 27.27%, or just over one quarter of the total (44 news organisations).

When creating these policies, it would seem necessary to get the newsroom employees' support, or at the very least their awareness. The responses received indicate that this may not be the case. Again, 15 respondents indicated that there were official policies at their outlets, and that to their knowledge everybody in their office was said to be obeying the newsroom's social media policy. However, three of the respondents expressed the opinion that the policies were neither reasonable nor useful. There also seemed to be some disagreement as to whether policies are official or not at the media outlets. The most noticeable case was perhaps that of *VTC News* - an on-line journal. A total of seven of its employees responded to our survey; four respondents indicated that the outlet did not have set rules for using social media, while another three indicated that there was a policy—and two of them said that it was an irrational and not very useful policy. This provides some indication that social media policies may not be uniform within the media outlets in Vietnam; further, that not all media workers may be aware of the specific policies that may be in place.

Providing training courses for the use of social media

Of our 71 respondents, 20 said that their newsrooms have held social media training courses. The respondents came from 10 on-line journals, 4 print newspapers, and 2 TV stations. These data show that on-line journals seem to be placing more emphasis and care on social media than other news organisations. This result carries prima-facie evidence, as one would suspect that on-line media outlets would indeed be more likely than their traditional counterparts to understand the importance of on-line social media and the care needed to use it properly.

Notably, 16 of the 44 newsrooms surveyed have provided some sort of social media training courses for their employees, and 12 of the 44 have designed their own social media policies and guidelines. However, there are only 8 organisations that have done both: *Dai bieu nhan dan* (print),

Quan doi nhan dan (print), *Ha Noi moi* (print), *VTC News* (on-line), *VnMedia* (on-line), *Gia dinh Viet Nam* (on-line), *Tuyen Quang TV station* and *Quoc hoi Viet Nam TV station.*

The behaviours of journalists

In Vietnam, social media is not solely popular as an entertainment vehicle and means to connect with friends. Vietnamese journalists at least considered social media as an important tool to help their journalistic profession. Among the 71 respondents, 6 (making up 8.45 %) refused to use social media in their journalistic activities. The majority, 65 (91.55%) confirmed that they have used social networks in their working life with many purposes and different frequencies based on each social networking site.

The stated purposes of social media use are plentiful, but concentrated on three phases: gathering information, writing, and disseminating news. Survey result shows that social networks are most often used by our respondents to ‘Check what other news organisations are reporting’ (81.54%), followed by to ‘Find new ideas for stories’ (80%). The use of social media as a channel to interview sources is the least common (accounting for only 24.62%). One thing worth noting is that, although social media is considered as a channel for sharing breaking news effectively because of its timeliness and widespread reach, only 43.08% of respondents said they use it to check and disseminate breaking news. The purposes of using social media according to the respondents are listed in Table 8B.

Time and Frequency

It was also important to examine the frequency and time spent with social media for the Vietnamese media workers. The percentages of respondents who chose levels of use ‘Less than once a week’, ‘Once a week’, ‘Several times a week’ and ‘Once a day’ are not too different (respectively 10.77%, 6.15%, 16.92% and 16.92%). The highest response in this category, 49.23%, indicated that they use social media for their work ‘More than once a day’.

Table 8B: The purposes of using social media in the journalists' work

	Frequency	Percentage
o Check what other news organisations are reporting	53	*81.54*
o Check and disseminate breaking news	28	*43.08*
o Find new ideas for stories	52	*80*
o Interview sources	16	*24.62*
o Verify information	29	*44.61*
o Find additional information	38	*58.46*
o Meet new people in my field of work	44	*67.69*
o Follow someone on social media I met in my field of work	36	*55.38*
o Investigate the audience's demands	44	*67.69*
o Investigate the audience's reactions to news that journalists report	42	*64.61*
o Share the stories to get the 'view'	31	*47.69*
o Share my own opinions	36	*55.38*
o Discuss the journalistic skills with colleagues	41	*63.07*

N = 65; Results from Social Media Survey, June 2015.

Among the social media platforms in Vietnam, Facebook is the most popular with Vietnamese users in general and Vietnamese journalists in particular. 65 respondents said that they have used social media as a tool to support their journalistic activities and all of them confirmed using Facebook (especially with 86.15% choosing the level 'regularly'). Audio-visual sharing sites (such as YouTube, Flickr, or Tumblr) were at the second rank with the percentage up to 81.54%. It is followed by 'Content communities and crowd-sourcing sites' (such as Wikipedia) with 75.39%; while the proportions for 'Blog', 'Microblogging sites' and 'Professional social networking sites' (such as LinkedIn) are much less.

Figure 8B: Frequency of using social media in the journalists' work

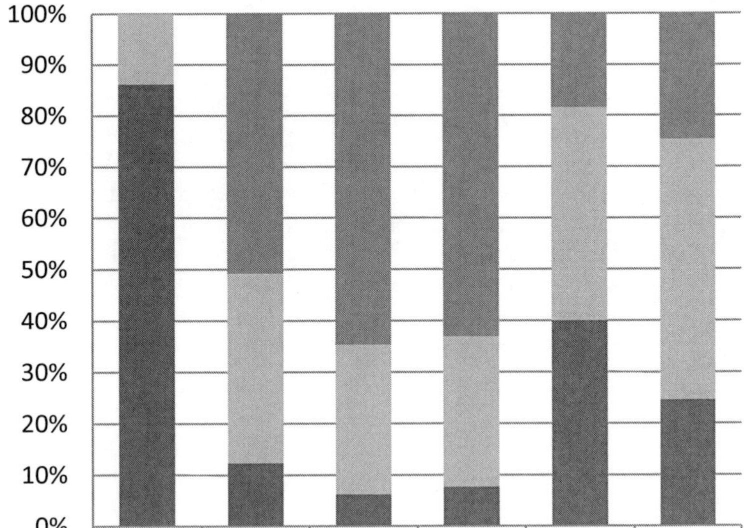

	Facebook	Blogs	Microblogging sites	Professional social networking sites	Audio-visual sharing sites	Wikipedia
Never	0%	50.77%	64.62%	63.08%	18.46%	24.62%
Occasionally	13.85%	36.92%	29.23%	29.23%	41.54%	50.77%
Regularly	86.15%	12.31%	6.15%	7.69%	40.00%	24.62%

N = 65; Results from Social Media Survey, June 2015.

The opinions of journalists about social media's impacts

The journalists' opinions about social media's impacts on their journalistic work

All 65 respondents who have used social media in their working life confirmed that social media is playing a significant role in their journalistic activities. The largest percentage (41.54%) chose 'very important' , 23.07% chose'extremely important' , while 30.77% agreed with the choice 'somewhat important'. The rest (4.62%) said 'not very important'. This shows that generally our respondents have positive thoughts about social media's role. By acknowledging the importance of this new media platform, they may thus be more concerned about how to use it reasonably and effectively.

Our respondents not only acknowledged the positive *role* of social media; they also said that social media has made positive *impacts* on their job. 10.77% who use social media in their journalistic activities selected 'very positive', while 30.77% chose 'positive'. However, many others have seen negative impacts as well the positive ones and it's the reason why a relatively high percentage (58.46%) chose 'both positive and negative'. No one thought that social media only has a negative impact on their work. Their detailed opinions are shown in Table 8C.

Table 8C: The impacts of social media on the journalists' work.

	Agree		Disagree		Total	
		%		%		%
Because of social media, I am more engaged with my audience	56	*86.15*	9	*13.85*	65	*100*
Because of social media, I communicate better with people relevant to my work	59	*90.77*	6	*9.23*	65	*100*
Using social media enhances my journalistic skills	50	*76.92*	15	*23.08*	65	*100*
Social media allows me to be faster in reporting	47	*72.31*	18	*27.69*	65	*100*
Because of social media, I am engaged with more journalistic issues	61	*93.85*	4	*6.15*	65	*100*
Using social media enhances my credibility as a journalist	27	*41.54*	38	*58.46*	65	*100*

N = 65; Results from Social media survey, June 2015.

The impacts of social media were also detailed in this study. As stated in Table 8C, up to 80% of the respondents have found new ideas for their stories on social media. But 93.85% of them acknowledged that, because of social media, they have been engaged with more journalistic issues. The gap between these percentages proved that besides active searching, the journalists could encounter the topics or ideas for their stories incidentally on social media. The issues could come from what their friends shared and discussed or even come from what other news organisations posted, etc. (and we consider this to be *ambient* in nature).

Moreover, social media is also the place for the journalists to learn more about their audience's needs and to know their audience's reactions to journalistic issues. It's the reason why many respondents agreed with the sentence 'Because of social media, I am more engaged with my audience' (accounting for 86.15%). Similarly, on social networks, journalists can 'meet new people in [their] field of work', or 'Follow someone on social media [they] met in [their] field of work'; so 90.77% who use social media confirmed that because of social media, they have communicated better with people relevant to their work.

Meanwhile, the response of 'Using social media enhances my credibility as a journalist' received the least agreement percentage from respondents (just 41.54%). This is reasonable because the reputation of the journalist is defined by many factors, which are primarily based on the quality of their work and the effects it creates, and are not only decided by the delivery channel.

The journalists' opinions about social media's impacts on the journalistic profession in general

The journalists who participated in the survey were asked about their views on the impact of social media on the journalistic profession in general. The highest proportion (64.79%) selected 'both positive and negative', (46 journalists in total) . Again here, no one said that social media only brings a negative or very negative impact on journalism. However, there is one person who chose 'no impact'; unfortunately, this lone respondent did not give reasons to explain this view.

Among 8 people (11.27%) who chose 'very positive' and 16 people (22.54%) who selected 'positive', there are 6 who did share their rationale on this topic. Their responses focused on the strong interactive nature and quick distribution features of social media, and many explained that social media had helped them a lot in finding the social issues or topics that would be relevant for their stories. They perceived social media as a useful tool to support their work in the modern communications era, especially in disseminating newsworthy issues widely.

Among 46 respondents who said that social media could have both positive and negative effects, 21 gave similar responses as to the negative impacts. Their responses indicated two main reasons why the impact is also negative: 1) the lack of accuracy of information on social media platforms, especially if the journalists use it for their stories without verifying; and, 2) the fact that audiences are changing their reading habits (instead of reading newspapers, they tend to read on social media – again indicating the ambient nature of the news). 'That is undermining the traditional journalism roles', one respondent said. These reasonable explanations indicate that many Vietnamese journalists hold rational and multidimensional views on the impact of social media on the journalistic profession.

However, among the suggestions we offered respondents to select, the highest agreement rate belongs to the following: 'Social media helps to disseminate journalism works widely', which made up 90.14%, followed by 'Social media makes journalism more accountable to the public' (83.1%). The opinion receiving the least consensus was 'Social media is undermining the traditional journalism roles' with 23.94%. But perhaps the most noticeable one was 'Journalism has sacrificed accuracy for speed' which received 26.76% agreement. This figure marks a concern about the fact that many journalists might put the *quality* aspects of a report behind the *speed* in reporting it.

Table 8D: The impacts of social media on the journalistic profession

	Agree		Disagree		Total	
		%		%		%
Social media is undermining traditional journalism roles	17	*23.94*	54	*76.06*	71	*100*
Using content that social media users create and share threatens the *quality* of journalism	36	*50.7*	35	*49.3*	71	*100*
Using content that social media users create and share threatens the *professionalism* of journalism	36	*50.7*	35	*49.3*	71	*100*
Journalism has sacrificed accuracy for speed	19	*26.76*	52	*73.24*	71	*100*
Social media makes journalism more accountable to the public	59	*83.1*	12	*16.9*	71	*100*
Social media helps to disseminate the journalism works (news, articles, TV/radio programs, etc.) widely	64	*90.14*	7	*9.86*	71	*100*

N = 71; Results from Social media survey, June 2015.

Conclusion

The news organisations in Vietnam have started to pay attention to the role and impact of social media on journalistic activities. It is for this reason that they are gradually interested in designing social media guidelines or policies and providing training courses for the use of social media for newsroom employees. However, these activities are not really popular in Vietnam because only a small percentage of newsrooms are involved in the implementation. The survey also uncovered that there is no uniform awareness, understanding or appreciation of such policies even when they are, in theory, being implemented.

Meanwhile, journalists themselves are very interested in social media. Most of them said that it is a useful tool in their journalistic work. More than 90% of the respondents have used the social media platform in their professional activities; over 50% indicated that they are using social media for their work more than once a day. The purposes are numerous but concentrated in three areas: gathering information, writing, and disseminating news. Notably, although social media is considered a channel for sharing breaking news effectively (owing to its timeliness and widespread reach), only 43.08% of respondents said they use it to check and disseminate breaking news. This finding shows that Vietnamese journalists may be quite cautious in using 'social media information' or they may have limited skills in exploiting 'social media information'. It is perhaps understandable because the survey has shown that there are not many newsrooms that provide their members the training courses for the use of social media.

In Vietnam, Facebook is still the most popular social networking site with the users in general and journalists in particular. All of the journalists who consider social media as a working tool have used Facebook in their journalistic activities. The audio-visual sharing sites, such as YouTube, and crowd-sourcing sites, such as Wikipedia, are also quite popular. However, not many journalists blog, use microblogging sites like Twitter, or use professional social networking sites like LinkedIn.

The Vietnamese journalists surveyed tend to have positive views of both the role and impact of social media, not only on their work, but also on the journalistic profession in general. Social media is the means to help them become more engaged with audiences or with people relevant to their work: enhance journalistic skills, engage with more journalistic issues, and be faster in reporting. Some even believed that using social media would enhance their credibility as journalists, but this proportion was not high (only around 40%). Certainly, their visibility would be higher – and if they are sharing good works, and making valid points, this could lead to a greater overall prominence. However, the respondents also mentioned negative aspects of using social media as a working tool. There were a few comments that the existence and development of social media will be a threat to the journalistic profession. There is also a significant percentage (over one in four) showing that 'Journalism has sacrificed accuracy for speed'. This figure marks a growing concern about the fact that many journalists might put the quality aspects of a report behind the speed in reporting.

There is no doubt that audiences are increasingly getting their news from their social media feeds. As a result, the relationship between journalists, the audiences, and social media will be an important one to watch, not only in the country of Vietnam. The ways that journalists use social media as an operational tool in their daily work contributes to the appearance of an ambient journalistic news environment, where more and more of the public gain exposure to news items through their social media feeds. In this context, Vietnamese news organisations and journalists themselves have to utilise the various social media platforms in their operations, together with holding more training courses on the use of social media in all of the media outlets and press agencies.

References

Ahmad, A. N. (2010). Is Twitter a useful tool for journalists? *Journal of Media Practice, 11*(2), 145-155.

Alexa. (2015). Top sites in Vietnam. *Alexa.com.* Retrieved from: http://www.alexa.com/topsites/countries/VN

Appota. (2015, January 22). Vietnam mobile market 2015 outlook. *AppotaCorp's Annual report 2014.* Retrieved from: http://www.slideshare.net/appota/vietnam-mobile-market-2014-annual-report.

Artwick, C. G. (2013). Reporters on Twitter: product or service? Digital Journalism, 1(2), 212-228.

Barnard, S. R. (2014). 'Tweet or be sacked': Twitter and the new elements of journalistic practice. *Journalism.* doi: 10.1177/1464884914553079.

Bastos, H., Lima, H. L. D. D., and Moutinho, N. (2010). *The influence of the Internet on Portuguese press.* Paper presented at the International

Association for Media and Communication Research conference, Braga, July 18-22. Retrieved from: http://repositorioaberto.up.pt/bitstream/10216/25241/2/PaperIAMCR2010000099499.pdf

Bird, S. E. (2011). Are we all produsers now? Convergence and media audience practices. *Cultural Studies*, *25*(4-5), 502-516.

Bosch, T. (2015). Research in African journalism: Trends and projections. *African Journalism Studies, 36(*1), 18-21.

Braun, J., and Gillespie, T. (2011). Hosting the public discourse, hosting the public: When online news and social media converge. *Journalism Practice*, 5(4), 383-398. doi:10.1080/17512786.2011.557560

Brock, G. (2012). *Out of Print: Newspapers, Journalism and the Business of News in the Digital Age.* London: Kogan Page.

Broersma, M., and Graham, T. (2013). Twitter as a news source: How Dutch and British newspapers used tweets in their news coverage, 2007–2011. *Journalism practice, 7*(4), 446-464.

Bruns, A. (2010). Oblique strategies for ambient journalism. *M/C Journal, 13*(2), n.p. Retrieved from: http://journal.mediaculture.org.au/index.php/mcjournal/article/viewArticle/230.

—. (2012). Journalists and Twitter: How Australian news organisations adapt to a new medium. *Media International Australia Incorporating Culture and Policy*, *144*, 97-107.

Bruns, A., and Burgess, J. (2012). Researching news discussions on Twitter: New methodologies. *Journalism Studies, 13*(5-6), 801-814.

Carter, S. (2014, October 17). Facebook Vietnam October 2014: Audience breakdown. *LinkedIn.com*. Retrieved from: https://www.linkedin.com/pulse/20141017074752-37571627-facebook-vietnam-october-2014-audience-breakdown.

Cooper, S. D. (2006). The blogosphere and the public sphere. In *Watching the watchdog: Bloggers as the fifth estate,* (pp. 277-303). Spokane, WA: Marquette Books.

Dickinson, R., Matthews, J., and Saltzis, K. (2013). Studying journalists in changing times: Understanding news work as socially situated practice. *The International Communication Gazette, 75*(1), 3-18.

Do, A (2012, December 18). Microblogging's Slow Start in Vietnam. Retrieved from: https://www.techinasia.com/microbloggings-slow-start-vietnam/

Do, A. (2013, November 20). Did Twitter just get blocked in Vietnam? *Techinasia.com.* Retrieved from: https://www.techinasia.com/twitter-blocked-in-vietnam/.

—. (2014, May 8). The real reason why Facebook dominates Vietnam but Twitter could never make it. Retrieved from: https://www.techinasia.com/vietnam-loves-facebook-not-twitter/

Donsbach, W. (2010). The Global Journalist: Are Professional Structures Being Flattened? In B. Dobek-Ostrowska, M. Glowacki, K. Jakubowicz, &Sükösd, M. (Eds.), *Comparative Media Systems. European and Global Perspectives,* (pp. 153-170). Budapest, Hungary: EU Press.

Earl, C. (2013). Saigon style: Middle-class culture and transformations of urban lifestyling in post-reform Vietnamese media.*Media International Australia, 147*, 85-97.

Franklin, B. (2012). The future of journalism: developments and debates. *Journalism Studies, 13*(5-6), 663-681.

—. (2014). The Future of Journalism: In an age of digital media and economic uncertainty. *Journalism Practice, 8*(5), 469-487.

Gainsborough, M. (2010). *Vietnam: Rethinking the State.* London: Zed Books.

Gill, P., Crete-Nishihat, M., Dalek, J., Goldberg, S., Senft, A., and Wiseman, G. (2015, January). Characterizing web censorship worldwide: Another look at the OpenNet Initiative data. *ACM Transactions on the Web, 9*(1), 4.1-4.29. Doi: 10.1145/2700339.

Hermans, L., Vergeer, M., and d'Haenens, L. (2009). Explaining the use of the Internet by work-related characteristics and professional opinions. *Journal of Computer-Mediated Communication, 15*, 138-157.

Hermida, A. (2010a). From TV to Twitter: How ambient news became ambient journalism. *M/C Journal, 13*(2), n.p. Retrieved from: http://journal.media-culture.org.au/index.php/mcjournal/article/viewArticle/220.

—. (2010b). Twittering the news: The emergence of ambient journalism. *Journalism Practice, 4*(3), 297-308.

—. (2013) #JOURNALISM. *Digital Journalism,* 1(3), 295-313.doi: 10.1080/21670811.2013.808456.

If a tree falls. (2015, April 18). If a tree falls…online, will the Communist Party hear anything? *The Economis*t. Retrieved from: http://www.economist.com/node/21648706/comments#comments

Internet Live Stats. (2014). *Vietnam Internet Users.* Retrieved from: http://www.internetlivestats.com/internet-users/vietnam/.

Internet World Stats. (2015). Asia marketing research, Internet usage, population statistics and Facebook information. *Internetworldstats.com.* Retrieved from:

http://www.internetworldstats.com/asia.htm.

Jordaan, M. (2013) Poke me, I'm a journalist: The impact of Facebook and Twitter on newsroom routines and cultures at two South African weeklies. *Ecquid Novi: African Journalism Studies*, 34(1), 21-35.

Kemp, S. (2015, March 11). Digital, social & mobile in APAC in 2015. *Wearesocial.net.* Retrieved from: http://wearesocial.net/blog/2015/03/digital-social-mobile-apac-2015/

King, V., Nguyen, P. A. and Nguyen, H. M. (2008). 'Professional middle-class youth in post-reform Vietnam: Identity, continuity, change'. *Modern Asian Studies, 42*(4), 783-813.

Kwak, H., Lee, C., Park, H., & Moon, S. (2010, April). What is Twitter, a social network or a news media? In *Proceedings of the 19th international conference on World wide web* (pp. 591-600). ACM.

Lewis, S. C., Zamith, R., and Hermida, A. (2013). Content analysis in an era of big data: A hybrid approach to computational and manual methods. *Journal of Broadcasting & Electronic Media, 57*(1), 34–52. doi:10.1080/08838151.2012.76170

Markoff, J. (2006, November 12). Entrepreneurs see a web guided by common sense. *The New York Times.* Retrieved from: http://www.nytimes.com/2006/11/12/business/12web.html?pagewanted=all&_r=0.

Marr, D. (1998). 'Introduction'. In D. Marr's (Ed.). *The Mass Media in Vietnam, Department of Political and Social Change, Research School of Pacific and Asian Studies*, pp. 1-26. Australian National University, Canberra.

McGrath, F. (2015, January 22). GlobalWebIndex informs WeAreSocial's new digital, social and mobile in 2015 report.*Globalwebindex.net*. Retrieved from: http://www.globalwebindex.net/blog/globalwebindex-informs-wearesocial-new-digital-social-and-mobile-in-2015-report

Newman, N. (2009). The rise of social media and its impact on mainstream journalism. *Reuters Institute for the Study of Journalism,* 8(2), 1-5.

Noguera Vivo, J. M., (2013). How open are journalists on Twitter? Trends towards the end-user journalism. *Communication & Society/ Comunicación y Sociedad, 26*(1), 93-114.

O'Reilly, T., and Battelle, J. (2009). *Web Squared: Web 2.0 Five Years On.* Retrieved from: http://assets.en.oreilly.com/1/event/28/web2009_websquared-whitepaper.pdf

—. (2012). What is Web 2.0? In M. Mandiberg's (Ed.) *The social media reader,* (pp. 32-52). New York: NYU Press.

Pavlik, J. (2000). The impact of technology on journalism. *Journalism Studies*, *1*(2), 229-237.

Pearce, H. (2014). Asian Beat #5: The Vietnamese mobile games market, welcome to Flappy Bird Land (guest post). *Applift.com.* Retrieved from: http://sumo.ly/5fx9.

Perlez, J. (2014, July 15). Chinese oil rig near Vietnam to be moved. *The New York Times,* A6.

Reese, S. D. (2001). Understanding the global journalist: A hierarchy-of-influences approach. *Journalism Studies, 2*(2), 173–187.

Russell, F. (2015). Journalists, gatekeeping, and social interaction on Twitter: Differences by beat and media type for newspaper and online news. *International Symposium on Online Journalism, 5*(1), n.p. Retrieved from: https://isojjournal.wordpress.com/2015/04/15/journalists-gatekeeping-and-social-interaction-on-twitter-differences-by-beat-and-media-type-for-newspaper-and-online-news/

Shoemaker, P., and Reese, S. D. (2013). *Mediating the message in the 21st century: A media sociology perspective.* New Jersey: Routledge.

Statista. (2015). Retrieved from: http://www.statista.com/statistics/193056/facebook-user-numbers-in-asian-countries/.

Van der Haak, B., Parks, M., and Castells, M. (2012). The future of journalism: Networked journalism. *International Journal of Communication, 6*, 2923–2938. Retrieved from: http://ijoc.org/index.php/ijoc/article/viewFile/1750/832.

Warf, B. (2013). Global Internet Censorship. In *Global Geographies of the Internet* (pp. 45-75). Amsterdam: Springer.

Wellman, B. and Haythornwaite, C. (Eds.). (2002). *The internet in everyday life.* Hoboken, NJ: Wiley-Blackwell.

Willnat, L., Weaver, D., and Choi, J. (2013). The Global Journalist in the twenty-first century: A cross-national study of journalistic competencies. Journalism Practice, 7(2), doi: 10.1080/17512786.2012.753210.

Worldometers. (2014). Vietnam population. *Worldometers.info.* Retrieved from: http://www.worldometers.info/world-population/vietnam-population /info.

CHAPTER NINE

NEW FREEDOM OF EXPRESSION IN MEDIA: AN ANALYSIS OF 'DISSENT' ON FACEBOOK WALL POSTS

PUSHPIKA KUMARI GANEGODA
AND NISANSALA SUBHASINI JAYAWARDHANA

Overview

- Vincent Miller (2008) hypothesised that much of the communication we do through social media is 'phatic', derived from Greek and Latin words that mean 'verbal togetherness' of speech that is used as social cement. These messages, sometimes called 'small talk', are not to communicate information, but to make one's presence felt.
- While governments attempt to suppress public protests on contemporary public issues, power of the president, and misconducts of political leaders, social media has given the public a new voice of dissent.
- This chapter scrutinises the dissent expressed by people in the wall posts of the Facebook and see whether they represent the public sphere envisaged by Habermas or do they come under 'phatic' communication or sentiments expressed to gratify users' multifaceted needs? What is the major content of these so called wall posts?
- The study indicates that although Sri Lanka has not experienced mass protest movements like the 'Arab Spring', wall posts on the internet have enough potency to inspire a mass protest moment in Sri Lanka.

Freedom of Expression and Digital Media

> 'Everyone has the right to freedom of opinion and expression; that this right includes freedom to hold opinions without interference and to seek, receive and impart information and ideas through any media and regardless of frontiers'
> —Universal Human Rights Declaration, 19th Article (2008).

In contrast to the traditional mass media often controlled by vested interests, the internet is seen as a force for 'radical democracy'. The internet is seen as helping marginalised groups develop their own deliberative forums, link up, and subsequently contest dominant meanings and practices. Scholars hail new media as a potential way to break away from the vertical information flow and 'top down' politics where most political decisions are made without negotiation or input from grassroots support. Instead, new media seems to provide means for the provision of political information. In a more radical way, by the new media, unlimited access to different voices is given and feedback between leaders and followers are established. New media promise new forums for the development of interest groups as well as the formation of public opinion. According to McQuail (2005), 'New media allows dialogue between politicians and active citizens and it provides an arena where public discourse can take place and public opinion, as its function, can be formed'.

Moreover, social media is credited for revolutions in the Arab World and political uprisings in Spain, Israel and Greece. The root causes, such as high unemployment, for these protests are similar, especially among young people, frustration over political corruption, corporate greed in the financial sector, and a general dissatisfaction with the political situation. In order to organise protests, new media provide views alternative to those of mainstream media; to spread their message, social movements have made use of social media tools. According to Fulya Şen (2012), social media provides a rapid flow of information to mobilise the social opposition. For the social opposition, the internet is first and foremost a vital source of alternative critical information to educate and mobilise the 'public' – especially among progressive opinion leaders, professionals, trade unionists and peasant leaders, militants and activists. Therefore, the internet is the alternative to the capitalist mass media and its propaganda, a source of news and information that relays manifestos and informs activists of sites for public action. More specifically, social media, such as Facebook, Twitter, LinkedIn, and YouTube, enable people to send messages, images and videos that can be read or seen by large numbers of people.

Vincent Miller (2008) hypothesised that much of the communication we do through social media is 'phatic'; derived from Greek and Latin words that mean 'verbal togetherness' of speech that is used as social cement. These messages, sometimes called 'small talk', are not to communicate information as much as indicate that people are present. Phatic communication, as Malinowski points out is a form of 'verbal togetherness'. According to him, the huge numbers of texted messages people send one another are caused more by the need to maintain our network of friends and consolidate our togetherness with one another than by the desire to convey information. However, the internet has also played a vital role in publicising and mobilising 'spontaneous protests' like the *indignados* (the indignant protestors), i.e. the unaffiliated unemployed youth in Spain, and the protestors involved in the US 'Occupy Wall Street'. In other instances, the organised trade union confederations played a central role in the mass general strikes in Italy, Portugal, Greece and elsewhere while the internet had a secondary impact (Petras, 2011).

However, with incoming reports of abductions and tortures of journalists, the use of 'any media' to freely express one's point of view is not always possible in countries within the existing power structures, especially under the existing theories of the press. In such a situation social media play an important role in creating space for the public to assemble, discuss and work together virtually to make changes in their political and social atmosphere. World history provides plenty of examples for the power of social media; social media contributed to the fall of regimes in the world such as the fall of Philippine president Joseph Estrada in 2001, the ouster of Spanish prime minister Jose Maria Aznar in 2004, the defeat of the Communist Party in Moldova in 2009 (Shirky, 2011), and so on. Furthermore, researchers have documented instances in which content generated by citizens through new media has been influential in forcing traditional media and governing bodies to shift their focus and to allow issues and concerns stemming from the civic grassroots into their agenda (Bakardjieva, 2011).

The Sri Lankan Media Scenario

In a speech at the Sri Lankan Defence University, Defence Secretary Gotabhaya Rajapakshastated asserted that social media was a threat to national security as it can be used to cause problems by 'propagating certain ideologies on-line and mobilising and organising people' (Gotabhaya Rajapaksha, 2013). This echoes a sentiment made by no less than Sri Lanka's President Mahinda Rajapaksha, who has labelled Facebook as a 'plague'. Under different circumstances, government has taken several actions to get new media under control. For instance, in December 2012, the Sri Lankan government announced that all the media web sites should be registered with the Ministry of Mass Media and several news websites such as <www.srilankaguardian.com> and <www.srilankamirror.com> were blocked.

Although they were unblocked later on, volatile conditions continue to exist for the local media (Colombage, 2012). However, despite the enormous actions taken by the government to exercise control over media freedom and freedom of expression, the increasing technological development, computer literacy and accessibility of public has made new ways to fulfil the public's need for information and has given them a space for free expression.

Catherine Jackson, from the French NGO Reporters without Borders, stated that with the growing censorship over media, a new uncontrolled medium must be found; that uncontrolled media are social media networks, which allow the opportunity for uncensored news to continue to filter its way to the people (Colombage, 2012).

Freedom of expression remains a controversial issue in Sri Lanka even as it is violated and/or interpreted differently from time to time according to the whims and fancies of the interpreters. In such context, the internet becomes the more accessible arena for people to express their viewpoints. Unlike traditional media, the internet has offered people plenty of opportunities to express, discuss and share their opinions freely and in a secured manner. Thus, it is important to find out how social media is used by the citizens of Sri Lanka in relation to their political discourse in the 'public sphere'.

One of the objectives of this research paper is to scrutinise the dissent expressed by people in their Facebook wall posts. Do they really represent the public sphere envisaged by Habermas or do they come under 'phatic' communication, or sentiments expressed to gratify a user's multifaceted needs? Moreover, the research focused on examining the way people use new media to express their point of view freely on public issues, finding out the gratifications users have fulfilled by using Facebook to express their views, and the content of the wall posts of the users.

Functionality of new media

Three major theories will be used as the basis of this research project. They are: Uses and Gratifications Theory; the theory of Democratic Participation; and, theory of the Public Sphere.

The Uses and Gratifications Theory is based on a functionalist approach to communication studies; it focuses on media consumers and their needs and behaviours rather than on the media channels through which they are communicated. The premise of the theory is that media users (viewers, listeners, readers, Internet users) are members of an active audience aware of their needs and the ways that those needs can be met; they select the means perceived to be the most appropriate in fulfilling these needs. People use media to assist them in addressing some of their needs, and their expectations lead to a deliberate usage of media and selective exposure to the content they transmit (Katz et al., 1974). Media can address a few types of needs, such as cognitive (information and understanding), affective (emotional and aesthetic experiences), escapist (disconnect from reality) and integrative (strengthening the sense of belonging and relationships with family/friends/community/state, as well as providing a sense of security, trust, stability and status) (Katz et al., 1974).

Several studies have applied the Uses and Gratification Theory to various on-line environments. Tewksbury and Althaus (2000) identified entertainment, monitoring/surveillance, and 'passing the time' as key gratifications obtained from the internet. Papacharissi and Rubin (2000) identified five motives for using the internet: interpersonal utility, passing time, information seeking, convenience (for example, to communicate with friends and family), and entertainment. Parker and Plank (2000) identified three such factors: companionship and social relationships; surveillance and excitement; and relaxation and escape. Kaye and Johnson (2002) found four motivations for political information web search: guidance, information seeking/surveillance, entertainment, and social utility. Song *et al.* (2004) found seven such motivation clusters: establishing a 'virtual community' (find companionship, meet new friends), information seeking, aesthetic experiences, monetary compensation (i.e. find bargains on-line), diversion (i.e. fun and entertainment), personal status, and relationship maintenance.

More recent studies have focused on the uses of and gratifications from social media; for example, Raacke and Bonds-Raacke (2008) found that social networking sites – Facebook and Myspace – address the social needs of users (for example, keeping in touch with old friends and making new ones). Leung (2009) identified four key gratifications from content generation on-line: satisfying recognition needs, cognitive needs, social needs, and entertainment needs. Quan-Haase and Young (2010) compared the uses of Facebook and Instant Messaging, and identified six key gratifications obtained: pastime, affection (for example to thank people and help others), fashion (i.e. to look stylish), sharing problems, sociability, and getting social information. The current study is unique in its application of the Uses and Gratifications framework to study the uses of new media in the contemporary media environment for political dissent.

'The public sphere' envisaged by Habermas (1989) designates a theatre in modern societies in which political participation is enacted through the medium of talk. It is the space in which citizens become deliberate about their common affairs and therefore, it becomes an institutionalised arena of discursive interaction. In the mind of Habermas (1989), this arena needs to be conceptually distinct from the state. It is a site for the production and circulation of discourses that can, in principle, be critical of the state. For Habermas, the 'liberal model of the bourgeois public sphere' is the rise and decline of a historically specific and limited form of the public sphere (Habermas, 1989).

It is believed that a new form of public sphere is required to salvage this arena's critical function and to institutionalise democracy (Fraser, 1990). Therefore, an urgent need for deliberative democratic public sphere theory is becoming increasingly popular in internet democracy research and commentary. In terms of informal civic practices, advocates of this theory see the internet becoming the expansion of citizen deliberations leading to the formation of rational public opinion. Therefore, to many internet-democracy commentators, researchers and practitioners, the internet is a deliberative public sphere that is ideal for citizen participation in politics.

In his writings, Habermas recognized three institutional criteria which act as the preconditions for a public sphere to exist. The first precondition is the *disregarding of status*. If status is disregarded, the influence of rank is absent and therefore the better argument will uphold against the hierarchy imposed by the society. In this way, the uniformity of 'common humanity' is asserted. The idea of the public sphere is established as an objective forum independent of the authority of rank and status.

The second precondition for a public sphere to emerge according to Habermas is that it needs to be a domain of *common concern*. Before the development of the public sphere, authority of interpretation lay in the hands of the state and the church. These two institutions had a monopoly of interpretation in the fields of literature, philosophy and art. The monopoly persisted even at the time that specific spheres adhered to the rational thinking, which flowed from the development of capitalism where more information was required. During this time, philosophy and literature, as well as works of art, became commercialised and were accessible to private citizens. These items no longer remained components of the churches' and courts' publicity of representation. As a result, the private individuals, for whom these cultural products became available, determined meaning to it by the use of rational communication with others, verbalised it and stated the implicitness for as long as they could assert its authority. Cultural products and information ultimately became the common concern of private citizens and this paved the way for other issues of common concern to be introduced as topics of deliberation (Habermas, 1989).

The final precondition is the idea of *inclusivity*. The process that commercialised cultural products and information made it inclusive. Even at times when the public strengthened its boundaries to exclude people, it was never able to fully close itself to disallow participation. The public sphere has always been immersed within a more inclusive public of private individuals. These private individuals could gain from this process. Issues discussed, which were previously confined to the debates amongst secluded groups, now became general in their significance and accessibility. Thus, everybody was able to participate.

The public sphere was not necessarily founded on an institution that constituted a stable group of discussants. It did, however, equate itself with being the mouthpiece of the bourgeoisie. Even when the first public spheres developed as specific groups of people, it was ever conscious of being part of a larger public and acted as a representative group of that larger public. The potential of it being a publicist body was evident as its discussions did not merely remain internal but could be directed to the outside world (Habermas, 1989). According to Fulya Şen (2012), to explain the Internet as public sphere, the institutional criteria as set forth by Habermas (1989) should be recalled, i.e. the disregarding of status, common concern, and inclusivity. Within the internet, these three criteria are, at least to some extent, present. People access the internet using virtual identities similar to their own. If an individual's socio-economic status allows it, he or she has the resources needed to access and use the internet; when individuals have access to the necessary network infrastructure, all people can use the internet. The internet is used by on-line journalists, web-based interest groups and other organisations to explore and use the information available on the internet. These groups are often ignored by mainstream media; thus, the internet reinforces the idea that new media can open up new channels of communication and instigate new forms of public discourse and ultimately public opinion (Debatim, 2008). Social media has the potential to form a public sphere for the dissemination of counter hegemonic discourses, or to mobilise public opinion outside the centralised authoritative state control.

In contrast to the mass media, the internet can be instrumental as a force for radical democracy. The internet is seen as helping marginalised groups—those groups associated with discourses excluded from the mainstream public sphere—develop their own deliberative forums, link up, and subsequently contest dominant meanings and practices. There are three parts to this argument. First, the internet provides communication spaces for members of groups associated with marginalised discourses to develop counterpublics—'alternative' discursive arenas constituted by a number of participants engaging in debate and criticism that strengthens and develops oppositional discourses (identities, interpretations, social imaginaries and languages) to those dominating the mainstream public sphere. Second, the internet's interactivity and reach assists politically diverse and geographically dispersed counterpublics in finding shared points of identity and forming counterpublic networks and coalitions (or articulations) of radical discourses, leading to the development of more powerful oppositional discourses. Identification is particularly found through common experiences of exclusion and domination. This articulation of identity and discourse gives strength to marginalised publics weakened by isolation. Third, the internet supports on-line and off-line counterpublic contestation of dominant discourses, and hence the contestation of the deliberations of the mainstream public sphere (Dahlberg, 2007:56).

Writings on the Facebook Wall

The wall posts carrying political messages of purposively selected Facebook profiles and the comments they carry for six months, from July to December 2013 (the time period of the provincial elections of three provinces, including the controversial Northern Province; the commonwealth conference; and the presentation of the 2014 budget) was content analysed qualitatively via textual analysis. Content analysis is a research technique for the objective, systematic and quantitative description of the manifest content (the literal meanings embedded in them) of communication (Mayring, 2000). Using textual analysis, the latent content (implied meanings embedded in them) of the wall posts was analysed. The gathered qualitative data were analysed using the constant comparative method for examining the common themes of opinions embedded in them.

According to the data, political issues addressed through the Facebook wall posts can be organised into ten major categories. They are:

1. Issues related to the government's attempt to suppress public protests. The major subject of the discussion was the Rathupaswala incident in which a young man and a student were killed by the Sri Lankan army while trying to control the protestors who were demanding to close a rubber production factory, which was deemed as the cause of water pollution in the area;
2. Power of the President and his family, especially nepotism in the government and misconducts of the President's sons;
3. Cost of living;
4. Opposition party and its leader. The primary subject of the discussion was the defection of a popular opposition party leader and parliament member, Dayasiri Jayasekara, to the government party;
5. Corruption in the government and corrupt officials;
6. Issues related to development and development projects; specifically, the controversial development projects in Sri Lanka such as the Hambanthota harbour, Maththala airport, Norochchole power plant, highway roads, newly proposed Casino clubs, and the commonwealth conference held in 2013;
7. Issues related to media freedom. Biasness of state media and government's unnecessary influence on media institutions;

8. Issues related to war and ethnic conflict. Major subjects in discussion are the activities of LTTE, Indian (Thamilnadu) influence on the Sri Lankan ethnic conflict, UN influence on Sri Lanka, and government's unwise reactions towards UN interference;
9. Misconducts of ministers, parliament members, provincial council members, local council members and their relatives; and,
10. Other issues such as religious extremism, election, education, and introduction of new rules and regulations (ex: banning full-face helmets).

By counting the number of people who liked, shared, and commented on the wall posts, the percentage of the level of attention gained by these issues are given in Table 9A.

Table 9A: Percentages of the levels of attention gained by the issues

No.	Issue	No. of likes	No. of shares	No. of comments	Total	%
1.	Government's attempt to suppress public protests	15697	15743	1312	32752	19.2
2.	Power of president and his family	18559	12419	931	31909	18.7
3.	Misconducts of ministers, parliament members, provincial council members, local council members and their relatives	11942	10157	645	22744	13.3
4.	Opposition party and its leader	12501	8010	725	21236	12.4
5.	Issues related to development and development projects	12357	6041	544	18942	11.1
6.	Other issues	8162	6862	442	15466	9.1
7.	Issues related to media freedom	5282	4329	294	9905	5.8
8.	Corruption of the government and its officials	4381	3766	305	8452	4.9
9.	Cost of living	3969	2241	160	6370	3.7
10.	Issues related to war and ethnic conflict	1463	1250	84	2797	1.6

The data in Table 8A show that the most popular issues in discussion are government's attempt to supress public protests, the power of the President and his family, and the misconducts of ministers, parliament members, provincial council members, local council members and their relatives. As the power structures in many Asian countries, including Sri Lanka, are person-centred, the governments formed are more authoritative than democratic. Within such an environment, it is difficult to criticise the president, ministers or parliament members as it becomes a criticism of a person rather than a position or a policy. In that sense, it is obvious to find people using social media like Facebook to do what they cannot do through mainstream mass media.

The majority of the respondents (45.2%) were seriously critical with their comments; 39.8% of the respondents commented on the issues with humour; 15% used aggressive and abusive language to express their viewpoints.

However, different issues received different emotional expressions from the respondents. Firstly, they were more serious and critical on issues like the government attempting to suppress public protests, corruption of the government and its officials, media freedom, war and ethnic conflict, misconducts of ministers, parliament members, provincial council members, local council members and their relatives, and other issues such as education, religious extremism, elections, among others. The respondents used humour when discussing things like the power of the President and his family, cost of living, the opposition party and its leader, and issues related to development and development projects; this humour, however, appears as sarcasm as it represents the unhappiness of the respondents towards the issues. Respondents were more aggressive about issues related to war and ethnic conflict. The results are given in Table 9B.

Table 9B: Issues and the percentage of emotions expressed

No	Issue	Humorous	Serious	Abusive
1	Government's attempt to suppress public protests	19.1	63.7	17.2
2	Power of president and his family	57.4	30.8	11.7
3	Cost of living	55.2	31.4	13.2
4	Opposition party and its leader	49.2	34.9	15.8

5	Corruption of the government and its officials	34.1	53.4	12.4
6	Issues related to development and development projects	60.2	29.7	9.9
7	Issues related to media freedom	33.4	55.2	11.3
8	Issues related to war and ethnic conflict	13.2	59.1	27.7
9	Misconducts of ministers, parliament members, provincial council members, local council members and their relatives	39.8	40.6	19.6
10	Other issues	31.2	52.4	16.4

Phatic communication

According to Vincent Miller (2008), much of the communications we do through social media are 'phatic'. However, this varies based on the issue in discussion. The issues discussed and the percentage of people who used phatic communication in the discussion is given in Table 9C.

Table 9C: Issues on discussion and the percentage of people who have used phatic communication in the discussion

No	Issue	phatic %	Non phatic %
1	Government's attempt to suppress public protests	16.6	83.4
2	Power of president and his family	62.8	37.2
3	Cost of living	75	25
4	Opposition party and its leader	50	50
5	Corruption of the government and its officials	45	55
6	Issues related to development and development projects	56.5	43.5
7	Issues related to media freedom	50	50
8	Issues related to war and ethnic conflict	10	90

9	Misconducts of ministers, parliament members, provincial council members, local council members and their relatives	56	44
10	Other issues	78.9	21.1

The majority of the people who have commented on Facebook wall posts have used phatic communication when discussing issues such as the power of the President and his family, cost of living, issues related to development and development projects, misconducts of ministers, parliament members, provincial council members, local council members and their relatives, and on other issues. However, they were serious and were building up constructive conversation on matters such as the government's attempt to suppress public protests, corruption of the government and its officials, and issues related to war and ethnic conflict.

The majority of the respondents (54.6%) expressed ideas opposing the government, whereas 33.7% respondents' responses were neither for nor against the government. A low percentage (11.6) of respondents expressed supportive responses towards the government.

Regarding LTTE and war related issues, majority of the respondents (43.4%) expressed comments supporting the government. However, all the other issues on discussion, except issues regarding the opposition party, contained anti-government comments. Comments about the oppositional party and its leader were neither pro-government nor anti-government. Data are given in Table 9D.

Table 9D: Political ideology towards government and the percentage of respondents

No	Issue	percentage of respondents		
		Supportive	Neutral	opposite
01	Government's attempt to suppress public protests	9.1	26.1	64.8
02	Power of president and his family	15.3	24.6	60.1
03	Cost of living	28	25.2	46.8
04	Opposition party and its leader	12.6	63.4	24
05	Corruption of the government and its officials	9.2	34.7	56.1

06	Issues related to development and development projects	20.1	22.2	57.7
07	Issues related to media freedom	6.6	46.4	47
08	Issues related to war and ethnic conflict	43.4	29	27.6
09	Misconducts of ministers, parliament members, provincial council members, local council members and their relatives	3.1	34.8	62.1
10	Other issues	6.1	37.7	56.2

The majority of the people who posted wall posts (82.9%) on Facebook have done that in order to fulfil their need for escapism, whereas 36% of the total wall posts fulfilled a cognitive need; 11.8% of the total fulfilled an integrative need; 10.4% of the total fulfilled an affective need and only 2.4% fulfilled their need for self-esteem.

As for the issues regarding the discussions, majority of the wall posts that meant to fulfil a cognitive need (28.9%) were about the government's attempt to suppress public protests; the highest percent of wall posts that meant to fulfil the affective need (22.3%) were about the misconducts of ministers, parliament members, provincial council members, local council members and their relatives; and the majority of the wall posts that meant to fulfil the need for escapism (17.7%) were about the power of the President and his family.

The majority of the wall posts that meant to fulfil an integrative need (32%) were about the government's attempt to suppress public protests; and 60% of wall posts that meant to fulfil the self-esteem need were the issues related to development and development projects.

According to the data, those who commented on Facebook wall posts were not reluctant to reveal their identity as they had their names displayed in their profiles. However, the profile owners were somewhat reluctant to display their photographs on their profile. The data are given in Table 9E.

Table 9E: Identity status and percentage of people who have commented on wall posts of different issues

No	Issue	percentage of respondents			
		Without name	With name	With photo	Without photo
01	Government's attempt to suppress public protests	4.6	95.4	63.6	36.4
02	Power of president and his family	6.6	93.4	64.1	35.9
03	Cost of living	5.6	94.4	64.3	35.7
04	Opposition party and its leader	6	94	63.4	36.6
05	Corruption of the government and its officials	3.9	96.1	75.4	24.6
06	Issues related to development and development projects	7.4	92.6	66.1	33.9
07	Issues related to media freedom	4.4	95.6	59.7	40.3
08	Issues related to war and ethnic conflict	6	94	59	41
09	Misconducts of ministers, parliament members, provincial council members, local council members and their relatives	5	95	60.2	39.8
10	Other issues	5.9	94.1	64.6	35.4

Conclusion and Recommendations

In contrast to the traditional mass media often controlled by vested interests, the internet is seen as a force for 'radical democracy'. Thus, this research focused on examining the way people use new media to express their point of view freely on public issues and finding out the gratifications users have fulfilled using Facebook to express their views. The findings reveal that the main issues that attracted the users to make a comment on the wall posts are about the government's attempt to suppress public protests on contemporary public issues, the power of the President, and the misconducts of political leaders. Moreover, while they were freely expressing their ideas with their Facebook comments, the majority showed no reluctance in revealing their identity as they displayed their names or photographs, or both. The majority of the respondents were fulfilling their need for escapism through these wall posts; their cognitive and integrative needs were fulfilled as well.

It is evident that a social media platform like Facebook creates an alternative platform for the citizens to voice their ideas regarding the political and social issues that have an effect on their life. However, future research should take place in order to find out the class, gender, age, educational and geographical differences of social media users that create a public sphere using social media; this would lead to findings about the real impact of such a virtual public sphere in changing the political and social setting of the country.

References

Bakardjieva, M. (2011). Reconfiguring the Mediapolis: New media and civic agency. *New Media and Society*. 14 (1), pp.63-79

Dahlberg, L. (2007). The Internet, deliberative democracy, and power: Radicalizing the public sphere. *International Journal of Media and Cultural Politics*. 3 (1), pp. 47–64.

Debatim, B. (2008). The Internet as a New Platform for Expressing Public Opinions and as a New Public Sphere. In: Donsbach, W. & Traugott, M. W. (ed), *The Sage Handbook of Public Opinion Research*. London: Sage.

Colombage, D. (2012). *Sri Lanka lagging behind in social media*. [ONLINE] Available at: http://www.thesundayleader.lk/2012/02/05/sri-lanka-lagging-behind-in-social-media/. [Last Accessed 2013.07.10].

Fraser, N. (1990). Rethinking the Public Sphere: A Contribution to the Critique of Actually Existing Democracy. *Social Text*. No. 25/26, pp.56-80.

Gotabhaya Rajapaksa (2013). *Gotabhaya Rajapaksa and National Security: The Kotelawala Defence University Lecture*. [ONLINE] Available at: http://groundviews.org/2013/06/14/gotabaya-rajapaksa-and-national-security-the-kotelawala-defence-university-lecture/. [Last Accessed 2014.03.24].

Habermas, J. (1989). *The Structural Transformation of the Public Sphere: An inquiry into a category of Bourgeois Society*, T. Burger and F. Lawrence (trans.), Cambridge, MA: MIT Press.

Katz, E., Blumler, G. and Gurevich, M. (1974). 'Utilization of mass communication by the individual'. *In:* Blumler, J.G. and Katz, E. (ed),

The Uses of Mass Communication: Current Perspectives on Gratifications Research. 1st ed. Beverly Hills: Sage. pp.19-32.

Kaye, B.K. and Johnson, T.J. (2002). Online and in the know: Uses and gratifications of the Web for political information. *Journal of Broadcasting & Electronic Media*. 46 (1), pp.54-71

Leung, L. (2009). User generated content on the internet: An examination of gratifications, civic engagement and psychological empowerment. *New Media & Society*. 11(8), pp. 1327–1347.

Mayring, P. (2000). *Qualitative inhaltsanalyse. Grundlagen und Techniken*. 7th ed. Weinheim: Psychologie Verlags Union.

McQuail, D. (2005). *McQuail's Mass Communication Theory*. 5th ed. London: Sage.

Miller, V. (2008). New media, networking and phatic culture. *The International Journal of Research into New Media Technologies*. 14 (4), pp.387-400

Papacharissi, Z. and Rubin, A.M. (2000). Predictors of Internet use. *Journal of Broadcasting and Electronic Media*. 44 (2), pp.175-196

Parker, B.J. and Plank, R.E. (2000). A uses and gratifications perspective on the Internet as a new information source. *American Business Review*. 18 (2), pp.43-49

Petras, J. (2011). *Social opposition in the age of internet: Desktop 'Militants' and public intellectuals*. Downloaded from: http://petras.lahaine.org/?p=1880. [Last Accessed 2014.02.25].

Quan-Haase, A. and Young, A.L. (2010). Uses and gratifications of social media: A comparison of Facebook and Instant Messaging. *Bulletin of Science, Technology & Society* .30, pp. 350–361.

Raacke, J. and Bonds-Raacke, J. (2008). MySpace and Facebook: Applying the uses and gratifications theory to exploring friend-networking sites. *Cyberpsychology and Behavior* . 11 (2), pp.169-174

SEN, F. (2012). *The social media as a public sphere: The rise of social opposition*. Downloaded from: http://www.cmdconf.net/2012/makale/92.pdf. [Last Accessed 2013.05.11].

Shirky, C. (2011). *The political power of social media: Technology, the public sphere, and political change*. Downloaded from: http://www.foreignaffairs.com/articles/67038/clay-shirky/the-political-power-of-social-media. [Last Accessed 2013.11.05].

Song I, Larose, R., Eastin, M.S. and Lin, C.A, (2004). Internet gratifications and Internet addiction: On the uses and abuses of new media. *Cyberpsychology and Behavior*. 7 (4), pp.384-394

Tewksbury, D. and Althaus, S.L. (2000). An examination of motivations for using the World Wide Web. *Communication Research Report*. 17 (2), pp.127-138

The Universal Declaration of Human Rights (2008). *The Universal Declaration of Human Rights*. Downloaded from: http://www.un.org/Overview/rights.html#a19. [Last Accessed 2013.10.15].

ANNEX

THE SOUTHEAST ASIAN REGION AT A GLANCE

This book primarily tackles issues in social media in the region of Southeast Asia. The region is composed of eleven countries that are diverse in history, culture, religion and socio-economic development. These countries include: Brunei Darussalam, Cambodia, East Timor, Laos, Indonesia, Malaysia, Myanmar (Burma), the Philippines, Thailand, Singapore and Vietnam. Except for East Timor (which gained its independence from Indonesia in 2002), the other nations also comprise the Association of Southeast Asian Nations or ASEAN, an economic bloc that seeks to have a free flow of goods and services among its members by 2020. Sri Lanka, which geographically belongs to South Asia (together with India and Pakistan) was included in this book because its social media environment is more similar to those of the ASEAN.

Official Government Website and Internet country code (cctld)

	Official Government Website	ccTld
Brunei	http://www.brunei.gov.bn	.bn
Cambodia	http://www.cambodiainvestment.gov.kh	.kh
Laos	http://www.mofa.gov.la/	.la
Indonesia	http://www.indonesia.go.id/en/	.id
Malaysia	https://www.malaysia.gov.my	.my
Myanmar	http://www.mofa.gov.mm/	.mm
Philippines	http://www.gov.ph/	.ph
Singapore	http://www.gov.sg/	.sg
Sri Lanka	https://www.gov.lk/welcome.html	.lk
Thailand	http://www.thaigov.go.th/	.th
Vietnam	http://www.chinhphu.vn/portal	.vn

Internet and Facebook Users Stats
(source: http://www.internetworldstats.com/)

	Population (2015)	**Internet Users** (2015)	**Penetration** (% of population)	**Facebook Users** (as of 2012)
Brunei	429,646	318,900	74.2 %	254,760
Cambodia	15,708,756	5,000,000	31.8 %	742,220
Laos	6,911,544	985,586	14.3 %	255,880
Indonesia	255,993,674	73,000,000	28.5 %	51,096,860
Malaysia	30,513,848	20,596,847	67.5 %	13,589,520
Myanmar	56,320,206	1,182,724	2.1 %	n/a
Philippines	109,615,913	47,134,843	43.0 %	29,890,900
Singapore	5,674,472	4,653,067	82.0 %	2,915,640
Sri Lanka	22,053,488	5,689,800	25.8 %	1,515,720
Thailand	67,976,405	23,716,968	34.9 %	17,721,480
Vietnam	94,348,835	45,579,922	48.3 %	10,669,880

Telecommunication Stats
(ITU 2012)

	Fixed-telephone subscriptions	Mobile-cellular telephone subscriptions	Fixed (wired)-broadband subscriptions
Brunei	70,933	469,740	19,849
Cambodia	584,475	19,105,115	29,734
Laos	112,000	6,492,000	93,200
Indonesia	37,982,855	281,963,665	2,983,000
Malaysia	4,588,900	41,324,700	2,459,900
Myanmar	556,000	5,440,000	5,400
Philippines	3,939,000	103,000,000	2,146,600
Singapore	1,989,500	8,063,000	1,371,000
Sri Lanka	3,449,391	53,624,427	423,194
Thailand	6,391,030	84,075,036	4,357,398
Vietnam	10,191,049	134,066,000	4,446,600

About Us

The book is primarily a compilation of selected academic lectures and papers presented during recent conferences organised by the Asian Congress for Media and Communication (ACMC).

The Editors

Azman Azwan Azmawati is an Associate Professor at the School of Communication, Universiti Sains Malaysia (USM) in Penang, where she was Deputy Dean for Research (2013-2015), Deputy Dean for Academic (2010-2012) and Journalism Chairperson (2003-2009). She is also the current President of the Asian Congress for Media and Communication (ACMC) Executive Council. She holds a Ph.D. in Economic Journalism from the USM and a Masters in International Relations from Boston University. Prior to academic work, she was a business journalist of *The New Straits Times Group Malaysia*. She is also on the Board of Women's Development Research Centre of USM. She was also a Visiting Scholar at the Department of Gender Studies, School of Society, Literature and the Arts of the University of Canterbury in Christchurch, New Zealand.

Rachel E. Khan is an Associate Professor of Journalism at the College of Mass Communication, University of the Philippines, where she is currently serving another term as Chair of the Journalism Department. She is concurrently an Associate Editor of *Media Asia*, a Hong Kong-based academic journal of the Asian Media Information and Communication Centre (AMIC) and the Chairman of the Board of the ACMC. She holds an M.S. in Journalism from the Columbia University in New York under the Fulbright Programme and a B.S. in Economics from the University of the Philippines. Prior to joining the academe, she was a multi-award-winning journalist working for *BusinessWorld*, a leading business daily in the Philippines. She is also the author of several textbooks in media literacy and journalism.

The Contributors

Chapter 3:

Khairiah A Rahman is Senior Lecturer and Programme Leader for Certificate Studies at the School of Communication Studies, AUT University in Auckland, New Zealand where she lectures in intercultural communication and public relations. She is also on the advisory board of the Pacific Media Centre at AUT University. She is Vice President for Communication and the New Zealand representative for ACMC (Asian Congress for Media and Communication). Khairiah has written articles, book chapters and presented on transnational identities, crisis miscommunication, intercultural trust relationships, cultural representations and stereotypes, Islamic perspective of dialogue and persuasion, and the impact of media on culture. She has worked in both the private and public sectors with specialisations in media and communication. Her PhD research is on Islam and communication.

Tracey Ann Jury holds a Master of Communication Studies with First Class Honours from AUT University in Auckland, New Zealand and a Bachelor of Arts with First Class Honours in Media and Communication from the University of Canterbury, New Zealand. She has worked in the private sector in public relations and in marketing, in agency and in-house. She has a strong interest in the research areas of communication, public relations and crisis, and has previously researched changing public-relations strategies following the 2011 Canterbury Earthquake and journalism ethics in disaster reporting. More recently, research interests have focused on the relationship between social media, emotion and crisis communication.

Chapter 4:

Karen Y. Varona teaches English, Communication, and Media courses at the University of the Philippines-Visayas campus (UPV) and has published a study on the media coverage of Overseas Filipino Workers. She is a Ph.D. in Communication student at the University of the Philippines Diliman, where she also earned her M.A. in Media Studies (Journalism). She has an M.Ed. in English (as a Second Language) from the UPV and was a curriculum developer in Temasek Foundation-Singapore's English Language Teaching Curriculum Development Project in Southeast Asia. Her research interests include media coverage of migrant workers, social media, and popular culture.

Chapter 5:

Jamilah Ahmad is a Professor at the School of Communication, Universiti Sains Malaysia in Penang, Malaysia. She was a visiting Professor at Universitas Gadjah Mada, Indonesia and was a visiting Professor at Yildiz Technical University, Istanbul, Turkey. Jamilah is an accredited member and Fellow of the Institute of Public Relations Malaysia (IPRM). She is dedicated to advancing research in the areas of Corporate Social Responsibility (CSR), Public Relations, Environmental Communication, Community Relations & Communication, Corporate Communication, e-Learning and New Media Technology. She also sits as Editor-in-Chief for GSTF Journal on Media and Communication, editorial board and issue reviewer for Asia Pacific Public Relations Review (APPRJ), Journal of Communication and Media Studies (JCMS), International Journal of Business Management & Research (IJBMR), Environmental Education Research Journal, Public Relations Inquiry Journal (PRI), InSITE (Informing Science and IT Education) and Social Responsibility Journal (SRJ).

Nurzali Ismail is a young and aspiring academic in the field of media and communication. At present, he is a Lecturer at the School of Communication, Universiti Sains Malaysia (USM). Prior to joining USM, he was a Visiting Research Fellow at the Wee Kim Wee School of Communication and Information, Nanyang Technological University (NTU), Singapore. In recognition of his academic excellence, Nurzali was awarded the prestigious Australian Postgraduate Award / Monash Graduate Scholarship by Monash University Australia. Nurzali has keen interest in research topics related to new media, youth, media and communication in education, branding and the communities of practice.

Chapter 6:

Chanon Adsanatham, a native of Bangkok, Thailand, is an Assistant Professor of English at the University of Maryland, specialising in cross-cultural rhetoric, digital writing, and multimodality. His works on digital delivery theory and multimedia assessment have appeared in *Computers and Composition* and *Multimodal Literacies and Emerging Genres*. He frequently teaches courses in histories of rhetoric, critical theory, multimedia composition, and academic writing. Currently, he is writing a book on how conduct functions as an important form of rhetoric in the Thai tradition.

Chapter 7:

Tony Chalkley is a Senior Lecturer at Deakin University, Australia and his research, irrespective of how it starts, always seems to bring him back to communication, be it in schools, teams, factories, government departments or on-line social worlds. He holds a Ph.D. from the Royal Melbourne Institute of Technology, where he worked as an organisational ethnographer and noticed that most people wanted to talk about 'communication' and, more than anything else, wanted to talk about what happens when it goes wrong. This simple discovery, teamed with an awareness of the power of new media, led to an interest in finding out more about 'the future of communication'. He is the author of a number of communication papers and is currently working on the second edition of his text 'Communication, Digital Media and Everyday Life'.

Chapter 8:

Bradley Freeman is an Associate Professor of Communication and Information Studies at the Mohammed Bin Rashid School for Communication at the American University in Dubai. He taught previously at the Wee Kim Wee School of Communication at Nanyang Technological University, Singapore. He holds a Ph.D. from Syracuse University, New York. Before moving to Asia, he worked at various media institutions in the USA and Germany; including as Television Research Associate with the ARS Group, Editorial Assistant for 'Communication Research,' and has contributed articles and papers on a broad range of topics in popular and academic publications. His research interests are varied but tend to deal with pop culture, new media, and news coverage and analysis. He brings a global, cross-cultural perspective, along with comparative insights to his research investigations.

Hoang Thi Kim Khanh is a lecturer at University of Sciences, Thai Nguyen University (TNU), Vietnam. She completed her Masters in Journalism at the Vietnam National University, Hanoi (VNU). Prior to joining academe, she was a freelance journalist for several journals, both print and on-line. Her research interests include on-line journalism and social media issues.

Chapter 9:

Pushpika Kumari Ganegoda is currently a Lecturer in Communication Studies, at Trincomalee campus of Eastern University, Sri Lanka. She holds an M.Phil in Development Communication and a B.A. Mass Communication (Upper Division) at the Post Graduate Institute of

Agriculture, University of Peradeniya, Sri Lanka. Her research interests are Interpersonal Communication, Cultural Studies, Film and Television, Communication research, Environmental Journalism, Bollywood cinema, advertising, global media and media representation. She has presented an individual research paper and three joint research papers at ACMC in 2010 and 2012.

Nisansala Subhasini Jayawardhana is a Lecturer in Communication Studies at Trincomalee Campus of Eastern University, Sri Lanka. Having obtained a B.A. Mass Communication, she is now a Visiting Lecturer in the Faculty of Humanities and Social Sciences at the Open University, Sri Lanka. Her research interests are New Media, Print Media, and Advertising. She has presented a research paper in GCRA International conference (2014) on 'Farewell to Movie Theatres: The Current tendency of Movie Viewers towards DVD movies (A Case Study)' in Sri Lanka.